VISUAL PEDAGOGY

VISUAL

DUKE

UNIVERSITY

PRESS

DURHAM

AND LONDON

2002

Media Cultures in and

beyond the Classroom

BRIAN GOLDFARB

PEDAGOGY

© 2002 Duke University Press   All rights reserved
Printed in the United States of America on acid-free paper ∞
Designed by Rebecca M. Giménez   Typeset in Sabon
with Futura display by Tseng Information Systems, Inc.
Library of Congress Cataloging-in-Publication Data
appear on the last printed page of this book.

For Carole and Ted,

and for Sabina and Danilo,

whose education is my education

CONTENTS

Visual Pedagogy would not have been possible without feedback and input from so many people—more than I can mention. I am grateful to Warren Crichlow, Douglas Crimp, David Rodowick, Sharon Willis and Janet Wolff at the University of Rochester for supporting the research that formed the basis for this book. Their guidance was essential to this project's development. Friends and colleagues in the Visual and Cultural Studies Program at the University of Rochester—especially Karen Kosasa, Walid Ra'ad, Phil Gentile, and Allen Topolski—provided a wonderful environment to study and work in. I thank Susan Cahan, Jerry Philogene, Claudia Hernandez, Rayna Lampkins Fielder, Dan Cameron, Marcia Tucker, and others at the New Museum of Contemporary Art in New York. Their faith in my ideas allowed me to incorporate my research into my curatorial and programming work at the New Museum in the mid-1990s. Numerous artists and media producers, including Almir Almas, Julia Meltzer, Greg Bordowitz, Steve Schiff, Mona Jimenez, Rebeca Odes and Ester Drill, provided me with important feedback and insights and gave me access to the material and interviews that form the basis of this book. Equally important to this project's development was ongoing dialog with media educators and collaborative groups including Steven Goodman and the staff of the Educational Video Center, Laura Vural and the staff at Rise and Shine, Chris Bratton and the members of Video Machete, Jubilee Arts, ARTEC, the Hetrick Martin Institute, and the Bay Area Video Collective. I thank Chon Noriega for editorial feedback for the chapter on local television in Brazil and N. Frank Ukadike for the insightful comments he offered during the editing of the chapter on African cinema, and to Amy Herzog for help researching illustrations. Thanks, also, to Aubrey Anable for her careful indexing of this book. I am grateful to have had the opportunity to work with editor Ken Wisoker. He and his expert staff at Duke provided thoughtful and clear direction throughout the revision process.

Finally and most significantly, I cannot thank Lisa Cartwright enough for her inspiration, feedback, editorial suggestions, and unfailing support throughout this project. More than anything, our close working relationship made this book possible.

An Ethos of Visual Pedagogy

The second half of the twentieth century was marked by the global expansion of communications media and a burgeoning visual culture, radically altering the dissemination and production of information and knowledge. Education, widely espoused as the principal instrument of social change, was fundamentally challenged and transfigured by this process. Visual media culture was perceived as a threat to literacy, but also touted as a potentially powerful tool for educators. Behind these variously phobic and euphoric reactions to communications technology was an increasingly undeniable apprehension that any stable conception of literacy was being eroded.

In a 1975 world conference organized by UNESCO (United Nations Educational, Scientific, and Cultural Organization), one of the central projects was the evaluation of recent literacy campaigns throughout the developing world. According to UNESCO's report, the success of these literacy campaigns related directly to the revolutionary transformations of the societies in which the campaigns took place.[1] In 1987, reflecting on his literacy work in postliberation Guinea-Bissau, where thirty languages and multiple discourses vied in a period of intensive globalization, Brazilian theorist of education Paolo Freire commented on the extraordinary role that "*reading* the world" played in various countries' reinvention of their educational and social systems.[2] Though no less true, the focus on language and literacy as the chief entities measured to chart progress in countries undergoing radical societal changes in the postwar period overlooks a crucial reality of that era.

To focus exclusively on language literacy and speech is to overlook the visual and graphic means of knowledge production and reproduction that played a major role in strategies of resistance and social transformation. Media and visual culture were extraordinary forces in contexts where education—broadly construed as a set of means of societal transformation—came under the influence of the global circulation of information and the means of knowledge and meaning production. The period in which Freire wrote was rife with projects devoted to experimentation in the use of new media and visual culture in the very sorts of contexts that concerned him: Third World cultures, colonized and postcolonial countries, and oppressed populations in the First World. The publication of Freire's *Pedagogy of the Oppressed* in 1970 spawned three decades of scholarship in education built on the premise that pedagogy is a form of cultural politics, not a science of knowledge transmission. It is by now a commonplace of education theory that pedagogy as cultural politics exists beyond the confines of classrooms and spaces where education is the explicit agenda. But today there is still only a limited understanding of the place of visual culture, and especially visual media culture.

Visual Pedagogy: Media Cultures in and beyond the Classroom steps into a breach in our understanding about the role of the visual and media in the broad cultures of education and pedagogy during the late twentieth century. The 1980s and 1990s saw an explosion of work in critical and feminist pedagogy—writings that theorized the class, gender, race, and cultural politics of schooling in light of previously underconsidered factors such as students' life experience and popular cultural forms, including television and new media. The explicitly pedagogical function of popular media in the daily lives of students became an object of particular focus in these writings, which were strongly influenced by cultural studies. But this work most forcefully put forth critiques of media, seeing the media as means of social indoctrination and inculcation into Western capitalist models of knowledge and citizenship. Witness the technophobic proclamation of founding critical pedagogy theorist Peter McLaren, writing in 1999:

> Communications networks—the electronic servo-mechanisms of the state—with their propulsions and fluxes of information that have grown apace with capitalism, make this hegemony not only a tenebrous possibility but also an inevitability as they ideologically secure forms of exploitation so furious that every vulnerability of the masses is seized and made over into a crisis.[3]

Visual Pedagogy takes as its starting point a blind spot, perhaps even a bias, in critical pedagogy that dates back to Freire's foundational work and extends forward into the body of work known as critical pedagogy that was produced in the last three decades of the twentieth century. This blind spot is the place of the art-media-technology nexus in the politics of pedagogy. The bias is that the visual is a more base, even primitive, and also untrustworthy form of knowledge transmission and production—a modality used by dominant forces to seduce naive populations into compliance. Freire's *Pedagogy of the Oppressed* put forth the argument that to acquire literacy is not simply to learn the techniques of reading and writing but to gain the ability to think critically and to use language—in the forms of reading, writing, and speech—as politicized action. Freire first formulated this agenda in a context of left agrarian reform, so his work emphasized speech and (secondarily) writing as modes of politicized action. But he wrote during a period when technologies of the word were being transformed through new media forms such as television and computers in public education and other public spheres of teaching and learning. These media supplemented the hallowed forms of the embodied and written word with electronic and digital image and text. Whereas embodied speech, for Freire, carried the aura of authenticity, electronic and digital image and text were viewed by his followers as seductive techniques of institutional and bureaucratic control. The visual media were disparaged for their perceived status, on the one hand, as "primitive" or culturally indigenous forms of communication, and, on the other, as the pedagogical tools of global capitalism.

The early transformation toward visual and media pedagogies globally and across areas beyond education remains relatively undertheorized in critical pedagogy, except with guarded interest. *Visual Pedagogy* zeroes in on this blind spot—the visual technologies of pedagogy—to

provide it with a history and a future. It corrects the bias of critical pedagogy by acknowledging those early instances where a pedagogical use
of media and visual education functioned more complexly than either
an oppressive tool of the state or a revolutionary technique of the oppressed.

The transition from voice and writing to media transmission and a
visual logic of knowledge production occurred not only in elite Western
institutions but also in the Third World settings that were the basis for
Freire's early ideas about pedagogy. It was in the latter settings that new
media became a venue for the long arm of global benevolence in education. From the late 1950s through the 1970s, the Third World was tapped
as a testing ground for the educational-technology systems that would
transform educational philosophy and practice in U.S. schools and institutions in the 1980s and 1990s. With the introduction of computers, television, and global communications networks in the postwar period, the
technologies of language literacy, tacitly understood by Freire to be reading and writing pure and simple, underwent a transformation that was
far from merely formal. New media technologies (and by *new* I mean
those that became ubiquitous following the Second World War, including television and computers) transformed what it meant to speak, to
read, to write, and to think—and hence to know and to have agency.
Visual and media forms came to be commonplace in producing and cir-
culating knowledge not only by and in the interests of the West but also
by and for the revolutionary, marginalized, and resisting cultures that
were the focus of Freire's attention.

It was not until the late 1980s that Freire would focus on media technology, with the opening of the Central Laboratory for Educational In-
formatics and the launching of a program to set up computers in public
schools of São Paulo, Brazil, during the years that Freire led the Bureau
of Education (between 1989 and 1991). Yet Brazil's innovative television
network TV Globo had played a key role years earlier in overthrowing
the dictatorship—during the very years that Freire wrote his influential
first book. (The pedagogical function of TV Globo is documented in
chapter 7.)

The generation of writers who took up Freire's work saw a direct application for his theories about the Third World at home in the urban
public schools of the United States. Peter McLaren, Michael Apple,
Henry Giroux, Ira Schor, and David Trend, among others, saw the ap-

plicability of Freire's theories of oppression and empowerment in these locales, and they used his work to introduce an advocacy model of critical pedagogy into education. David Trend, more than any of these authors, has noted the role of media technology in furthering left critical pedagogy within and beyond schools. He describes experiments with media technology in the U.S. public schools of the 1970s as a brief period of liberal formalism, a period when the structure of learning was emphasized over culturally specific content, downplaying differences of race, class, and gender.[4] Hands-on work with media technology, he suggests, made it possible for students to understand and engage in the technological means of knowledge production and reproduction. But in the 1980s, Trend explains, the period when students engaged in the means of production was short-lived. The Reagan administration's policies and budget cuts resulted in a climate where hands-on student participation in educational media process and production was reduced to simple classroom media viewing.

The research that supports *Visual Pedagogy* complicates and challenges Trend's account of this shift, taking the story back to the 1950s and forward to the digital revolution of the 1990s. Some of the U.S. schools where hands-on media systems were piloted were test sites for the same sorts of media education systems that had already been tried in more distant sites such as American Samoa. In the latter sorts of places, the goal was to streamline and cost-cut the delivery of education, and in some instances to reduce discourse to the global common denominator of images, not to level difference through students' hands-on knowledge production. The visual and technology-heavy pedagogy that informed these experiments strove for uniformity and ease of information delivery, aiming as well to circumvent the necessity for native teachers and human interaction in the process of preparing subjects for a world in information and culture that was newly global.

In this era of globalization, these Third World media education experiments were both testing ground for, and counterpart to, similar experiments in U.S. public schools populated by poor, immigrant, and African American student bodies. This is not to say that the U.S. foundations and government entities that influenced education policy and practice globally saw these two populations as alike; rather, they saw them as posing similar problems in their overall economy of forging a global economy of pedagogy. The desire for cost-efficient ways to educate large numbers of people for the benefit of serving larger and more diverse populations in a globalizing economy was one factor that motivated the testing of educational media locally and at a distance. This was true not only in schools but in public institutions such as museums, where the mission to educate had become an explicit agenda. Another view that held sway was that language difference and illiteracy could be surmounted using graphic and visual symbols to introduce "more complex" discursive forms. This concept was supported by Jean Piaget's popular theories of child psychology, which considered symbolic language acquisition as a more primitive, basic precursor to the complexities of learning written language. This point is explained at length in chapter 6 that is not about education per se but about the pedagogical mission of African colonial and postcolonial cinema. What Third World and marginalized cultures "at home" shared in common, then, according to education funders and policy makers, was their "primitive" relationship to the world of the symbolic. One of the interventions *Visual Pedagogy* will make in later chapters is to challenge the belief that the visual occupies a lower level of knowledge than writing. This view held sway not only in mainstream educational policies at midcentury but also in the theories of media in education (like McLaren's, quoted earlier) that condemn visual media as the tools of capitalist seduction.

Even if we were to focus on the U.S. context alone, it is not clear that leveling difference is what the 1970s experiments with learning technologies in U.S. schools were all about. We need to look not only at the training of students to use media systems but also at the influx of technologies designed to streamline and cost-cut in education delivery. The philosophy of the electronic classroom intersects complexly with the philosophy of hands-on media production training. As Ira Shor explains, a pedagogical philosophy of vocationalism under the name of career education blossomed in the U.S. public school system in the early 1970s.[5] Hands-on experience with media was one of the career skills worth cultivating in public school workforce training. Technological know-how did not replace book learning. Rather, it was a class-based register of knowledge that ran beneath the academic track. The liberal view of media production's potential to transform the politics of difference in schools forwarded by David Trend comes up against the class, gender, and race biases inherent in both the "vo-tech" imperative and the idea of the television as a cost-effective teacher substitute. The value of both systems for training a global workforce was not lost on educators involved in transforming education in Third World settings.[6]

I do not mean to downplay the radical potential of programs that engage students in the visual, the popular, or the technical means of media production. *Visual Pedagogy* takes a strong advocacy position throughout regarding the activist and even revolutionary potential of technical hands-on practice in classrooms. I write as a media educator who was involved in public education reform and projects that encouraged marginalized students to gain agency within their communities through hands-on media production. I do, however, want to complicate the politics of agency implicit in much left critical pedagogy, as well as to challenge the overarching suspicion of engagement with popular media and mainstream institutions that runs throughout that body of work. The agency and voice gained through the labor of challenging the "culture of silence" (Freire's term) in education is always articulated through institutions and the technologies they sponsor and use. The pedagogical uses of media described here demonstrate the degree to which engagement in media technology and its institutions is not a choice but an inevitability of life in a late-twentieth-century culture shaped by an ethos of the visual and of media pedagogy.

No situation better illustrates the conditions of the culture of media pedagogy in which this book was written than the digital transformation of schools in the 1990s. During that decade, schools became only one of numerous institutional sites where networked computers were introduced, ostensibly to democratize information and knowledge for the broad U.S. populace. Schools are the focus in the discussion that follows, but they are paradigmatic of the media pedagogy mind-set that escalated in public cultures of the late twentieth century. If the link between technological and pedagogical intervention was suddenly and dramatically instilled in the national political imagination at the height of the Cold War, it was more thoroughly transformed into a cultural imperative over the decades that followed. When digital technology emerged at the center of the national culture and economy in the 1990s, it was almost unquestioned that digital media would be central to pedagogy, and that pedagogy would be the key to the potential of a new democratic media form that would go beyond education proper. U.S. president Bill Clinton made this assertion in 1996, at the height of a much publicized wave of attention to the promise of digital and computer media in the classroom and beyond: "We know, purely and simply, that every single child must have access to a computer, must understand it, must have access to good software and good teachers and to the Internet, so that every person will have the opportunity to make the most of his or her own life."[7]

The idea that computer access is every U.S. schoolchild's right—that this is something "we know, purely and simply"—came into its own in the 1990s. By the end of the decade, media and communications technology had become ubiquitous in classrooms across the United States. Debates shifted from the question of whether computer and audiovisual technology belonged in educational settings to how it should be used. Indeed, the idea of computer access as every citizen's right in a democratic society was a motif that characterized not only the Clinton administration but also the platforms of countless politicians and educators right and left of Clinton, including Freire during his leadership of São Paulo's Bureau of Education. The U.S. call for a computer on every schoolchild's desk is rooted in a vision of the United States as world leader in an information-based global economy. But it is a call that issued from the smallest and most vulnerable of nations as well, representing for them a basic condition of survival in a global economy. This vision finds its paradigmatic expression in schooling but extends beyond education to stand for new visions of society, global and local. Witness the U.S. Education Department's 1996 report "Getting America's Students Ready for the 21st Century: Meeting the Technology Literacy Challenge": "Computers are the 'new basic' of American education, and the Internet is the blackboard of the future. . . . If we help all of our children to become technologically literate, we will give a generation of young people the skills they need to enter this new knowledge- and information-driven economy."[8]

In the 1990s, information technology was transformed from a useful resource to the key to literacy and, indeed, to success in the "knowledge- and information-driven economy" of the twenty-first century. The Internet replaced the blackboard as the symbol of the schoolchild's mind as virtual tabula rasa waiting to be inscribed with the knowledge needed to survive in the world of the future. In the same year that this Education Department report was released, a national poll reported that "U.S. teachers ranked computer skills and media technology as more 'essential' than the study of European history, biology, chemistry, and physics;

than dealing with social problems such as drugs and family breakdown; than learning practical job skills; and than reading modern American writers such as Steinbeck and Hemingway or classic ones such as Plato and Shakespeare."[9]

This embrace of new media technology as the heart of the educational system coincided with the penetration of personal computers and the Internet into all corners of everyday life and commerce. It is easy to see that the late 1980s and 1990s were a watershed period in the incorporation of new media technology as an essential element not only of education but also of all sectors of everyday life for the upper- and middle-class populations of the United States. Education played a pivotal role in this process of making computer technology ubiquitous in everyday life and symbolic of that cornerstone of cultural survival, literacy. Certainly many of the parents of the upper- and middle-class children who used computers at school were themselves simultaneously encountering computers and the Internet at work. But children raised on video and home computer games were crucial participants in spreading the computer from facilitator of mundane everyday transactions and mindless home recreation to core educational and communications technology. Their school experiences led them to carry the skills and enthusiasm about the "enriching" aspects of living life on the screen and on-line into the private space of the home, affording home computers for children a degree of acceptability they had not previously held. The incorporation of computers into mainstream education unlinked the technology's image relative to youth from the mindless repetition and violence that was the received view of video game systems such as Nintendo. The question was no longer whether children should own or use a computer but how their (necessary) encounters with computers should be regulated. Networked computers, by the century's end, had become a ubiquitous feature of the image of the good life of middle- and upper-class American families.

The impact of these transformations was not limited to middle- and upper-income populations. As Clinton's assertion suggests, in the 1990s computer access was a goal—indeed, a symbol—of the mission to educate the broader U.S. public, to prepare all citizens for life in the twenty-first century. Computers and the Internet were introduced to the lives of the poor and working classes through initiatives to make computer use commonplace in public schools, libraries, and museums—institutions shaped by a mission to educate the broad public. Children attending public schools transmitted the idea of the computer as symbol of learning and literacy to their parents, whose experiences with these technologies were more likely to have occurred through depersonalized forms like bank machines and the supermarket checkout line. In the mid-1990s, computer information systems and the Internet were introduced to public libraries, community centers, and even clinics, where video and computer kiosks were set up under the auspices of the consumer self-health initiative, which was an outgrowth of the media education ethos of the decade. Previously employees of the government, university, and business sectors and those who could afford home networked computers had access to the personal side of computer use, even if only through illicit work-time activities. Subsidized institutional access, through plans such as the National Information Infrastructure, linked the poor and working classes to the personal side of computer use.

The media technology ethos that characterized the last decade of the twentieth century was not as sudden or new as it may appear. This book traces some of the events and circumstances in the media and education sectors that led up to and made possible these transformations. In the late 1950s and 1960s, television was a major feature in discussions about the classroom of the future. The era of Sputnik, space technology, computer experimentation, and broadcast television brought us an array of experiments in which media technology was introduced as a pedagogical tool in classrooms across the United States and its postwar protectorates. During this period, proponents of media education saw a flip side to the image of television as mindless mass entertainment. Television held the potential to usher in a new sort of pedagogy and cultural knowledge that would be in keeping with a future in which technology would be integral to work and life for citizens of the world leader in democracy. The roots of the information-technology-democracy nexus so apparent in Clinton's technology access platform can be found in this earlier way of thinking about television's potential. During the early years of the medium's success as a consumer technology and its incorporation into the American home, television was at the center of a discourse that made media literacy a core component of postwar literacy and knowledge. The massification of education and cultural survival in an era of globalization and technological transformation and connectivity necessitated experiments with new communications technologies, including television, in institutions where public education was mandated.

This book will trace an ethos of media pedagogy in and beyond schools after the Second World War. I will not, however, make the claim that media education originated with media technologies that rose up during this period—broadcast television and computer technology. In tracing the roots of media education, we could easily look back to the origins of the printing press. Pictorial and graphic illustrations in books can be cited as part of a history of media education. Motion picture films were used as educational tools before the rise of television; there is abundant evidence of an explicit, organized media education movement that gave rise to the educational film markets that existed in the United States and Europe well before the Second World War. Professional discussions took place through a transnational society devoted to film education that began publishing its own journal in the 1930s. One could argue that media education's origins coincide with the cinema itself, with the *actualité* films of the mid-1890s. Certainly educational films were a feature of European and American public classrooms well before classrooms were equipped with televisions or computers. Film has been a crucial pedagogical tool in the political and cultural reeducation of illiterate peoples in countries undergoing political revolutions and cultural transformations.

The chapters of *Visual Pedagogy* are grouped in two parts. Part 1 is generally concerned with projects occurring in, or closely linked to, school settings. Part 2 takes as its focus the pedagogical techniques and strategies of media projects in sites outside of formal educational institutions. I have made an attempt to maintain a historical chronology in ordering my examples, but the theoretical orientation of this division has led to some inevitable exceptions. It is important to note that although this book addresses work in film, television, video, and computer-based media, I do not propose a close link between shifts in media and the developments I am considering. As history has shown, the advent of newer electronic media doesn't merely displace and preempt the continued use of older media such as film or radio.

Chapter 1 considers an educational television project carried out by the U.S. government in the South Pacific territory of American Samoa from the early 1960s to the early 1970s, and its relationship to the broader educational television movement engineered by the Ford Foundation on the U.S. mainland. The Samoa educational television initiative is an important but underconsidered moment in the history not only of education but also of broadcast television. It stands as a striking example of government and private-sector collaboration on a project that could be deemed paternalistic media education imperialism. The project also provided the model for later educational public television initiatives by the U.S. cable and broadcast industries (e.g., Educational Television, or ETV; Instructional Television, or ITV; and Networked Educational Television, or NET). The Samoa project, within the history of the Ford Foundation's broader educational television initiatives on the mainland, reveals the crucial connections among education, media, and state power in the postwar period.

The early educational television initiatives led by the Ford Foundation were part of its efforts to foster greater federal involvement in public education. Their ETV projects were an attempt to use technology to alleviate what educators, the government, and the public perceived as a postwar crisis in education—a crisis that was blamed for U.S. inadequacy in the global race for technological, and thus military, superiority during the Cold War. Motivated by this Cold War ideology, the Ford Foundation's vision of television as a tool for reducing school staff needs and standardizing curricula drove the foundation to play a central role in the battle for federal regulation of broadcast television, culminating in the Public Broadcasting Act of 1967.

Educational television became implicated in social regulation and the centralization of authority through overtly pedagogical techniques exercised beyond the boundaries of the educational institution proper. Although the Ford Foundation's efforts to apply media technology to education were largely geared toward increasing efficiency, an indirect outcome was that pedagogical techniques were transported into the public sphere as educational programming was broadcast not only in schools but in public and domestic spaces. Sites previously out of reach of the pedagogical arm of the state (the home, the community center) were transformed into virtual classrooms. Hence the discussion of the Ford Foundation's media education projects is crucial to understanding the pervasive role of media pedagogy beyond schools.

The chapter's main argument is that testing televisual education projects in "remote" sites such as Samoa was crucial to instituting media education as a viable pedagogical approach on the U.S. mainland. Moreover, federal involvement in education policy and federal regulation of the media were parallel developments driven by the country's rapidly changing role in the global economy after the Second World War. These two developments were increasingly harnessed to each other through the intersecting interests of social and economic bodies, including private foundations and government entities. Examining the Samoa project provides insight into how pedagogical authority became central to shifting relationships of power within an increasingly technological and global society.

Chapter 2 examines the place of mass, popular, and subcultural visual media in the classroom. I begin with a review of the extensive literature critiquing popular culture, beginning with the legacy of the Frankfurt School in theories of pedagogy and media literacy. I then turn to more recent theories that propose that popular media is a legitimate source of knowledge and culture, and that students make productive use of popular media texts in their social formation. Finally, I consider whether these latter approaches do in fact provide an adequate model for challenging hierarchies of pedagogical authority. I ultimately suggest that these approaches, though important, provide limited potential for intervention in conventional models of pedagogical authority. The missing link in these approaches is a way of positioning and understanding the student as media producer or author. Media production is an important means of generating student engagement in questions of agency, authority, and knowledge production, and the primary aim here is to advocate for a particular pedagogical approach that maximizes the potential of student media production to address issues of gender, sexuality, and national and cultural identity. Its arguments draw on Stuart Hall's critical observation that cultural identity is a productive and political process equally about imagined futures and imagined pasts—a process that is severely limited when classroom discourse is confined to mainstream broadcast media or media texts that fall within the academic canon.

Chapter 2 thus aims to expand the debates about media pedagogy to include three intersecting projects. The first is to acknowledge the importance of teaching techniques of media analysis in schools. The second is to emphasize the value of popular and subcultural (locally produced, alternative) media in the classroom. The third is to promote the introduction of students to techniques of media production. Central to this chapter is a consideration of the relationship of this overall agenda to the history and development of culturally diverse and inclusive curricula. It advances a theory of media pedagogy that shows the crucial links between a specifically visual pedagogy and the challenge to conventional relations of pedagogical authority in and beyond the classroom.

The latter part of chapter 2 considers the work of a variety of alternative educational media projects set up in and for schools, including the Educational Video Center (New York City), Rise and Shine Productions (New York City), Strategies for Media Literacy (San Francisco), and the Community Television Network (Chicago). These institutions participate in a highly productive institutional border crossing with schools, helping to institute new media pedagogies—a point that is central to the particular cases examined in the next two chapters.

Chapter 3 considers media productions by HIV/AIDS advocacy and social service agencies during the early 1990s. In a sense, these are case studies extending the arguments made in the previous chapter. The focus is videotapes intended for use in the New York City Board of Education's "Children of the Rainbow Curriculum." This was a set of guidelines for creating diverse and inclusive multicultural grade school curricula that included, among other things, safer-sex education guidelines. Proposed in the early 1990s, the Rainbow Curriculum was hotly debated and eventually shelved. I consider how video production and distribution worked with this set of guidelines and helped progressive educators negotiate relationships across institutional borders. These videos brought together like-minded independent media producers, health care service providers, students, educators, and activists in powerful alliances. Like the previous chapter, chapter 3 considers the ways that independent media organizations engage with young people and youth culture at the grassroots level, strategically working with schools to reach youth audiences at their own levels—a theme that will be developed more extensively in chapter 4.

The conflict over the Rainbow Curriculum provides the basis for my consideration of disparate forms of community media intervention in complex pedagogical struggles. Effective pedagogical media strategies must be formulated in relation to particular institutional discourses. In this instance, though, pedagogy is at the center of an extremely broad public debate about authority (over, in this case, children's sexuality and lives). The public crisis about curriculum that ensued from the Rainbow documents occurred because the community recognized that pedagogy is, in the case of sexuality, so clearly also in the hands of authorities who operate outside the school and the family—health educators, community organizers, activists, and so forth. This chapter thus drives home the point, made throughout this book, that the dispersion of pedagogical authority is not always such a bad thing—that is, pedagogical authority can be deployed from a range of social positions to accomplish a range of effects.

In chapter 4, I expand on the discussion about the conjuncture of participatory or peer education and new media technologies in progressive education by analyzing educational video projects and computer programs based on the peer education model. The range of examples extends from in-school peer education participatory video projects, such as those described in chapters 2 and 3, to computer interactives produced by and for youth through nonprofit organizations working in conjunction with, or through funding from, federal, state, and municipal government agencies. These agencies include boards of education and health and welfare entities. I conclude by discussing educational computer programs designed for communities outside the limits of schools, to demonstrate the impact of the peer education model beyond the education system and into other areas, including public health and social welfare.

I continue to expand on the argument in earlier chapters that alternative work with new media in education cannot take place outside institutional boundaries. This work is ideally suited in organizations that exploit their marginal or ambiguous relationship to entities such as schools, government programs, and official education channels. The projects described here exploit the contradictions among their various funders, sponsors, and institutional frameworks, evading oversight and long-held policies in the process. This situation harks back to the discussion in chapter 1 about the foundation of an ambiguous relationship among government, schools, and educational entities—a relationship that has become typical of education broadly conceived in the late twentieth century. Such situations often enable visual media to play a therapeutic role in the classroom, allowing students to work through issues (sex, drugs, violence) more often elided from the curriculum.

Chapter 4 scrutinizes utopian concepts of democratizing knowledge through new media technologies by launching a critical dialogue about the increasingly pervasive presence of instructional technologies in the broader culture. Interactivity, the buzzword of instructional technology discourse, is considered at length. Some advocates of interactivity have argued that this modality is potentially a more democratic, less didactic educational form than the unidirectional instructional broadcast model. I challenge this simple equation of mechanical choice and increased agency in knowledge production in order to propose an understanding of interactivity that is at once more broad and more limited. I suggest that "interactive" media incorporate a range of techniques beyond those that involve mechanical selection. In many instances, television or video can be said to have been made to function "interactively," if we understand interactivity to mean an engagement of the user in the production of knowledge and meaning, and not simply in the mechanics of making "choices."

The programs described in the second half of the chapter—those originating outside schools—have something in common with the museum education programs described in the next chapter. Much of the work covered here is known to me through my experience as curator of an art museum education program from 1994 to 1997.[10]

Chapter 5 considers contemporary museum exhibition technologies as they parallel the local-global nexus of educational television described in chapter 1. The museum, an institution whose emergence is wedded to the rise of the modern Western nation-state, is an exemplar of the historical connection between visual modes of knowledge in Western science and social science, on the one hand, and political rule, on the other. As an institution of the state, the colonial museum traded on both the material spoils of colonial endeavors and the discourses that surrounded these endeavors. This process had its reciprocal form in visually oriented modes of education in the colonial setting (this point is discussed in detail in chapter 6).

The opening of museums to the general public coincided with the institution of public, and eventually mandatory, schooling in the United States. Indeed, in this country, education was a major motivating factor in the development of the public museum and has remained a core, though in many cases understated, element of museum policy. As Tony Bennet, Pierre Bourdieu, and others have shown, the museum has played a major role in the reproduction of classed, gendered, racial, and national identities and communities. Bourdieu emphasizes the contemporary public museum's ability to exclude and include subjects on the basis of class distinction—a function inherited from the institution's royal origins.[11] However well the late capitalist museum maintains its function in the reproduction of upper- and middle-class taste, though, the transformation of many museums into public institutions around the turn of the century entailed the formation of cultural programs meant to encourage the education of a broader audience. As Bennett points out, the nineteenth-century museum was more generally an institution for organizing working-class people around nonthreatening cultural practices.[12]

Although the twentieth-century museum culture explored by Bourdieu and others does function on some level to exclude the working class to reproduce differences of class, race, and sexuality, the dynamic described by Bennett nonetheless remains an important pedagogical agenda of the contemporary museum. "Education of the general public" continues to be a critical disciplinary mandate, especially when it becomes a subtle and implicit agenda in museum policies and structure. This mandate is exemplified in museums' recent attempts to "democratize" and broaden their audiences through large-scale educational curatorial practices (e.g., blockbuster exhibitions). I situate these recent practices in the history of museums' construction of ideologies of national identity among a broad museum-going public. This is an explicitly pedagogical and media-dependent set of practices.

The second nonschool instance of pedagogical authority that I consider is the paternalistic program of media education in colonial and postcolonial West Africa. In chapter 6, I look at the use of documentary and fictional cinema by French colonial forces as means of educating and indoctrinating West African subjects, and the strategic appropriation and transformation of these techniques by postliberation West African directors. Popular and liberation West African cinema may not seem an obvious choice for this book, but these cinemas were grounded in an explicit discourse of visual pedagogy. This discourse extended from nineteenth-century European anthropological and missionary practices in West Africa to the twentieth-century ethnographic documentary. It bore explicit links to Western child development theory—that is, to theories of education and child rearing used widely in Europe and the United States. The basis of a central portion of Western teacher training was also the basis of colonial educational strategies.

Chapter 6 brings full circle the work begun in chapter 1 on the Ford Foundation by taking up once again the relationship among colonial practices, techniques of pedagogical authority, and media culture. Pedagogical techniques traverse disciplinary and national boundaries, and the work here uncovers some surprisingly direct ties between pedagogical theory (theories of child development) and colonial techniques of social discipline (developmental policies and colonial educational programs). This chapter offers the book's most detailed analysis of theories of visual culture and literacy—precisely because these theories "grew up" in joined discourses of colonial and pedagogical authority.

Chapter 7 considers an example of postwar media technology in São Paulo, Brazil, a city that was far from technologically underdeveloped but was nonetheless designated "Third World." Brazil developed a relatively huge television industry despite its lack of development in other areas (education, resources, health, and so on). The chapter focuses on a municipally sponsored collaboration between community-based videographers and mainstream television in São Paulo. This is TV Anhembi, a hybrid political-pedagogical performance and video project that emerged out of the unique political and media landscape of São Paulo in the late 1980s and early 1990s. These years were also pivotal in the formation of a new media pedagogy in the United States. TV Anhembi came into being through an unlikely alliance among local video activists, government agencies, and the mainstream Brazilian television industry. I use the example of TV Anhembi to stress the particularity of the Brazilian media landscape and its various distinct groups.

TV Anhembi also provides a useful comparison or counterpoint to alternative media projects in other regional and national contexts. In light of the reconfiguration and reregulation of communications networks (including the information superhighway and the cable and telephone conglomerates) faced by U.S. community media organizations in the late 1990s, the example of TV Anhembi can help to rethink terms such as "community" and "alternative media."

Why a Transnational Approach to Reading Visual Pedagogy?

The case studies that make up *Visual Pedagogy* focus mainly on U.S. media education and a broad national ideology of media pedagogy. However, the ethos of visual pedagogy did not develop only or primarily in the United States. Examples of it in other countries provide important information and insight into the broader culture of pedagogical media. Moreover, the U.S. media context of the late twentieth century includes examples of transnational, global, and cross-cultural initiatives. A discussion of the role of the United States in forging a global educational mediascape is therefore a necessity. In two of the three non-U.S. based cases I consider, American Samoa and West Africa, the contexts were chosen because they provide instructive examples of the stakes of the United States and France in establishing themselves as benevolent leaders in introducing media technology—and hence knowledge and status in the global market—to underdeveloped regions. Chapter 6 considers U.S. and European education and child development theories that both drew from and informed colonial techniques of education and indoctrination in the 1950s. The instances of colonial and postcolonial pedagogical media that I consider in the first and last chapters of this book, then, underscore the pervasiveness of the visual- and media-based techniques of pedagogical authority that I attempt to theorize. These techniques cannot adequately be considered within their apparent national or institutional boundaries. The third case that is not U.S. based, TV Anhembi in São Paulo, Brazil, was selected because it provides useful insight into the potential for creating a community-based high-tech media education agenda in the Third World through a local and progressive government.

Media Culture and Visual Pedagogy

Audiovisual media have played a pivotal role in the development of pedagogical techniques that have organized and disciplined cultures in and beyond schools.[13] I have noted that visual communication has historically been viewed in a somewhat disparaging light relative to textual reading and writing. Visual literacy has been an inadequate trope for the study of visual culture and media pedagogies because it misidentifies looking and visual modes of knowledge and communication as forms of language and literacy. One does not become "literate" in visual media in anything other than a metaphorical way. The complex and diverse visual modalities that contribute to media cultures require analytical tools and terminology specific to these forms. Jacques Derrida has given us a salient account of the primacy of writing in Western culture.[14] The visual, historically, takes its place alongside oral culture as a signifier of underdevelopment. In chapter 6 I address the low status of the visual in pedagogical theory. The point to be made here is that educational policies and practices of the second half of the twentieth century figured importantly in the emergence of a vaunted public agenda of education through visual media. The museum, the television industry, the cinema, and public health are just a few settings where the visual came into its own as a respected and even a preferred mode of educational representation. Visual media were regarded as practical alternatives in contexts where low literacy levels were seen as a barrier to education (a factor still sorely underestimated in many public education campaigns). But the turn to the visual, especially in the late twentieth century, has been remarkable even in settings where high levels of achievement in writing and reading are assumed to be the norm. The visual has become a modality of choice, not just a fallback strategy. Linked to emergent state-of-the-art media technologies, visual images and graphics increasingly took on a new cachet relative to coveted knowledge and status during the latter half of the twentieth century. To have media literacy in the late twentieth century was to have privileged access to knowledge. *Media* literacy was, by and large, a vaunted form of *visual* literacy.

Public institutions where pedagogical models are at play have been important sites for the formation of new configurations of community and identity, and also new examples of political agency and resistance. The narratives of media use that make up this book help to support this proposition relative to the two more central theses framed earlier: that in the mid-twentieth century the art-media-technology nexus became central to the politics of pedagogy and that, contrary to the bias within the literature, the visual is a positive force in critical pedagogy. Writing and reading occupied a space of privilege in the Western tradition of education and literacy for most of the twentieth century, making these skills key factors in subjects' identity and status relative to community. Images and graphic representation have since become integral aspects of writing and reading (as in hypertext and the rise of digital over analog modes). And images have earned a new status in some educational contexts, becoming a representational mode of choice with nuances well beyond their previous status as illustration—as visual icing on the textual cake. The visual has thus taken on a new importance not only in the scheme of knowledge representation but in the formation of identity and community relative to how knowledge is accessed and lived. We identify with and through the visual (an immediate example is the use of brand logos as identity signifiers); we increasingly experience our everyday lives through media in which visual and sound-based representations predominate. The chapters that follow lay out cases in which communities coalesce around new media, in which populations are organized and disciplined around visual principles, and in which resistance is enacted through new media's cultures of image and sound. In all of these cases, the visual is linked to the new. It breaks from the tradition of the textual, that icon of older educational values. Implicit in the ethos of media pedagogy is an elevation of, and allegiance with, the visual as a way of thinking and a way of organizing life, identity, and community. The visual is a renegade form, but one that, by the twentieth century's end, is elevated to being a paradigm of knowledge of the future.

Pedagogy beyond Schools

The claim that pedagogy is not limited to schooling alone deserves further explanation, especially with respect to the proposition that there exists a pervasive and transinstitutional ethos that can be captured in the term "media pedagogy." Schooling no longer represents an isolated period of life coincident with preparatory learning. Continued learning has become a necessity for maintaining one's place in the hierarchy of the global information economy. An array of approaches to learning is integrated with all aspects of living, from work to entertainment to leisure. It is not surprising that debates in North America, Europe, and England about the human right to education underwent significant changes in the late 1990s relative to the information economy. Viewed in the context of media education, the idea of education as a "right for life" must take on the questions of where entertainment media culture ends and media education begins—what it means when leisure and learning coincide. As education becomes integral to the missions of health care, civic life, and cultural activities (museum going, for example), we begin to see the obsolescence of education in the narrow sense—as something that takes place in schools alone.

Visual Pedagogy, then, is not solely about media per se, or about education narrowly speaking. It begins with the premise that the science of pedagogy is not limited to schools but is enacted across a range of institutions that draw, sometimes tacitly, on educational theories or work in conjunction with schools to produce and regulate subjects and communities. I argue, along with education theorist David Lusted, that pedagogy

> draws attention to the *process* through which knowledge is produced. Pedagogy addresses the "how" questions involved not only in transmission or reproduction of knowledge but also in its production. Indeed, it enables us to question the validity of separating these activities so easily by asking under what conditions and through what means we "come to know." How one teaches . . . becomes inseparable from what is being taught and, crucially, how one learns.[15]

Subjects "come to know" in institutional settings that rely increasingly on media forms to produce knowledge. As the twentieth century progressed, media became an integral part of any discussion about the "how" questions in education. How do we teach? Certainly *with media*. How do media function? Certainly *as modes of pedagogy*. Throughout the intensified globalization of the second half of the twentieth century, media technology made a firm union with the science of pedagogy broadly applied, and this union has come to symbolize technological life in the industrialized nations of late capitalism.

PART ONE

Historicizing New Technologies

in the Classroom

CHAPTER ONE

Media and Global Education

Television's Debut in Classrooms from

Washington, D.C. to American Samoa

In 1961 the popular press (notably *Reader's Digest*) pointed to the impoverished conditions in American Samoa as an example of the hypocrisy of the Kennedy administration's social welfare, foreign aid, and development policies. The administration's relative nonintervention in the indigenous cultural practices of other nations drew particularly sharp criticism.[1] The unincorporated South Pacific territory, ceded to the United States by Samoan chiefs in 1900, was governed under the authority of the U.S. Navy until 1951, when the Department of the Interior took over responsibility. The plight of the islands, according to the *Reader's Digest* article, was the result of sixty years of neglect. Negative media attention to the administration on this issue, it was noted, promised to be exacerbated by the attention that American Samoa would draw as the site of the first meeting of the South Pacific Commission, an organization of representatives from territories and recently or soon-to-be independent nations, in 1962.[2] This publicity, coupled with negative congressional reports about social and economic conditions in American Samoa, spurred the U.S. Congress and the Department of the Interior to seek swift changes in its administration of this small South Seas territory.

In response to the situation, President Kennedy appointed a new governor to the islands, H. Rex Lee, an Idaho-born government officer and farm specialist from the mainland who had established his reputation through his work at the Office of Indian Affairs. Shortly after taking office in Pago Pago, Lee and his staff proposed an educational reform project in American Samoa with the goal of overhauling the nation's entire school system. Their vision was to implement an educational television system based on the newly developed models that Lee had observed in his work on the mainland United States—projects largely sponsored by the Ford Foundation in poor urban neighborhoods of Washington, D.C., New York City, and Philadelphia. Congress and the Department of the Interior endorsed Lee's plan, which led to the construction of a broadcasting system in American Samoa that, in 1964, was the largest educational television infrastructure in the world.[3] The system was designed to serve all students in all grades of the territory's primary and secondary schools.

Framed by its architects as a model program, the Samoan Educational Television Project was a part of a movement to replace traditional teaching with televised broadcast lessons. Educational television (ETV) was one of numerous responses to the highly publicized crisis in U.S. public schools during the 1950s and 1960s—a crisis that included a shortage of qualified teachers, overcrowding of schools, concerns about the quality of education (specifically as a means of supplying the nation's scientific brainpower), and debates about busing in response to the ruling on *Brown v. Board of Education* in 1954. The media-generated shaming of the government for its "neglect" of its unincorporated territory was matched, if not outstripped, by the media's attacks on the nation's inadequate public education system, which, in the early 1950s, was still almost exclusively the domain of state and municipal governments. Following the height of this crisis, the Samoa project marked a turning point in the use of educational technology and the transfer of educational responsibility to the federal government.[4]

The Samoa project followed a decade of rapid growth of ETV projects in urban settings throughout the United States. It was the first attempt to introduce educational television on such a massive scale, as the centerpiece of the wholesale restructuring of schooling. Government adminis-

Typical schoolhouse in Tutuila, American Samoa, circa 1960.

Governor H. Rex Lee puts American Samoa's second of three instructional television channels on air. Government and education officials look on (September 1965).

trators and progressive educators alike embraced the project as a model for improving education in territories, developing nations, and public school systems throughout the United States. The project was immediately followed by the founding of a number of large-scale ETV initiatives in developing nations, most notably in Niger (1964), El Salvador (1967), the Ivory Coast (1971), Brazil (1970), and India (the site of the 1975–1976 Satellite Instructional Television Experiment).[5]

These early experiments in the use of televisual technology in schools to centralize curricula and alleviate teaching loads proved unsuccessful; most of these projects, including the one in Samoa, were dismantled or scaled back by the late 1970s. In subsequent years, television was incorporated into U.S. schools and overseas educational reform projects in much more modest doses and with less regularity, functioning generally as an addition to preexisting print media. The Samoa project, however, does serve as an instructive example of how an ideology linking new technologies and pedagogical reform became pervasive in the later part of the century. The project is an early example of the export of communications technologies and ideologies in overseas institutional settings including education, health, and business—a relationship that would become emblematic of the postwar globalization of U.S. technology that saw its apex in the formation of the Internet.

In this chapter, I examine the social, economic, and institutional forces behind the Samoa ETV project. I consider how nascent communications media became identified as instruments of global discipline and cultural indoctrination. For the United States, federal involvement in education policy and federal regulation of the media were parallel developments driven by the country's rapidly changing role in the global economy after the Second World War. These two developments were increasingly harnessed together through the intersecting interests of social and economic bodies that might otherwise have seemed strange bedfellows—private foundations and government entities, for example. By examining the project, I hope to provide insight into how pedagogical authority became central to relationships of power within an increasingly technological and globalizing society.

The Samoa ETV project was proposed as a solution to an immediate crisis in U.S. diplomacy. It was introduced in part to stave off further bad publicity surrounding the conditions in American Samoa, but more centrally to develop models for improving education on the mainland.

Television teachers recording lesson programs for later broadcast at the Kirwan Educational Television Center, Utulei (1964). Lessons were prerecorded to videotape for later transmission.

Although nominally aimed at improving the image of the influence of the United States on the developing world, the project was a maneuver to promote technological solutions to the widespread educational crisis in public schools. This crisis was understood as potentially threatening to U.S. leadership in relationship to other world powers (most notably the Soviet Union). The Cold War ethos of intellectual leadership, driven by a fear of Soviet technological and scientific superiority, fostered a heightened interest in educational reform. Technological advancement, then, was viewed as both the goal and the method of educational reform.

The Samoa ETV project is a starting point for thinking about how power was conceived and enacted through pedagogical programs within and across national boundaries in the second half of the twentieth century. ETV in Samoa brought about ideological changes not only in the schools but in the broader culture as the technology that made the educational system viable also made possible new patterns of consumption and everyday lifestyle. As one source reports, in El Salvador the introduction of ETV brought about minimal changes in the broader society because television and general services already existed there. In Samoa, educational television represented the first introduction of technology on a broad scale. Electrical appliances began to appear in stores as villages were wired to accommodate the school television system. People changed their lifestyles and recreation habits. Media pedagogy thus was the impetus for the introduction of a Westernized culture of consumption and leisure.[6]

The project received extensive press coverage from its launch in 1962 through 1971, after which changes in the political administration led to a swift reduction in economic support to the program.[7] *Life, Look, Ebony,* and other mainstream magazines ran upbeat stories about the young American teachers who became the first tele-educators on the remote South Pacific island.[8] The project was widely studied and observed by visiting scholars and delegates of educational and political entities. Professional journals such as *American Education* ran features with titles like "TV Goes Way Out and Brings the World to Samoa."[9] Although these articles generally toed the prophetic techno-utopian line of the program's promoters, academic journals and government-sponsored studies debated and closely scrutinized its efficacy and its implications for other, similar projects—particularly on the mainland.

Following its media moment in the 1970s, the project was forgotten. The scant attention it has received since has been limited to a few scholarly essays on education or media, and one book. Armand Mattelart provides what is perhaps the most in-depth critical analysis of the project in his book-length study of multinational corporations. He views the project as an experiment in the indoctrination of Third World peoples into American consumer culture:

> Just as Puerto Rico from 1937 on was converted into a contraceptive testing laboratory where the neo-Malthusian policies reserved by the Empire for the Third World were developed, so Samoa became a guinea pig for the Ford Foundation to study the reactions of an undereducated population to its tele-educational projects. . . . All the conceptions that inspired U.S. research into a model for tele-education for the proletarian nations were revealed by the Samoan project.[10]

Mattelart's analysis of the program is exemplary of a broader late-1970s critique of cultural imperialism of which he was one of the key proponents. This school of thought drew on the Frankfurt school critiques of ideology, suggesting that Third World countries were prey to a form of calculated dominance by Western proponents of global capitalism. In this framework, the Samoa ETV project is an example of the power of nations to control foreign markets through corporate control of social and cultural resources such as education and entertainment. In his short account of the project, Mattelart attributes leadership of the project to the Ford Foundation alone.

His assumption is not only mistaken but allows for a misconception about a crucial and complex relationship among government, private foundations, and professional entities—a relationship that characterized such initiatives in technological development in schools and other social institutions. It is true that until the time of the Samoa project, nearly all U.S.-based work in ETV was done under the auspices of the Ford Foundation. The Samoa project, however, was monitored by the Ford Foundation but carried out by the National Association of Educational Broadcasters (NAEB), under federal contract with Governor Lee. It is clear from documents that appropriations from Congress funded the project; hence the Ford Foundation's financial role is unclear. As a funder of the NAEB, the foundation exercised significant influence on that organization's projects. But records do not tell us whether the foundation's say in this project stemmed from its direct financial support. More significant than the exact economic relationship, however, is the fact that the project illustrates the complex interplay among private foundation, government, and professional cooperation in the postwar development of media pedagogy as a global enterprise.

Mattelart identifies the project as one among many examples of U.S. cultural imperialism following the Second World War. Citing Ford Foundation experts, Mattelart suggests that the program aimed to expose Samoans to modern-day conveniences of consumer culture: washing machines, mopeds, automobiles, and foreign foods. The main object of the ETV project, he suggests, was to break Samoans of their traditional lifestyle and bring them into the fold of the Western market economy. The introduction of modern Western consumer culture may have been one of the achievements claimed by some proponents of the ETV program, and this type of cultural imperialism was undoubtedly an effect of projects like this one. Cultural indoctrination, however, was by no means the central objective of those who masterminded and implemented the Samoa project. In fact, its purported objective of educational reform was unclear with regard to the issue of economic and cultural assimilation. What appears quite significant, in retrospect, is that such a sweeping educational reform initiative was enacted without any unified resolve among the project's authors and educators about what the Samoans should or would gain from this program, much less what benefit would accrue to the United States. Moreover, the motivation for effecting cultural indoctrination was unclear. A typical motivation during this period would have been to create a cultural climate amenable to the introduction of U.S.-mainland goods, services, and industries. Annual reports to the secretary of the interior suggest that American Samoa presented little in the way of economic prospect for U.S. businesses, suggesting that this motivation was minimal, if not absent. The territory remained largely of military strategic interest.

Another explanation for the intense interest in American Samoa as a site for ETV is that the territory provided a convenient "remote test site" for programs that might aid the troubled mainland public school systems. Taking place within a community that was small, isolated, and contained, the project could be instituted and controlled, and its success measured, with relative ease. Moreover, the literature on the project tacitly constructs parallels between the lives of American Samoans and those Americans living in inner-city ghettos on the mainland where similar educational technology systems had been tried. Both groups were poor, technologically underdeveloped, and "remote" in both a geographic and a cultural sense (from the normative perspective of suburban middle-class America). And both groups were experiencing shortages of teachers and teaching supplies. Discourse on educational reform in the United States was, at the time of the Samoa ETV project, closely tied to the understanding of what it meant to be an educated American within the global context. Hence it was not far-fetched for the media to link inhabitants of a territory with disenfranchised citizens of mainland cities.

Education and technology were linked in a Cold War ethos of leadership in a world economy. The education-through-technology of the Samoan people modeled on a microcosmic scale what could also be put into effect in mainland schools, ostensibly to rectify the educational crisis that could make the country lose its hold on world leadership. Paradoxically, a poor, remote, and largely unindustrialized territory marginal to U.S. interests became the test case for technology-linked educational advancement, determining the future use of technology in the industrialized urban communities of the country's central cities.

The Project's Goals and Structure

In 1961 the Senate Committee on Interior and Insular Affairs presented the newly appointed Governor Lee with a complete study of conditions in American Samoa along with recommendations for improving the territory's economic and social conditions. The Samoan school system was described in this report as seriously impoverished and subject to protracted neglect. The United States was spending less than fifty dollars per pupil each year on education in American Samoa, a small percentage of the money spent per pupil on the mainland. Teachers were described as poorly prepared and downright unqualified, testing on the average at the fifth-grade level. The school infrastructure was minimal and outdated. There was enough space in the existing high schools to accept only one-third of the graduates of the territory's primary schools. The committee recommended large appropriations for buildings, teacher training, curricular improvement, equipment, supplies, and other teaching aids, and the extension of universal public education to all children between the ages of six and sixteen. Along with this call for increased resources, and in tune with the policies of the Kennedy administration, the report stressed that changes in the educational system should be attuned to the needs of American Samoans.[11]

Governor Lee used this report to support his own recommendations, which included the institution of an educational television system. Lee had observed this sort of system on the mainland. (It can be inferred that he had encountered prior Ford Foundation experiments.) Lee secured $40,000 from Congress to conduct a feasibility study for the use of educational television in Samoa's schools. The study, conducted by the NAEB under the leadership of Vernon Bronson, proposed to use television as a rapid and economical means of upgrading teaching standards and unifying curriculum. More than a program for integrating television into an existing structure, the plan called for a complete overhaul of the school system. Redesigning, rebuilding, and restaffing the schools around the use of television was central to the entire proposed curriculum. It was a large-scale project that would encompass all public schools and extend education to all children ages six to sixteen.

One of the key arguments for the plan was that it would allow for the upgrading of the educational system with a minimum of personnel imported from outside Samoa. Lee, the NAEB, and others suggested that

Classroom equipped for instructional television, American Samoa.

the most viable alternative plan for rapid reform would be to bring in a large corps of better-trained teachers to replace the current Samoan faculty. His plan, however, favored introducing a smaller group of imported teachers to serve as tele-educators. They would work out of a Samoa central broadcasting system, providing the core content of the curriculum, while other teachers (indigenous Samoans) staffed classrooms in remote villages, overseeing the televised lessons in the classrooms and providing follow-up exercises. The tele-educators, initially imported from mainland U.S. schools, would gradually be replaced by their Samoan counterparts. A $1.5 million centralized broadcast facility was set up with the primary aim of facilitating this process. It included six channels and two-way radio capability. The channels were dedicated to programming lessons for classrooms throughout the day and switched over to adult education in the evening. There was no entertainment programming on the side. The bulk of the core curriculum for all grades was televised; this took up about one-third of each school day.

There were clearly economic motives for the implementation of ETV in Samoa: Televised lessons were conceived as a means of quickly unifying the curriculum across the island and providing in-service training to Samoan educators. But Lee's decision to use television to make a more localized and centralized educational program (by bringing in fewer non-Samoan professionals and standardizing the program) was a political as much as an economic move. His thinking was in line with U.S. policies geared toward preparing Samoans for self-governance and self-sufficiency. Beyond being economical and efficient, the television system presented a unique means of achieving the government's mandate of tailoring education to Samoan needs.

The system made it possible rapidly to replace the outdated textbooks developed for U.S. populations and used around the island with locally produced broadcast lessons and mimeographed worksheets.[12] This change was not without its progressive effects: because they were locally determined, lessons became more in tune with indigenous concerns and ways of knowing. Media commentary emphasized this benefit. Moreover, the system allowed for more flexibility and interactivity than the textbooks had afforded. Unlike the more static conventional texts, television instruction was produced and consumed in a continuous flow that could easily be interrupted, modified, and updated in response to what was happening in classrooms.

It is difficult to evaluate the perception of this educational system by Samoans and the effects of this attunement to culturally specific knowledge on life in Samoa; reports from the island are mediated through the U.S. press and Western professional journals. Nonetheless there is some evidence that the system did enact, even if tacitly, progressive ideas about culturally specific education that are the cornerstone of contemporary liberal education theories today—theories discussed at length in later chapters. One clear benefit is that teachers imported from the mainland were eventually replaced by Samoans. Many of the progressive ideals tacitly embodied in the project, as we shall see in later chapters, also link community-based education to new technology use. For now, I want to focus on the issue of cultural indoctrination raised by Mattelart.

Mixing Oil and Water: Assimilationist and Preservationist Policies in Postwar American Samoa

Teachers may have been Samoan, but what of U.S. ideology had they taken on in adopting U.S. technologies? There is strong evidence that defining the needs of Samoans was at the heart of a protracted crisis in U.S. colonial education in Samoa. How did these new technologies aid in the process of U.S. cultural indoctrination as a means to self-sufficiency in a global context? Defining a culture's needs in terms of a need for technology and for communications in a globalizing world economy was a classic strategy in the transition out of colonial rule and into paternalistic oversight. But cultural indoctrination cannot completely explain the situation in postwar American Samoa. Ideas like self-government and the preservation of indigenous culture are not fully subsumed within assimilation.

What was meant by "self-government" is not made clear in the planning documents and evaluation reports relating to the Samoa ETV project. What is clear is that neither the paternalistic model of assimilation nor a hands-off policy dominated. The certain failure of colonialism created a situation for colonial powers in which the value and efficacy of assimilationist policies had to come into question if influence was to be maintained in former colonies and existing territories. The relationship of the United States to its possessions during the 1960s and 1970s was one of denial and ambiguity—denial that they were even colonies as such, and ambiguity with regard to what exactly these territories were. What resulted, for territories like American Samoa and Puerto Rico, was a perpetual state of decolonization that has yet to resolve itself in the first decade of the twenty-first century as the statehood and independence debates in Puerto Rico continue. The concept of self-governance implicit in the Samoa project documents included the idea that Samoans must acquire knowledge of the West, and the directive that they should develop a more in-depth awareness of Samoan ways of knowing, culture, and values. In other words, the process of perpetual decolonization involved an acceptance on the part of U.S. personnel of hybridization and creolization—or a mixing of assimilation and essentialism. Acceptance of indigenous Samoan culture was not motivated solely by benevolence: the United States stood to benefit from the otherness of its unincorporated territories. By providing enough cultural space to forestall outright resistance to U.S. paternalism, the United States has been able to maintain power over (and strategic military sites in) both Samoa and Puerto Rico. To a large degree, the conflict in creating an educational policy hinged on whether officials in charge of the educational program could productively negotiate the relationship between modernization and economic development (assimilation), on the one hand, and cultural authenticity, on the other. In an insightful essay on U.S. colonial educational policy in

Samoa produced at the tail end of the Samoa project, educator Edward Beauchamp wrote:

> There has never been a rationally designed, consistent American policy toward American Samoa. Since 1900, American policies, particularly educational policies, have been noted for their contradictory nature and their singular lack of success. This is not to charge that American rule in Samoa has not been well-intentioned, but only that absence of a well-defined and consistent policy has resulted in seventy-five years of starts and stops, new policies tending to follow each governor, and not infrequently completely contradictory objectives being sought simultaneously.[13]

Beauchamp points out that the Samoan educational system was always rife with contradiction, especially with respect to policy on assimilation of Samoans into American ways of life. This failure of assimilation in particular, Beauchamp argues, should be understood as a failing of the U.S. government, resulting from its lack of clarity with respect to the status of its territorial possessions. Samoans, like Puerto Ricans, are nationals but not citizens of the United States. Unincorporated territories thus occupy a position in limbo between colony and statehood. Beauchamp's insightful history of educational policy in American Samoa underscores the ideological gymnastics that U.S. administrations have performed to maintain the appearance of a benevolent world power in relationship to these possessions. Among the abundant evidence of inconsistent and strained educational policy on the island, Beauchamp picks out two goals of a 1938 Department of Education report to illustrate this familiar contradiction:

> 1. To give all children of American Samoa an elementary education in the English language, which will open them to the vast field of knowledge which the Samoan language at present cannot and perhaps never will touch, and
> 2. to make them increasingly conscious and proud of their Samoan heritage of arts, crafts, customs and culture, in the hopes that these may not disintegrate under the influence of increasing contact with the world beyond them. (25)

The tension in educational policy between preservationist and assimilationist approaches described in this document of 1938 was still in place when Beauchamp presented his critique nearly four decades later. He convincingly argues that American policy on the island has reflected persistent denial of its colonial rule and abnegation of its pedagogical authority. Yet he concludes that the United States must now decide on a unified policy. His recommendation is clear: Given what seems to be the inevitable dissolution of traditional ways of life in the face of Americanization through economic pressures, it would be best for the Samoans if the United States pursued an active process of Americanization through its educational initiatives. "In this the United States will have at last arrived at a colonial policy which is recognizable and logically consistent with the reality of the colonial situation" (28).

What Beauchamp fails to see is that a colonial policy is not appropriate to the postwar period and that, moreover, ambiguity of U.S. educational approaches in Samoa was precisely the sort of neocolonial policy that the United States needed to maintain its hold on Samoa. It was a policy that effectively allowed the United States to maintain some form of rule through its unique combination of allowance for local autonomy with provision of select means of assimilation.

Although Beauchamp does not cite the ETV project specifically, his critique comes more than a decade after it was first implemented. Designed to overturn sixty years of neglect, the project nonetheless manifests many of the same contradictory goals with respect to assimilation that Beauchamp and others have blamed for the continued failure of U.S. educational policy. Proponents of the project issued strong statements about the need to reform the educational system so as to bring it in line with the Samoan way of life alongside statements championing the introduction of English (which was a primary goal of the project) and the exposure of students to Western technology. The latter goals are those cited by Mattelart to support his thesis of cultural indoctrination. But the former statements—those emphasizing support of indigenous culture, as well as the project's clear commitment to teaching in the Samoan language for a fair portion of the school day—cannot be disregarded. The NAEB's initial recommendations for the ETV project, for example, authored by Vernon Bronson, indicated that one of the clear shortcomings of the system in place before the ETV project was its insensitivity to Samoan culture and traditions. Bronson emphasized that in the new system, "every effort should be made to fit the curriculum to Samoan experience and needs, and illustrations from Samoan life should be substituted for the illustrations from United States suburban life typically found in the cast-off text books then in use. . . . The prohibition of the Samoan language in the classroom should be eliminated and first reading should be in Samoan."[14]

In some respects, the policies suggested for American Samoa paralleled those implemented by governments of newly independent nations following the widespread decolonization of Third World countries after the Second World War. As I show in chapter 6, which discusses film pedagogy in West Africa, governmental support of modernization in previously colonized West African nations was accompanied by efforts to preserve indigenous language and cultural traditions as key elements of national identity. The negritude movement is an example of this approach. The simultaneous embrace of these contradictory and seemingly incompatible policies forged the conditions of creolization or hybridity that have become characteristic of postcolonial societies. Beauchamp wrote from the standpoint of a modernist framework that saw pure assimilation as the means to maintaining colonial power, overlooking the more complex power relations between the previous colonial rulers and the emergent postcolonial nation-state. This relationship featured the legacy of education as a means to the former colonizer's maintenance of influence. Beauchamp's alternative rests on a nostalgic view of colonial paternalism that holds "the United States cannot have it both ways in American Samoa; either we preserve the traditional values and culture (and all that that implies), or we encourage the substitution of modern, technological values."[15]

Beauchamp's criticism of "U.S. neglect of Samoa" stems from his assumption that the United States should still rightly occupy the role of colonizer—or not: "Like oil and water," he argues, "the traditional and the modern do not mix well, and it is a fraud to tell the Samoans that they can have both the *Matai* system and a competitive, free-enterprise economy."[16] The contradictory policies Beauchamp described, which were maintained for three-quarters of a century, might be said to form the basis of an administration in search of precisely that mix of oil and water.

The Samoa ETV project was marked by an increase in ambivalence with respect to assimilation, an ambivalence that had existed to some extent during the colonial period. Tied to the introduction of the project was the lifting of a ban on teaching native Samoan in schools. Classes in the lower grades were taught primarily in Samoan. The project emphasized English acquisition in the later grades, and included lessons geared toward exposing Samoans to Western economic and cultural forms, but also included continued instruction in the native Samoan language.

Mattelart's portrayal of the program as an experiment in cultural assimilation is certainly overstated. By emphasizing the assimilationist side of the curriculum, he describes the Samoa project as putting into effect exactly the plan Beauchamp proposes for U.S. educational policy: outright cultural indoctrination. But the ideological forces and institutional structures that came together to make the project a reality were not unified in their position regarding this matter. Politicians, educators, and the Samoan population all demonstrated ambivalence regarding the benefits of indoctrination into American culture and economy.

In the 1990s, theorists of global media have presented a more nuanced view of transnational mechanisms of cultural domination. Mattelart himself more recently suggests that it is no longer possible to maintain the argument that power is centralized through either the nation or multinational corporate entities: "The era of information society and industry is also (when we look beyond the myopic gaze of its prophets) the production of mental states, the colonization of the mind."[17] He maintains a critique of the consolidation of power through transnational flows of information, suggesting that it is no longer possible to envision that process as the colonization of the world by a single nation-state or even a unified class. Cultural indoctrination (Mattelart's concept of "colonization of the mind") is figured as a process of hybridization rather than homogenization or assimilation. The mechanisms of domination and acculturation lead to the creation of new cultural forms as Western products and ideologies are appropriated and transformed by Third World peoples. Mattelart quotes Arjun Appadurai:

> The globalization of culture is not the same as its homogenization, but globalization involves the use of a variety of instruments of homogenization (armaments, advertising techniques, language hegemonies, and clothing styles) which are absorbed into local political and cultural economies, only to be repatriated as heterogeneous dialogues of national sovereignty, free enterprise and fundamentalism in which the state plays an increasingly delicate role.[18]

The seemingly contradictory educational objectives taken on in the Samoa ETV project reflect the disorder that accompanies this logic of cultural hybridization. The project proclaimed its goal as maintaining Samoan cultural identity at the same time that it stressed "competence in a world language" as "a doorway to understanding."[19] The teaching of English was understood as a tool for Samoan self-governance, a goal not necessarily at odds with maintaining a separate Samoan identity.

Earlier in this chapter, I claimed that the most significant issue at stake in the Samoa project was not cultural indoctrination per se but the project's status as a model for U.S. educational technology on the mainland. Let me clarify my claim before providing substantive evidence for it. I have described Samoa's status as one of model or test site, and this in particular deserves some clarification. For officials like Lee, Samoa seemed to provide a field of least resistance, and as such an optimal representative showpiece, for a national technology that had met with resistance in the troubled schools on the mainland where it had been tried. Success in Samoa would be judged by its media representation as a model school, not its success within the broader context of Samoan society. The territory seemed a perfect opportunity for providing a shining representation of American primacy in educational technology, thereby establishing the United States as a world leader in education without risking the turbulence encountered in the educational system on the mainland. By "world leader," I mean not just that the U.S. domestic education system could outshine that of the Soviet Union, for example, but that the United States could emerge as a leader in the global economy of education—including, and indeed featuring, educational techniques involving advanced military technologies such as television. The Sputnik crisis is emblematic of an era in which American education became a world politics issue, not just a domestic affair. This is true in at least two senses: The status of the U.S. educational system as having implications for the education of citizens of the world was explicitly linked to the country's ability to maintain its place as a world power, and the education of U.S. citizens was seen as vital to the production of a workforce with the skills, knowledge, and technological prowess to maintain the country's status as a world power. In both senses, world domination involved a mix of education and technology. By the end of the 1950s, "technology" and "brainpower" had become intricately linked terms that characterized the advanced educational policies of the era to come—a concept that lingers into the twenty-first century.

The Samoa ETV Project as a "Trip to the Possible"

The ambiguous status of Samoa as part of the United States, but marginal to it geographically, culturally, and economically—indeed, its image as remote in every way—made the region an alluring site for fantasies of what new educational technologies could do if unencumbered by the considerable problems of the mainland educational system. Samoa was portrayed by the project's enthusiasts as a kind of tabula rasa, an ideological vacuum owing to the absence of a recognized educational policy and its relative isolation. It stood ready to be filled by something new and different. I quote from Lewis Rhodes, an educator who drove this point home quite clearly in an essay tellingly titled "A Trip to the Possible":

> Sitting geographically protected 8,000 miles from the violent conditions eroding the structures of American education, the school system of the unincorporated territory of American Samoa recently provided the opportunity for a group of America's top school administrators to see in operation a system of education that effectively employs many of the principles of comprehensive change that are still only being discussed back home.[20]

The isolation and size of the island suggested ease of implementation across an entire educational system, and ease of monitoring. The latter point is crucial: evaluation of the project for possible use elsewhere required controlled studies of its effects across a given, traceable population. A geographically contained and isolated population made this task easier. The monitoring of the press's response to the project could similarly be controlled. Visiting reporters, educators, and scholars would be flown in and escorted as if through an island amusement park of sorts, allowing careful planning of photo opportunities and demonstrations. And indeed, a view of Samoa as an idyllic vacation resort for educators is repeated throughout press coverage of the project, as in the following passage from an article about "a barefoot teacher from Oklahoma" in Samoa: "Two Oklahoma winters ago, Dolores 'Dee' Tidwell was just another low-paid teacher—a single woman raising an adopted child on

$4,500 a year. Now she winters in warm Samoa, a barefoot principal with double the salary."[21]

Beginning in the late 1960s, teams of school superintendents, the head of the Department of the Interior, and scores of other professionals were flown into Samoa by Bronson to view and attend meetings about the project. Articles about their trips draw heavily on the tropes of exotic travel and idyllic paradise lands. This view of Samoans as outside culture is expressed by Norma Anderson, a tele-educator who taught math on public television in New York City. Anderson was recruited by Bronson to work in Samoa. Identified as a black woman, her experience is described in *Ebony* as follows: "Although there are many races represented on the islands, Norma has yet to encounter racial prejudice. She has noticed, however, that some Samoans have accepted her somewhat more quickly than they have *Palagis* or Caucasians. 'They think I am from Fiji or the Tonga Islands,' she says. 'They know so little about the outside world.' "[22]

The view that "they know so little of the outside world" was essential to the establishment of Samoa as a logical follow-up to projects such as the one in which Anderson had participated in New York City, where Norma presumably encountered the racial prejudice she did not experience on the island. Those visitors to the Samoa project familiar with the messy and large grade school tele-education projects in urban areas fraught with racial tension must have appreciated the fantasy of isolation and control that came with rebuilding an entire educational system from scratch. They clearly appreciated working among people unexposed to the cultural battles raging in "the outside world." A chief aspect of this fantasy was the ability of the project to elide the historical relationship of discrimination against blacks by whites in place on the mainland. This relationship came to the fore in mainland school systems during the years of the Civil Rights movement and was being negotiated in the very schools the Samoa educators had escaped. Power struggles between Samoans and mainland educators were marked neither by the same political urgency nor by the same degree of self-conscious struggle over rights and authority among the Samoans—or so the Western report would have it.

The project must also have seemed idyllic to the government. Plagued by humiliation by the press for its "neglect" of the territory, and its education system in particular, it is not surprising that Congress and the Department of the Interior embraced Lee's proposal and the media coverage that ensued from it. As it was probably the only project on the table to address the exact predicament publicized by the press, one can only imagine the relief with which Lee's plan must have been viewed by officials anxious to change the image of the United States as neglectful patron. The project was certainly a "trip to the possible" for the government in the sense that it provided one means of building up the country's postwar stature as benevolent leader in developing regions.

The response of Samoans to the project is grossly underreported. One source, however, does chronicle the experience of a Samoan educator involved in the project, the sole book-length documentation of the project of which a Samoan educator, Mere T. Betham, is the third of three authors listed. The authors write that the school system prior to the Samoa project appeared to have been "neglected, backward, and very much in need of change."[23] The Samoan public system, preceded by missionary schools, got started in 1921 and reached its prewar apex in 1943 with forty-six schools, only two of which went beyond the fourth grade. This system was undermined during the war. When the ETV system was proposed, education took place in small, unadministered village schools where students learned from textbooks discarded from the mainland about urban issues and concerns far from those of the Samoan subject. Betham is quoted recounting the positive experiences offered in the old system—the teaching of arts and crafts skills and banana planting, the individual and personalized attention teachers gave to their students before the institution of the television as lead teacher. According to this tele-educator's memories, the pre-TV Samoan school was a warm and happy place (23–25).

Betham and her coauthors recount that with the institution of the new system, familiar patterns were broken as new *palagi* (mainland) teachers and principals arrived from the mainland to train indigenous teachers on limited two-year contracts, and the television dictated the pace of lessons. One of the palagi teachers involved in the project recalled the televisual regimentation of lesson duration and flow. There was never time to finish an individual experience or linger with a topic when a student needed more time, she explained. "The TV just kept coming!" (71). Clearly it was not just students who were regimented by the standardized flow of the lesson plan; teachers were also subject to the disciplining temporality of the medium. Indeed, it was the training of the teachers that was most essential to the success of the system.

The authors of the volume on the Samoa project indicate that enthusiasm declined among participants for multiple reasons. The sporadic presence of administrators such as Vernon Bronson from the mainland and the changing cycle of mainland teachers generated resentment. The project was implemented in schools except the one institution that serviced the Stateside population on Samoa. In other words, the one school attended by U.S. mainland citizens and catering to the college-bound Samoan population was exempt from the program, underscoring its remedial and social-control orientation (a theme already rife in the limited world of ETV). This two-tiered system understandably generated resentment and lack of compliance. Grumbling about the regimentation of the curriculum by teachers, it is suggested, gave students the sense that it was OK to resent the television as teacher. One educator is cited as stating that if the system had not been so unbendingly rigid, and if local teachers had been given more say and control over the television flow, the system might have survived. Pulled from the high schools where teachers (reported to have higher levels of education) objected most forcefully, the system was eventually shut down entirely (73).

But this was not before the system had instituted change in Samoan culture islandwide. Before the introduction of the ETV project, Samoa lacked television and electricity. Towns had to be wired for service. This resulted in an influx of technologies and media beyond the ETV system. The introduction of ETV brought about changes in everyday life and, most significantly, in patterns of consumption and leisure. The question of ideological inculcation was clearly not limited to schooling but extended to the technologies and practices made possible indirectly by the introduction of technologies for the new school system. Media pedagogy was the impetus for Samoa's entry into the global market as consumers of the goods and services offered to the industrialized West.

One of the most obvious services introduced through the ETV system was home television. From the system's beginning, it offered home television service. *The Mickey Mouse Club, Bonanza, and Hawaiian Eye* were standard fare, peppered with a few examples of local informational and educational programming in the project's early years. Television in Samoa remained within the Department of Education, shifting over to the Samoan government for a brief period after the demise of the project. It then became a commercial enterprise entirely before the close of the decade. By 1976, there were about 3,800 televisions on the island, or one for every eighty people. This startling turnaround is largely attributable to the ETV initiative.[24] One study reports that over the period of a few years during which American Samoan youth were exposed to television, they became less conservative, less enamored of success, less inclined to respect authority and value family, and more competitive than their Western Samoan peers who did not have access to television. Media pedagogy was clearly at work beyond the schools (165–69).

In order better to understand where the Samoa project fit into the larger picture of U.S. educational technology, it is necessary to consider the project's economic and practical structure in relation to the general place of education in national policy. We also need to consider the urban mainland programs that preceded it. The use of television as an agent of school reform was not a new idea in the early 1960s. Numerous pilot projects had been carried out throughout the United States, largely under the auspices of organizations and agencies set up and funded by the Ford Foundation and the Carnegie Institute. In the following two sections, I describe the general scene in which these projects emerged, and some of the mainland predecessors and parallels to the Samoa project.

"One Great ETV Station Shining like a Beacon": The Education and Technology Race

If Mattelart's 1970s assessment of the Samoa project as a pilot for cultural imperialism is reductive with respect to the reality of educational initiatives in the Third World, it also falls short of analyzing the meaning of the project within the larger context of struggles over education and communications technology on the U.S. mainland. Mattelart frames the Samoa project as one of three major pilot ETV projects launched by the Ford Foundation (the other two projects referred to were in Hagerstown, a Washington, D.C., suburb; and New York City's Chelsea). Unlike these privately funded ETV projects, the Samoa project was actually a federal initiative, implemented by a congressional vote, funded through U.S. budgetary appropriations, and administered by the government. Authority over the program, however, was almost entirely ceded to the NAEB, a longtime Ford Foundation affiliate and recipient of Ford funding. The NAEB was contracted to carry out the program, and it maintained almost complete control over the restructuring of the school system in Samoa. Its work included the hiring of principals, teachers, and technicians. The scale of previous and continued funding of the NAEB by the Ford Foundation, along with its close administrative ties to the organization, suggests that the NAEB was only semiautonomous from the foundation. As one account explains, this relationship is crucial because it established the NAEB as a key player in the nascent field of educational technology:

> The NAEB was used initially to encourage the development of a network and, as a lobbying force, to handle matters vis-à-vis the FCC. Before the Ford grant, the NAEB had been an impoverished and practically defunct group of early advocates of educational television; as a result of the influx of more than $640,000 in the four-year period 1951–1955, the NAEB had become the trade organization for the industry, perhaps its most powerful lobbyist in Washington.[25]

The first project of its kind on such a large scale, the Samoa project marked a transition in the role of the Ford Foundation as well as the NAEB. For one, the project signaled that the foundation had gained a foothold in national policy issues. The Samoa project was tied, even if indirectly, to Ford initiatives to promote centralized federal education policies and the development of a national public television network. Indeed, in perusing the documents devoted to each of these areas, it becomes difficult to discern where the government leaves off and Ford begins in policy decisions, funding, and management.

Ford's involvement in these "federal" matters of culture and education dates from the beginning of the 1950s. By far the largest foundation in the United States, the Ford Foundation began spearheading efforts to shape public educational policy in 1951, when it established the Fund for the Advancement of Education and the Fund for Adult Education. The scale of the foundation's efforts during the fifties and early sixties was enormous. The foundation spent hundreds of millions of dollars in this area.[26] And the effects of its initiatives were remarkable: within the first half decade, the Fund for Adult Education had used its financial leverage to set up or take control of a half-dozen influential trade, lobbying, and citizens organizations dedicated to the cause of educational television.

Through these organizations, they were able to unite disparate constituencies, from academics to grassroots groups opposed to the representation of violence on commercial television. Their efforts had helped to influence the Federal Communications Commission (FCC) to set aside frequency allocations for 242 educational stations, and by 1954 the foundation had spent $3.5 million on the construction of at least 35 educational stations throughout the United States.

The Fund for the Advancement of Education was more directly involved in developing school-based applications of educational television. In 1957 the fund published a report by Alexander Stoddard, titled *Schools for Tomorrow,* which laid out the foundation's arguments for the use of television in schools. Stoddard stressed the teaching of very large classes to alleviate classroom crowding and limit numbers of teaching positions needed. He also argued that broadcast lessons would bring a wider range of subject matter and a higher caliber of teaching to remote and rural schools. The report was presented to superintendents of districts throughout the country to solicit their cooperation in pilot teaching projects as part of Ford's national program. Based on this effort, the foundation funded modestly sized experiments with the introduction of ETV in more than eight hundred primary and secondary schools in municipalities throughout the United States, along with several more comprehensive studies. Approximately 200,000 students were involved in these projects. Along the lines suggested in *Schools for Tomorrow,* almost all of these projects employed television to reach exceptionally large classes: up to 175 in elementary classes, and from 200 to 500 in junior and senior high schools.[27]

Among the comprehensive projects that encompassed entire districts, municipalities, or schools dispersed across entire states, the closed-circuit television projects in Hagerstown, Maryland, and in the Chelsea district of New York City stand out as the most significant precursors to the Samoa project. In these cases, unlike in Samoa, closed-circuit television was chosen over broadcast. This decision was determined on the basis of limited available licensed bandwidth—an obstacle that did not exist in Samoa and that the Ford Foundation was busy trying to overcome through the efforts of the Fund for Adult Education.

The Hagerstown project began in 1956 and was funded by the foundation through 1961, when it was taken over by the state board of education. It actually served a larger student population than the Samoa project (21,000, as compared with 10,000), though with fewer televised hours of instruction per capita. Hagerstown was selected as a district representative of severe teacher shortages throughout the United States and the world. The main goal of the project was to use centrally broadcast programming to increase the student-teacher ratio. As in Samoa, exemplary teachers were selected to serve as tele-educators. Lessons were broadcast to classrooms in both rural and urban areas of the county. In many cases, the programming was viewed in auditoriums housing hundreds of students, who were then split into ordinary classroom-size groups for follow-up instruction. Touted features of the system were standardization of instruction and the evening out of disparities between regions with differing resources and staff, as noted in evaluations of the program by the Hagerstown officials: "Television has become a pacing device, a means whereby all students at a given grade level receive the same basic amount of instruction in a given subject area, regardless of school size or composition of teaching staff."[28]

The questionable benefits of standardization aside, the immediate goal of the project was to alleviate an expanding school population accompanied by a paucity of adequately trained educators. The production-oriented ethos of the project comes across strongly in the official's statement of enthusiasm about its efficient use of capital: "In the words of one high school principal, television has made it possible to house an excess of students in buildings originally intended for smaller numbers; e.g., one high school now serves 2,250 students in a plant built for 1,500."[29]

On the whole, the project proved cost-effective, and according to evaluation reports, student test scores rose significantly with its implementation. One of the most significant conclusions of the evaluations of the Hagerstown project, however, was that television instruction was most effective in limited doses, and that it should not take up a major portion of any pupil's school day—an insight not taken up in planning the Samoa project.

The Chelsea project, which was undertaken in 1957, was an experiment in consolidating the in-school and broader community use of educational television. It was the first project aimed directly at an ethnic inner-city population, and it was also explicit in its orientation toward community social work and therapy. The community served by the district was made up of fairly equal numbers of poor and working-class

Latino (largely Puerto Rican), black, and Euro-American residents. In the words of the foundation's own evaluations, the project was "a means of meeting the challenge of the small urban area containing a high concentration of people with hard-core educational or cultural problems." Use of television in the schools extended beyond consolidation of curriculum to include teacher training, examinations, and administrative functions. Programming for the community, which was a component of the project, was conceived as "an instrument for the development of community leaders, and . . . as a form of psychotherapy."[30]

An important shift was taking place with regard to federal intervention in U.S. educational policy during these years. From the nation's founding until the 1950s, educational policy had been the largely unchallenged province of state governments. The push toward national intervention in what was perceived as a crisis in education began in the years immediately following the Second World War. Developing communications technologies became both the central impetus and the vehicle for consolidating pedagogical authority at the national level by mid-century. The goal of remaining competitive, if not dominant, in an increasingly global culture was the cornerstone of arguments for shifting power over education from the local and state governments to the federal level. The struggle for a technological edge in the Cold War provided pedagogically based justifications for centralizing authority. Technological competitiveness with the Soviets thus contributed to the mandate for a national educational policy; the space race was paralleled by a race for superiority in national education standards, a race in which using technology was also a crucial factor.

Through this linking of technology to better education emerged a rationale for federal regulation of the media and partial ownership of television bandwidth at precisely the moment when television was emerging as a major national interest, and hence a major market and industry. The hard-won battle over regulation and bandwidth pitted the government and foundations (along with grassroots advocates of educational television) against the major networks, who struggled for corporate self-determination. The latter had steadfastly fought against any form of national or public ownership of the broadcast spectrum since the advent of the medium's commercial viability in the 1940s.[31] Federal regulation, even in the name of education, was anathema to the industry; it smacked of communism.

The image of educational technology as a weapon of national defense was widespread by the early 1960s. When in July 1961 the Soviet Union attempted to seal off East Berlin, John White, president of the National Educational Television Network, wrote to President Kennedy: "As the nation makes plans for its defense . . . the facilities of the educational television stations are an important national asset, ready to play an important role in conveying information to youngsters in school and adults at home, as well as for training of specific civilian groups."[32] A true national education network did not yet exist (individual stations were not wired together like the major network station affiliates). White's rhetoric nonetheless suggests a fantasy of a tele-educational system that could be transformed in an instant into a wartime command unit—an idea that would soon see more direct manifestation in the founding of the Internet through government research and development initiatives.

Efficiency was another aspect of the introduction of television as a pedagogical tool serving a larger national agenda. During the 1950s and 1960s, the promotion of efficient schools was one of the Ford Foundation's principal concerns. This agenda was carried out through numerous projects with two general objectives: the introduction of new administrative and managerial schemes, and the automation of education through the introduction of new technologies. These two directions bore the mark of Henry Ford, the technocrat who was still quite involved with the foundation's policy decisions. Thus it is not surprising that automation and the division of labor that had brought success to the Ford Motor Company and the mogul's other businesses would also form the basis of the foundation's panacea for a national educational crisis.[33] Ford's initial image of ETV as a centralized entity—undoubtedly with Ford at its core—is unmistakably clear in the foundation's published vision of "one great ETV station, shining like a beacon over the country to show the light to others."[34]

In keeping with this ethos of centralization and efficiency, the Ford Foundation was also highly involved in the development and institution of national standardized testing—a goal shared with its close collaborator, the Carnegie Institute. The institution of standardized tests was in line with the foundation's general push for centralized control of education. The push for centralized national educational policies was thus linked to the techniques of standardization and automation.

Why automate education in the late 1950s? Fordism and the related industrial philosophy of Taylorism are more typically associated with the interwar period, during which U.S. industry expanded its sites and increased production through design and labor efficiency programs involving industrial technologies. Education was faced with particular demands and crises in the 1950s—needs that made the familiar practice of automation seem a logical move at that moment.

This situation of demands and crises merits some description. At the beginning of the 1950s, it had become apparent to educators and politicians that the United States was facing a national shortage of teachers. It was widely understood that this shortage was symptomatic of a broader educational crisis that would require more than stepped-up recruitment or educator training. Against a backdrop of internal and external threats to the system, educators and politicians began to paint a picture of imminent decline—an image in which young people were depicted as an endangered national resource. Social unrest and the much-publicized image of urban American violence were increasingly tied to images of youthful delinquency and resistance to authority in civil rights and student demonstrations. The political unrest and racial tension that marked the civil rights movement were conceived by many as a problem that was fundamentally pedagogical in nature. The Elementary and Secondary Education Act of 1965, the legislative expression of this increasingly dominant train of thought, dedicated significant national funding to the so-called educationally disadvantaged.[35] The act can be read in part as a means of bringing under control potentially "rebellious" sectors of the populace (most notably the emergent underclass) through education.

Fueled by a concern that the Soviet Union was gaining strategic advantage in the areas of science and technology, pressure mounted on the Eisenhower administration to institute a national education policy. This reached a peak when media coverage of the Soviet launching of the Sputnik satellite in 1957 ignited a rash of public debate about why the United States was falling behind in the space race and losing the Cold War. Sputnik became a symbol of imminent U.S. scientific and technological inadequacy. Sputnik itself had no functional military capabilities, but it was harnessed to a missile launching system that signaled the ability of intercontinental striking capability. Sputnik's combination of technologies that merged civilian and military objectives made it a particularly apt icon for linking education, communications technologies, and military superiority.[36]

The rallying cry for educational reform following the announcement of the Sputnik launch was enormous. Famous figures from all sectors of society spoke out as authorities on educational change. Critical appraisal of the U.S. educational system had been widespread throughout the 1950s, but the media portrayal of the crisis framed the problem in a way that precluded opposition to national intervention. Mainstream publications including the *New York Times, Life Magazine,* and the *Saturday Review,* along with a study by the Department of Health Education and Welfare authorized by the president, all suggested that the failure of U.S. educational policy was responsible for a national shortage of technological brainpower. The document, titled "Education in Russia," openly suggested emulation of Soviet educational strategies.[37] The most emblematic national response to the crisis was the passage of the National Defense Education Act of 1958, a bill that dedicated federal funds to support of a range of initiatives aimed at ensuring the necessary brainpower for future military and technological superiority of the nation. Significant portions of the fund were dedicated to uses of technology for teaching and were used in large part for the development of instructional television projects.

Criticism of the existing system of education in the 1950s was closely linked to the competitive nationalism of the Cold War, making education into an ideological battleground of global importance. Liberal educational movements were scapegoated as the cause of deficiencies in the educational system. Although there was heightened discussion of educational imperatives on a national level, there was also strong resistance to federal involvement in education. States had seen their authority undermined by desegregation and other liberal reforms. On the whole, they did not welcome further federal control of their turf.

The emphasis on technology and automation in education appeared in this context. It was based on a number of distinct but related rationales and motivations. The oft-proclaimed need to invest in the brainpower of future generations was rationalized by an overall linking of national defense to the scientific research-and-development industry launched a decade earlier.[38] At the same time, public discussion seemed to reflect a need for elevating educational standards for the entire population. Policies and initiatives were instituted that sought to increase the number of elite technocrats as a product of schooling. And finally, technology was also regarded as a key to alleviating the shortage of teachers through mass education techniques such as tele-education. These two objectives, though portrayed as unified, had discrete goals. Producing a corps of elite technocrats required ensuring that educational resources were concentrated toward a select few; the introduction of testing and merit scholarships aimed to achieve this. Improving education on a mass scale was a way of reducing the costs of education overall.

The Soviet threat was not the only impetus to these shifts in views about education. U.S. middle- and upper-class groups were increasingly threatened by the media specter of expanding economically disenfranchised populations, both in U.S. urban centers and in colonies and developing nations. Communications technology was conceived as an economical means of delivering mass education to these groups. Its purported advantages were not only efficiency of distribution but also centralization and standardization. Education was seen as a means of regulating these populations, as well as a tool for the sort of indoctrination that would guarantee their compliance with the status quo. The latter benefits were significant with respect to fears about the fostering of revolutionary thought within the academy.

The early history of educational television in the United States is closely linked to the Cold War and a growing need to redefine the role of education in relation to domestic and global politics that followed the Second World War. Television was first showcased at the World's Fair in 1939. The technology was being implemented commercially in the United States by 1947. The struggles over the implementation of educational broadcasting that began shortly thereafter culminated in what we now know as Public Television or the Public Broadcasting Service.[39] Early experiments with educational television out of which the Samoa project emerged were bound to, and shaped by, the conflicting ideologies (public versus private, and egalitarian versus elitist) that vied for primacy during this period. But the Samoa project is notable for its strategic importance as the first large-scale commitment of the U.S. government toward an educational broadcast system.

The Ford Foundation's introduction of television into schools as a labor-saving device and a mechanism of standardization shaped a lasting understanding of the role of communications technology in education. In effect, this conception of what television had to offer was short-sighted, and its implementation fell short of the utopian goal of the technique's proponents—to educate the threatening masses. Television proved limited in its effectiveness with large groups over the long term and was met with opposition by teachers, whose critiques included the view that the technology was socially alienating for them and their students. Despite all of this, the Fordist view of educational technology has remained prominent. Alternative approaches to educational technology were eclipsed by this position—for example, a greater emphasis might have been placed on programming new curricular content rather than replacing teachers. As a communications technology, television presented unprecedented possibilities for bringing students in contact with educational content remote from their daily lives.

Conclusion

The Samoa project took place within a broader setting that included these elements: a federal government anxious to improve its image as benefactor to developing regions, and to take central control of the educational system on the mainland; a national crisis in curriculum and widespread teacher shortages; heightened attention to race politics in and beyond schools; and a Cold War–era tying of technology to world leadership in education. The Samoan Educational Television Project presents more than an instructive case study of the complexity of U.S. postwar educational practices. It was conceived as an opportunity for dealing on a mass level with the types of problems arising in disparate settings in which poverty was a feature across an increasingly global society, from large urban centers to dispersed rural communities. Economic support for the U.S.-based ETV projects that paved the way for the Samoa project as well as the political lobby for ETV in general was provided by private philanthropic organizations, principally the Ford Foundation. These entities were concerned with finding ways to manage through corporate benevolence what their leadership saw as the threat of a growing underclass. These foundations also had an interest in opening up foreign markets for business, technology, and culture. The project is a crucial case in point, then, not only of U.S. postwar assimilationist policies regarding its possessions, but also of the role of media and technology in assimilation schemes. It is a case that reveals the complex network of issues that have contributed to the current stature of educational technologies in a global context.

In the 1990s as in the 1950s and 1960s, supremacy in educational technology was a driving force in educational reform. The goal of a computer in every classroom so often cited by the Clinton administration—a view broadly supported across the political spectrum—descended directly from the circumstances and motivations described in this chapter. In the chapters that follow, I consider other cases in which media, technology, and education come together as a force with vast ramifications for the cultural and political futures of countries and communities ranging from postliberation Senegalese nationals to New York City schoolchildren in the early 1990s. The Samoan ETV project, though an "isolated experiment," sets the stage for understanding how uses of technology in education, from the most repressive to the most progressive, are related in important ways to a much larger ideological nexus of media-technology-education. This network has become astonishingly complex and extensive in the first decade of the twenty-first century.

CHAPTER TWO

Students as Producers

Critical Video Production

Well, one can talk of course of education—of arming people's minds against
that kind of [mainstream] journalism. But there's now been a sustained cultural
attempt to show how this manipulation works, which has hardly impinged on
its actual power. I don't see how the educational response can be adequate. The
manipulative methods are too powerful, too far below the belt for that. These
people have to be driven out. We have to create a press owned by and responsible
to its readers.—Raymond Williams, "The Practice of Possibility"

Debate over which texts should be required in the K–12 curriculum
reached a heated pitch in the United States in the 1990s. Typically, debates centered on the questions "Which books in use continue to merit
inclusion?" and "What sorts of books should be generated to reform the
canon?" As the previous chapter indicates, this discussion shifted gears
as educators and theorists of education began to consider the role of
electronic media not only in art classrooms, where visual media would
seem an obvious alternative, but also across the curriculum. The Samoa
project demonstrated the appeal of television as a medium that could
transform the structure of the teaching and learning process while also

reforming content. By the 1980s, classroom media was no longer limited to television alone. Public art, advertising, video, popular television, and music videos had all made their way into the classroom, either as vehicles for learning or as objects of textual analysis. Computer programs designed specifically for educational settings were becoming more familiar items by the end of the decade (for example, interactive science learning programs with images, graphs, charts, and models).

In some education circles, questions about books and the canon were complicated by the challenge to the written word posed by electronic media. A conservative fear voiced in the 1990s was that the move to incorporate visual art and popular visual media across the curriculum was tantamount to asking, Why use books at all? For this constituency, to question the place of books was to attack the very foundation of academic knowledge. This fear was not unfounded. Implicit in the consideration of visual culture and media's role across the curriculum is the challenge to books (from great books to the stalwart textbook) by audiovisual and hypertext media in core curricular areas. Moreover, the World Wide Web, with its extensive database of educational texts and research materials, conjures a new relationship between written and visual communication, as well as between popular and academic cultures. The idea that media might migrate from extracurricular activity to the center of the curriculum posed a fundamental challenge to traditional education. This challenge was not immediately anticipated by the founders of televisual education who were experimenting with the medium in the early 1950s, before television assumed its place as a dominant form of popular culture.

Debates about classroom curricular reform over the past decade have included three intersecting projects: the development of multicultural curricula; the incorporation of mass, popular, and subcultures in the classroom, either as objects of study or as techniques of cultural expression; and the diversification of media forms, specifically those incorporating visual elements, in classroom materials and methods. This chapter analyzes these intersecting projects and considers a curricular model that engages all three. After analyzing the goals of a variety of alternative educational models, I make a case for the use of student video production as a pedagogical strategy. I also argue that artists and media producers, working alone or in teams with classroom teachers, can be strong resources in programs aiming to build a culturally diverse educational program that moves beyond the classroom and into the community. My argument will draw on writings in the cultural study of education by authors including Stanley Aronowitz, Henry Giroux, and John Fiske on the place of mass, popular and subcultures in the classroom. The work of the Educational Video Center and Video Machete, two nonprofit organizations that involve youth in critical media production, will form the basis of this chapter's argument for student-based production as an alternative approach to media education. The approach I advocate features developing students' skills not only in visual textual production and analysis but also in media production. These skills are commonly taught in art and media studies classes. I propose that they be taught, like literacy, across and beyond the curriculum, as part of a plan that is sensitive to the diverse concerns, knowledges, and experiences of students.

The experiments in media education described in chapter 1 ended in the mid-1970s. As popular media forms such as television, radio, and electronic media were introduced to schools, they were met with public and parental criticism. The rise of organizations such as Action for Children's Television (founded 1968) was just one expression of a broader sentiment that media and popular culture were simply incongruent with quality education.[1] The Frankfurt School's articulation of mass culture as an ideological force operating solely in the interests of capital happened to coincide with a period of backlash, even in progressive sectors, against media experimentation in schools. In the mid-1990s, scholarship in cultural studies began to question the totalizing critique of the culture industry launched by Theodor Adorno and Max Horkheimer in the 1940s and more fully elaborated by a range of theorists following the republication of their book *Dialectic of Enlightenment* in 1969.[2] A body of work in cultural studies emerged in the 1990s around the ideas of resistant spectatorship and the use of popular media texts to affirm marginal subject positions, or to strengthen local community bonds. Raymond Williams, Stuart Hall, John Fiske, Dick Hebdige, and Janice Radway have all contributed substantially to the literature on oppositional and resistant uses of popular culture and media.

The embrace of the popular as a site of resistance has entailed a reconsideration of visual media texts as potential sites of progressive culture building rather than as objects for passive consumption.[3] Stanley Aronowitz and Henry Giroux brought these debates about popular culture and media into the field of education with the publication of *Postmodern Education*. The essays in their book focus on mass, popular, and subcultural discourses in schools. They revise and challenge some of the tenets of previous theories of the culture industry and education. Some of the issues Aronowitz and Giroux take up are the dichotomy of high and low culture, the association of academic knowledge with book learning rather than with everyday sources of knowledge and experience, and the condemnation of popular media as mindless trash.

Of particular interest to my discussion is the chapter in *Postmodern Education* titled "Working Class Displacements and Postmodern Representations." Written by Aronowitz, it focuses primarily on mainstream visual media. Aronowitz considers the place of television, film, and rock music (a subculture with a strong visual component) in education. Because the most familiar of mass media forms are largely image based, this chapter is central to Aronowitz's and Giroux's broader claims throughout their book about the place of visual media and culture in the politics of education.

Aronowitz and Giroux on the Reclamation of Mass Media

Aronowitz proposes a pedagogical model that acknowledges the importance of mass media in marginalized communities. Mass culture, he argues, is an arena of everyday resistance in which educators can perform the potentially utopian act of reclaiming what he calls the "authentic expression," or genuine articulation, of students' interests and class and cultural identities. Rejecting the Frankfurt School's emphasis on the culture industry's relation to the state, Aronowitz draws on theories of audience reception to emphasize that consumers of popular media texts produce diverse, culturally situated textual meanings. For Aronowitz, mass culture performs a unique and liberatory function for the communities and classes of people who do not have access to "traditional culture" (by which he means the classical, Anglo- and European-based high culture of Western society). The mass media, he suggests, are the agents that "[reach] down to the erotic dimension of human character," allowing for a kind of cultural expression that is otherwise suppressed.[4] Following from this view, the mass media are a potential site for the formation of an emancipatory pedagogy and must thus be reclaimed from theories that would condemn them as a tool of state oppression.

Clearly, for those who want to generate an emancipatory pedagogy the task has changed since the days when the judgments of the Frankfurt School dominated their thinking about mass culture. It is not a question of unmasking television or rock music as forms of domination that reproduce the prevailing set-up. Instead, we are engaged in a program of reclamation, to rescue these forms as the authentic expressions of generations for whom traditional culture is not available.[5]

It is not clear from Aronowitz's discussion why certain generations would have a more authentic relationship to the popular than others, or why access to traditional culture would make one's relationship to mass culture less immediate or authentic. Class and generational status are complexly interwoven subject positions in the context he considers, urban public schools. I will put aside the association between age, class, and authentic (and erotic) relations to mass culture, though, to follow a more productive thread of his argument: the question of how the reclamation of cultural forms is put into effect in the classroom. Aronowitz's premise, which seems to draw on reception studies, is that audiences do not simply consume television, magazines, and popular music; they make readings that situate these texts as politically relevant entities and privileged means of expression in their everyday lives. Through them audience members gain meaningful knowledge of self-identity and community. Industry media texts are appropriated to make personal and political meaning. This argument is a useful step forward from the critique of mainstream media. However, we do not learn how audiences use these texts—that is, how media texts are consumed and reclaimed by students, and particularly by students who occupy marginalized class positions. Mass culture's exclusion from the academic canon is aligned with the cultural disenfranchisement of marginal peoples, but there is little evidence of how this alliance is effected by students relative to particular texts. Moreover, Aronowitz does not provide us with data on schools or educators that have incorporated media texts in their classrooms, and the impact of this incorporation of the popular into the classroom on teaching and learning. Without this evidence, his theory of cultural resistance and his model of media pedagogy remain speculative. My point echoes that of education theorist Warren Crichlow, who has written that Aronowitz and Giroux would have been more convincing if they had started with a discussion of actual pedagogical practices. Citing writings on alternative educational programs such as New York City's Central Park East, Crichlow argues that the positions and strategies proposed in *Postmodern Education* are not new and untried:

> Anyone familiar with the exemplars of thoughtful school reform will recognize this strategy as little more than what a number of public school educators have been working to implement in existing schools for nearly two decades. Such progressive pedagogical and curriculum practices are not hypothetical; they are already in practice.[6]

Aronowitz's essay shares many of its basic ideas with communication scholar John Fiske's well-known work on popular culture. Fiske explains his theory of media consumption as follows:

> Texts that meet the criteria of popular discrimination are cultural resources rather than art objects. Michel de Certeau uses the metaphor of the text as a supermarket from which readers select the items they want, combine them with those already in their cultural "pantry" at home, and cook up new meals or new readings according to their own needs and creativities. This sort of text is the product of a completely different reading practice. The reader of the aesthetic [high art] text attempts to read it on its terms, to subjugate him or herself to its aesthetic discipline. The reader reveres the text. The popular reader, on the other hand, holds no such reverence for the text, but views it as a resource to be used at will. . . . [Popular readers] are undisciplined.[7]

Fiske's concept of popular media representations as "cultural resources" is a welcome alternative to the textual determinism of much media criticism of the 1970s and 1980s. The idea that a given media text produces in its viewers a particular ideological effect has left little room for acknowledging the agency and potential for resistant modes of spectatorship among audience members or consumers. According to Fiske, the culture industry, no longer the agent of totalizing state power, caters to its popular reader by producing media texts that are "generic." The generic text is an open text, facilitating multiple interpretations and uses across a range of political and cultural positions. Ostensibly, this textual conventionality ensures that there is "plenty of space for different readers to produce different forms of popular culture" out of the same texts.[8]

Fiske's theory, like Aronowitz's, is compelling. Both Fiske and Aronowitz see great potential for agency in the interpretive acts of viewing communities. Fiske provides examples (although based on hypothetical, not actual, case studies) of his theory in action. In the following passage, he describes political alliances drawn across disparate disenfranchised communities through alternative readings of mass media positions and identities:

> Young urban Aborigines in Australia watching old westerns on Saturday morning television ally themselves with the Indians, cheer them on as they attack the wagon train or homestead, killing the white men and carrying off the white women; they also identify with Arnold, the eternal black child in a white paternalist family in *Diff'rent Strokes*—constructing allegiances among American blackness, American Indianness, and Australian Aboriginality that enable them to make their sense out of their experience of being nonwhite in a white society. They evade the white colonialist ideology of the Western to make their popular culture out of it.[9]

Fiske's thesis that industry mass media become popular culture through productive readings that facilitate social struggle, exemplified in this passage, indirectly supports Aronowitz's claim that "appropriation entails production as much as critical analysis." There is reason to wonder, though, whether the mass media text is really so flexibly open to the interpretations and uses Fiske's hypothetical subjects engage in. His vision of a transcultural alliance among American black, Australian Aboriginal, and Native American identities molds cultural difference into a binary world of multicultural others, on the one hand, and unspecified dominant subjects, on the other. Meaghan Morris has written an insightful critique of Fiske and other media critics who construct affinities among cultural others to redeem them from the position of passive consumers, "cultural dopes." There is a problematic identification, she suggests, between critics themselves and the cultural informants to whom they attribute critical insight. For the authors she discusses, a range of ethnographic others constitute a collective subject, "the people." Morris proposes that "in the end they are not simply the cultural student's object of study and his native informants. 'The people' are also the textually delegated allegorical emblem of the critic's own activity." Ultimately, the critical project runs the risk of becoming circular and narcissistic.[10]

Although Fiske does give us an example of his theory in action, he has little to say about how the supposed process of transcultural identification takes place, and which communities might be joined in this alliance. His idea of transcultural identification, not unlike Aronowitz's notion of authentic expression, rather patronizingly imputes a sense of authenticity to the (ironically generic) cultural other, suggesting that the possibility for identification outside of class status or into dominant culture is morally or psychically off-limits for any disenfranchised subject.

Although their positions do acknowledge important strategies of resistance, Aronowitz and Fiske place an inordinate emphasis on the reader's act of morally uplifting reception or appropriation in the larger framework of media production. James Donald, in a critique of Fiske's *Understanding Television,* makes a quip that succinctly identifies not only the shortcomings of Fiske's theory but its patronizing tenor: "No need to reform television, then. The People's 'resistive' viewing habits mean that 'cultural democracy' exists already. All the radical media theorist needs to do is to pat them on the head."[11]

Exactly how does the Aborigine's spectatorial evasion of white colonial ideology constitute political action in his or her community and beyond? How is one subject's oppositional reading of a text extended and reproduced in the broader community? Fiske points to the crucial fact of shared political meaning but does not acknowledge his own ethnographic enterprise in doing a "productive reading" of this viewing experience (which he has in fact read about in an anthropological text). Even more troubling is the idea that readers of the popular are "undisciplined" in their textual reading habits, linking lack of discipline (schooling) with resistance. This assumption evokes the pejorative labeling of indigenous peoples as primitive, as unschooled in the ways of the dominant culture. Objections to Fiske's analysis aside, his example elides analysis of the processes and contradictions involved in resistant reading strategies. For example, how does character identification by Australian Aboriginals with African Americans or Native Americans constitute political unity across these groups? (Certainly political coalitions require some actual communication among groups.) Situated popular readings do constitute a means by which groups shape social and political identities among themselves. However, conversation across communities requires something more than a shared "minority" mode of reception based in fantasy.

My discussion of Aronowitz and Fiske suggests that perhaps textual reception alone does not constitute resistance in any sustained or consistent way, and moreover, attention to the (resistant) reading habits of students cannot in itself constitute reform in education. Fiske and Aronowitz are right to a degree: mass culture involves a more complex process than passive acquiescence to a state-serving cultural apparatus. However, we need a more sound theory of what constitutes media intervention, political alliance, and action within and across communities. As Stuart Hall points out, engaging in ideological struggles must involve a broad network of interventions: "To deploy only one strategy and to put all one's eggs into a single tactic is to set about winning the odd dramatic skirmish at the risk of losing the war.[12]

Aronowitz seems to sense the limitations of his position. At the end of a lengthy discussion about mass media and received textual meaning, he closes his chapter with the prescriptive statement that "a curriculum in popular cultural studies would be required to include at its center video and music production and performance. Students would make videos that express their own ideas—writing the scripts, producing the documentaries, learning how to write and perform the music, and so forth."[13]

The link between resistance and production was expressed by Walter Benjamin in 1934, when he published his famous call for the disappearance of "the conventional distinction between author and producer" in the popular press. Benjamin proposed intervention in the means of bourgeois newspaper production, making way for a "reader [who is] at all times ready to become a writer."[14] He used the term "production" in a more literal sense than Aronowitz and Fiske do when they describe the television viewer's production of meaning. Politicized newspaper writing, not just productive reading, is what Benjamin had in mind.

Benjamin's call for authors as producers has been a springboard for some of the most exciting theories and applications of educational media use and production. Raymond Williams's proposal for "a press owned by and responsible to its readers" rather than the educational strategy of "arming people's minds" against the popular press is very close to Benjamin's original formulation and provides another rich resource for this model. Educators have been slow to respond to this idea, however, choosing instead to "arm" students against media messages with writing and speech as the weapons of choice. However, some educators have been involved in schooling students in the art and media skills needed for this approach to media reform. Surprisingly, these educators and the programs they have launched have been overlooked by media education and cultural studies scholars like Giroux and Aronowitz, who focus instead on the more conventional strategy of textual or oral critique.

This advocacy of production as political intervention has a long history, carrying over into debates about education in the form of discussions about youth-produced media in classrooms since the 1970s, with the advent of consumer-grade video equipment. Aronowitz probably intended such forms as televised music videos in his reference to video, music, and performance. I want to use his concept here, however, in a manner that is in keeping with Benjamin's more conventional understanding of access to the means of production, to emphasize the potential for increased transit between the roles of media consumer and media producer. In the following section, I consider student video production as an alternative to the consumption-centered model of media-based emancipatory pedagogy proposed by Giroux and Aronowitz in *Postmodern Education*.

From Student as Viewer to Student as Producer

Advocacy of video production in political activism dates from the late 1960s, when portable video recorders first became available. The accepted account of this period is that artists such as Nam June Paik experimented with the new medium, taking it to the streets to record spontaneous footage of action in, and bystander commentary about, antiwar protests, civil rights activism, and public events.[15] Portable video's introduction coincided with a period of intense optimism about the potential for artists to effect social change by producing works that performed social critique. The introduction of consumer-grade video equipment in the 1970s coincided with a federal mandate that the rapidly growing commercial cable networks provide community access to cable broadcasting. Art and media historians will be familiar with media-critical video in the vein of Richard Serra's 1973 *Television Delivers People,* a tape that was essentially a scrolling textual critique of the industry. Also known to art historians are the media-critical video collectives such as

TVTV (Top Value Television), which produced vérité documentaries of the 1972 U.S. political conventions, and Videofreex, which unsuccessfully attempted to get airtime for *Subject to Change*, the collective's 1969 documentary about the counterculture.

In the 1970s, without the same fanfare, community activists launched cable access centers and video collectives in urban and rural centers across the country, supported by the meager access to facilities and airtime mandated by federal cable regulations. Nonprofit community television collectives and centers staffed by volunteers or low-paid staff members provided training in production skills to community members whose interests and views were typically not represented in the mainstream medium, from the networks to public television. It is important to note that these collectives were not driven by the same ideals as those that spurred public television's growth. The Public Broadcasting System was founded on a mission to educate the public and provide quality programming as an alternative to the advertising-driven programming offered by the commercial networks. It supported educated middle- and upper-class demands for "quality" media alternatives.[16]

Whereas community television initiatives were in many cases launched in alliance with the left critique of mainstream media politics, public television was more typically grounded in a liberal perspective organized around the standard of taste and a disapproval of low culture. Community access served people who would not necessarily seek out "quality" television or see themselves as entitled to such alternatives. The most important distinction is that whereas public broadcasting provided educational and quality broadcasting as a viewing alternative, community access groups promoted involvement in production. Sometimes this amounted to mundane sorts of productions: church groups, community organizations, hobbyists, and adult education services all found venues for expression in cable public access television. A few examples: Appalshop, a collective founded in 1969, supported community access television production among poor and low-income people in Appalachia. Downtown Community Television (founded in 1972) and the Paper Tiger Television Collective (founded in 1981) provided training and broadcast access to progressive activists and community members in New York City, generating programs that performed criticism and analysis of institutions ranging from city government and business to the mainstream media.[17]

Aired late at night on public television and local cable channels, the programs produced by these collectives received limited distribution and attention. But they nonetheless allowed marginalized communities to have airtime—and they provided a venue for alternative community-based education. It is important to note that this idea of media production in the service of the community was an idea that existed long before the video era. The Cambridge Community Art Center's Teen Media Program, which started out working with 8 mm film and photography in 1970, is just one example of a media education program that came into existence before the video wave. What made access television different was the broadcast potential, and the creation of a virtual, if relatively local, community of viewers. Like the Samoa project, with its closed-circuit network, cable access community television forged a dispersed local community of viewers.

The 1980s and 1990s saw the beginnings of video education programs that drew inspiration from the broader community access television movement. The founders and staff members of these organizations had been trained in community access centers like Appalshop, Downtown Community Television, and Paper Tiger Television. Their pedagogical philosophy was informed by the didactic style of the left critique of the mainstream media that informed the work of some of these organizations. But pedagogy was at issue in a more structural way: production skills had to be taught, even in programs not explicitly set up to educate. The turn to education proper was a natural outgrowth of the effort to teach media skills as means of political expression.

In 1977 James Donald advocated for the convergence of media activism and education. Production, he argued, is an underconsidered but important component of media criticism. He proposed combining the teaching of critical-analytical skills (what he called the "cultural undoping" of students) with education in media production techniques, with the aim of teaching students to be critical producers rather than passive consumers.[18] In the classroom, this would involve a combination of exercises in production and critical discussion:

> [It] is . . . through the practice of learning (for example) how to use a video camera, record an interview, prepare a script, or reach a joint editorial decision that the first crucial step of revealing the human construction, the non-naturalness of the products of the media will

be achieved. . . . Thus the object is to reveal how the ideological messages of the mass media are put together (*encoded,* to use Stuart Hall's term), and to seek effective codes for the students' own messages.[19]

Donald's essay was written during a period when attention to the materiality of the medium and analysis of the means of production were popular approaches in left media criticism. To put these ideas schematically: ideology is embedded in the material aspects of the medium; to uncover the means of production behind the media text is to reveal key aspects of the mechanisms of power and oppression. Donald's approach takes this focus on the means of production a step further. By learning the production techniques that go into the making of a given text, students can understand the mechanisms of ideological construction at the level of the medium. By producing media texts themselves, students learn that there is an alternative to resisting interpellation through mainstream media, or critical reading alone. They can appropriate the means of production to produce new sorts of meanings. His idea is a prescient expression of the "author as producer" ethos of the 1990s, the decade that brought us desktop publishing and personal Web sites. The figure of student-as-producer was frequently invoked during this period when even the most underfunded public schools aimed to offer students access to the means of production.

The student-as-producer of the 1990s inhabited a spectrum from left media-critical positions like Donald's position of 1977 to the liberal democratic belief that new technologies could enhance individual expression. The remainder of this chapter chronicles the work of specific organizations that practiced a left media production approach in conjunction with schools. By returning to this video moment in the history of media pedagogy, we can arrive at a more grounded understanding of the spectrum of approaches represented in the contemporary ideal of student-as-producer in the computerized classroom.

Video Production across the Curriculum:
"Critical Vocationalism" or Progressive Pedagogical Reform?

Production skills have typically been taught through the curricular areas of art or vocational training. Advocates of production in the classroom inevitably encounter long-standing debates about class, race, and gender relative to the history of vocational, or vo-tech, educational programs. Typically, vocational education has existed as an alternative for students who are not expected to achieve the status of a white-collar profession, or to go on to university, for combined reasons of class, race, gender, and assessed intelligence. British educators Ian Connell and Geoff Hurd make a case for vocational training in the polytechnic setting. Marketable media production skills are proposed as an alternative to critical analysis in college-level curricula. "Critical vocationalism" is the term they use to describe their approach, which is based on their teaching experience at a polytechnic in West Midlands, an area of high unemployment and poverty.[20] They take a stand against the cultural elitism of left media theorists who focus on texts and spectatorship and steer clear of the mundane level of technical production. Their essay explicitly addresses the need for this class of students in particular to have training in useful skills, and to have access to the means of production. These are skills polytechnic students can use in their future lives in the workforce, Connell and Hurd suggest. Critical thinking skills are armchair luxuries for the privileged students of universities. They don't equip polytechnic students with a crucial necessity: a means of survival.

Critical vocationalism is an extremely useful concept because it implicitly recognizes the agency of industry workers and management in transforming social relations and ideology. The concept recognizes that students are potential future arbiters of social change through their day-to-day practical work in industry production. But the concept also threatens to fix the long-standing class-based educational divide between vo-tech and academic tracks. In the United States, an academic education has long been regarded as one of the means through which lower- and working-class youth can transcend the class positions of their parents, become more worldly, and acquire access to a better job, a better life. Critical vocationalism threatens to reify class boundaries by consigning the working classes to an education path that precludes the academic side in favor of training for the workplace, whether that training is purely practical or a mix of practical and political.

The concept of critical vocationalism is especially relevant to the history of U.S.-based video pedagogy, because the best-known and most enduring programs in the United States have served poor and minority students, particularly those labeled "at risk"—those in dropout prevention or teen mothers programs, for example. In the United States, vocational training is at the core of a long-standing debate about education in African American communities of the early twentieth century. These debates revolved around the opposing educational strategies of Booker T. Washington, who advocated vocational training, and W. E. B. Du Bois, who emphasized the need for blacks to gain access to academic venues. Paula Giddings notes that the boundaries between vocational and academic program advocacy were by no means clear-cut, as demonstrated in the position of educator Anna Julia Cooper on the issue. Cooper asserted, "I believe in industrial education with all my heart. We can't all be professional people"; yet her insistence on an academic curriculum for African American students drew charges of insubordination from the Washington school board.[21] In these debates about vocational (industrial) versus academic training, class issues were clearly integral to race issues.

This situation resonates in contemporary debates over vocational and technological (replacing industrial) tracking policies. Contemporary U.S. media educators who support media production as an educational strategy among culturally, politically, and economically disenfranchised communities need to consider how the history of this debate resonates with this legacy of industrial or technical tracking. To frame this in a question: Will media across the curriculum be the cutting edge of progressive pedagogy, or the newest vo-tech track for a class of workers?

My response to this open question is to propose that we rethink the split between the technical or vocational and the academic ("book learning"). Since the 1980s, media and education activists have stressed the importance of challenging these institutional distinctions. The question "Why only literary texts?" not only leads to the study of mass media as "low culture"; it also begs the questions, "Why the hierarchy among literature and mass media forms?" and "How can we begin to break down the high-low culture divide that separates books from media texts, writing from image making?" I am not proposing that we elevate educational media texts by infusing them with content from the classics, or that we teach students to produce media that reproduces certain standards of quality and value. Rather, the idea is to merge the process of critical thinking about existing texts—both those produced for classrooms use and those consumed in everyday life—with the skills of media production, and to make critical thinking something students can enact in the process of producing their own tapes. Some educators have incorporated media production into their curricula through programs and courses that do not compartmentalize vocational or technical skills in art or media production classes, combining video production with the teaching of area subjects. But overall, programs devoted to media pedagogy have tended to form around after-school or special short-term intervention programs serving low-income students or Latino, Chicano, and African American students in underfunded urban public schools. Neither training in vocational skills nor the acquisition of area knowledge is the primary goal in these programs. The objective is to use video production to provide a means for working through the social and psychological issues that play a role in these students' ability to make it through the school system and life, and to help students make meaningful connections to their communities through the production process. In these programs, production is something like a therapeutic technique—a point elaborated in depth in chapter 4. Skills training and, or versus, curricular learning take a backseat as the more pressing issues that these students face in everyday life become the focal point of the production process. The projects tend to be exercises in political consciousness-raising, addressing less overtly the agendas of workforce preparation and academic learning that are nonetheless intended outcomes of the curriculum.

The Educational Video Center (EVC), based in New York City, was founded by Steven Goodman in 1984 to bring together artists and media producers with teachers and students in school settings. The aim of the nonprofit center (which is still in existence) is to encourage the use of video and documentary techniques as expressive and interactive teaching and learning devices in the classroom. Inspired by Goodman's experience producing and directing a documentary about a South Bronx youth gang in 1981, EVC started out by working specifically with youth designated "at risk" in their schools. Media education, according to Goodman, "has a central role to play in the revitalization of schooling as [an] intellectually rigorous and democratic practice." It is a means of "transgressing the boundaries that separate school from community, artist from audience, thought from practice." [22]

Some EVC projects have not involved production at all but have instead encouraged students to develop critical reading skills that can be called on in later production exercises. In one such instance, students were asked to view mainstream television texts that represented stereo-types within their own cultural groups. They were encouraged to have a dialogue about their perceptions of these representations. The point was to generate a discussion about racism in the television the students routinely watched. As media educator Diana Agosta explains,

> Overwhelmingly, these kids are dealing with racism: in society, in the media's images of them, in their relation to each other, and in their neighborhoods. EVC encourages students to analyze media content critically in order to confront false images, and it teaches them pro-duction techniques so that they can create truer images of themselves and their worlds.[23]

The idea that there are representations of culture and identity that are "true" or "false" may sound naive. But it should be noted that the participants in this case are young students, and in these basic concepts, Agosta provides for them a useful shorthand description of the com-plex process through which they can begin to read media portrayals in more nuanced ways. The EVC project she describes also involved teach-ing the students about some of the basics of media production—the formal strategies of framing, editing, and sound recording.

Agosta goes beyond the conventional boundaries of television criti-cism and analysis, offering her students production skills and access to equipment as a step in the analytical process. Using video capture and editing, her students undid and remade the texts they had previously viewed and analyzed. In dissecting and remaking their own media texts out of these found texts, students were offered a distinct form of ac-cess to the production of media meanings. Granted, their remakes were slated for an audience no bigger than the class. But the process itself was meaningful insofar as students learned that they can have an impact on what they see on the television screen.

These examples of media pedagogy as practiced by EVC person-nel have taken us into territory well beyond the consumption-based spectatorial experiences of resistance and expression outlined by Fiske and Aronowitz. But this is not to suggest that media production—and pedagogical strategies based in it—necessarily provides students with a greater degree of agency or a sharper critical perspective. Rather, ex-perience with production can offer a different perspective from which to understand how meaning is produced, what functions media texts serve. It also offers a new approach to fostering dialogue among students. Authorship of media texts cannot be equated with agency, but the techniques of production can be applied to forms of critical analysis that open up alternative positions from which students can think, debate, and act.

How "truths" about identity and culture can be interrogated and even constructed by critical readings and by independent and classroom production was the focus of Yvonne Hilton, a teacher of African American history who used media in her alternative public high school curriculum of the early 1990s. In an interview with Agosta, Hilton explains the integral relationship between critical analysis of media and knowledge of production technique:

> Nine times out of ten, with our students, what they see and hear in the regular media has been true for them. When they start seeing (or reading) alternative stories, one of the questions they ask me is, "Why didn't I see this particular fact in the *Daily News;* why didn't I see that particular fact in the [New York] *Post;* how is it that these people have the information and those people don't?" And I throw the question back, what do you suppose happened; why is that? And they begin to think of the possibility of editing, filtering and deciding, and they look at the reasons editors would decide to do this sort of thing. (Agosta, 6)

Hilton's emphasis on "editing, filtering, and deciding" about mainstream media is meant to give students insight into how media stories are put together as well as to make a viable option of "editing" and "deciding" in the literal sense—that is, to make available the experience of composing media texts. Projects like this present a range of methods for analyzing the cultural nature of "technical" media production as a preliminary to production. As in the project Agosta describes, learning to take apart media texts provides students with ideas about how to compose their own texts. In the process, intellectual skills associated with a range of disciplines become an integral part of learning the "technical skills" needed to compose one's own media. Likewise, technical processes such as publishing, printing, and editing become points of focus in students' critical readings of their studies in more typically academic areas. Texts are no longer regarded as fixed products. Rather, students

Students from the Educational Video Center out on a shoot.

learn to see them as moments in a process of meaning production—a process that neither begins nor ends in their reading of the text.

Media education projects supported by EVC and other educational video organizations are sometimes integrated into the core curriculum of public schools. The media project Hilton describes was part of a history curriculum. This is not surprising, since media analysis is at home in the humanities. However, the approach Hilton describes has also been adapted for use in math, social science, and science curricula. Mario Chioldi, a colleague of Hilton's interviewed by Agosta, describes math projects in which statistical analysis of media representations shifts the focus from abstract problem solving to concrete social concerns:

> We've developed a work sheet with which you look through a magazine or watch a TV program and check off, "I saw this many males, of which x number were Latino, x number were Caucasian, x number were black; I saw x number of females," and you start to tally them up. It becomes very obvious that there are shows with no people of color. (Agosta, 7)

The project of cataloging media representation is one means of generating discussion about race in a class on statistics. Pam Sporn, who taught at the Schomburg Satellite Academy in the Bronx, relates how one of their media productions was structured around a lesson in close reading of the news:

> To go line by line through a magazine article to see what types of words they're using—if you just presented that as a project to young people, it doesn't sound very interesting, but that's the whole middle section of *Torn Between Colors* (a student production), and it's the part people like the best. In this article about the youths accused in the Central Park rape, they used the words "wolf pack" 10 times. They use "breed," which is usually associated with animal mating, and "roaming"—well, that's another word associated with animals. (Agosta, 7)

These reading strategies are productive for students and teachers on one level because they reveal the encoding of racism, sexism, and so on, providing tools to challenge media representations through discussion and written analysis. On another level, these exercises also teach about methods of production. In analyzing such a text, students and teachers learn how metaphor, narrative, planning, scripting, acting, shooting, and editing are used. This kind of analysis can facilitate a keener awareness of the choices that go into the collaborative production of media texts by students and teachers later, when students move on to production exercises. Students begin to see how decisions throughout the creative process determine the final form and meaning of their own work, whether that work takes the form of a paper or a collaboratively produced video.

EVC has been especially attentive to the class and race divide that separates the urban public schools whose students the organization tends to work with from more affluent institutions. Goodman listed some key concepts that EVC personnel share, among them the belief that the mass media "cross the fault lines of race and class," effectively becoming a universal experience for students, whose worldviews come from media representations, with television as the master text. He capitalized on this capacity of the medium in a yearlong project with a student team that resulted in the documentary *Unequal Education: Failing Our Children* (1992). Aired on PBS in 1992, this project engages directly in the class and race divide that grounds the vo-tech–academic split.

Goodman reports that he and colleague David Murdock followed

Students from the Educational Video Center conduct an interview.

Paolo Freire's "problem-posing" pedagogical strategy in this project. They proposed to four young people (two Hunter College students, a high school student, and a high school graduate) that they focus on their own educational experiences. Each was a product of the New York City public school system. Each had gone through either an EVC training workshop or a school program affiliated with EVC. Their project was supported by, and produced in consultation with, Bill Moyers for his series *Listening to America*. The group, which called itself YO-TV (Youth Organizers Television), worked on the project part-time, and members were paid a stipend.

The group observed various high schools in preparation for their production. They visited a South Fordham urban high school in dire disrepair in a neighborhood populated by crack dealers and prostitutes. They noted the school's chaotic atmosphere and witnessed a confrontation between a teacher and student and another teacher using verbal humiliation in his classroom to manage the predominantly black student body. This was juxtaposed to conditions at a school they visited in Riverdale, a middle-class suburban sector of the same district. This school was clean and bright, had a well-equipped library, extensive curricular choices, and a calm and positive atmosphere. The principal of the former school denied the group permission to use footage that they shot there, and so they turned to another school in a nearby black and Latino neighborhood plagued by unemployment, drugs, and street violence. The tape they ultimately produced compares the experiences of James, a white thirteen-year-old boy of Jewish and Irish descent who attended the more affluent school, and those of Lonnie, an African American boy of the same age attending the latter school.

The tape clearly played a role in educating the student producers about race and class issues in the school system. Traveling between these two schools, Goodman explains, they "could not help but gain a deeper understanding of how race and class shaped the contours of Lonnie and James's experiences."[24] But the tape also served an important function in the communities in which it was filmed. Lonnie's mother, Goodman reports, was outraged to see the disparity between her son's school and the Riverside institution only three miles away. School administrators and board members accused the producers of distorting the truth and refused to address questions about the unequal distribution of resources across the district. The airing of the tape on PBS sparked a public forum about an issue that had long been buried in this community, and opened the issue to debate in communities around the country where similar disparities existed.[25]

To return to the issue of vocationalism and career training: it is worth noting that it is schools like the one James attended, and not Lonnie's, that are more likely to have acquired video and computer equipment in the half decade following the production of *Unequal Education*. If anyone was going to be trained for the media industry labor force, it was more likely to be students like James, not Lonnie. It is worth speculating that vocationalism as it existed before the 1990s is no longer in place with the emergence of a class of workers trained on the newest and best equipment. The MITs of the world, and not the working-class polytechnics, are producing the technical workforce with the most control over the means of production. Technical training may not be a part of a classical education, but the value and class association of a technical education shifted dramatically as media technology became a respected and even an essential component not only of education but of everyday life in the second half of the 1990s.

At least one of the student producers of *Unequal Education*, Carol, is reported as having been inspired by the experience to change her career path, in her case from anthropology to community video teacher.

Whether or not she acted on this goal, we must recognize a clear distinction between it and the industry career path that is a more typical outcome of vocational media training. "I'm gonna be a teacher in a quote 'undesirable' neighborhood," Goodman reports Carol as saying. "I wanna be a video instructor, to teach young people to do video in their neighborhood."[26] This aspiration is sharply distinct from the goal of working in the mainstream industry, or even working in the mainstream school system in any conventional manner. Carol is quite explicit in her intentions to work in the margins: "I want to start now. I don't want to wait till they certify me. I wouldn't be teaching science though" (68). The disclaimer about science is crucial. It suggests that Carol sees her pedagogical mission as existing outside the realm of the conventional curriculum. Rather, she wants to practice, in Goodman's language, a "liberating pedagogy" that teaches students "to bear witness," to "look at the world as if it were otherwise" (68). At issue is not *what* curricular area Carol will teach in but *how* she will teach it, and how students will process lived experience through that curriculum. From this perspective, media pedagogy is a philosophy with a political mission, not a set of techniques geared toward achieving curricular goals.

Students don't always approach media production with the altruistic ideals expressed by Carol at the end of her project. Teachers may not view the media pedagogy project as skills-based training, but this does not prevent students from being drawn to the approach for precisely this kind of training and exposure. Maria Benfield, cofounder of Video Machete, a Chicago nonprofit youth media production organization, notes that "while many of the youth are attracted to our workshops because of the allure of technology and the promise of a professional career, the workshops are designed to get young people engaged on other levels. We want to foster in them a consciousness of being community media producers."

Video Machete was founded in 1994 by Benfield and Chris Bratton, a former participant in Paper Tiger Television and Rise and Shine Productions (discussed in chapter 4). The organization brings together students, community activists, artists, and video producers in after-school workshop settings in a neighborhood with a large Chicano community to produce videos about community issues, primarily focused on youth. The organization's workshops raise awareness of the potential for using media as a form of testimonial, to present the stories and points of view of local communities and individuals not represented in the mainstream media. Testimonials, Benfield explains, "are so important . . . since they provide an important moment of making oneself present in the educational process."

Central to Video Machete's pedagogical philosophy is an understanding of video (and more recently Web-based) production as a tool for sustained involvement in social change. In 1994 the organization sponsored a video workshop in collaboration with the organization Youth Struggling for Survival, a group dedicated to addressing the role of gangs in the lives of urban youth.[27] Discussion of the treatment of urban teens by police became a departure point for a production aimed at broadening public awareness of the complexity of relationships among young people that are wrongly perceived and labeled as gang activity. Working closely with gang members, former gang members, and their families, Video Machete produced a series of tapes that give depth to the portrayal of gangs. These tapes acknowledge the violent side of gangs but also show how these groups provide support and serve as surrogate families to young people who have nowhere else to turn. The tapes provide a sharp contrast to the images of gangs on television news.

Intergenerational collaboration is an important aspect of the group's approach, leading its organizers to favor out-of-school over school-based workshops. The project described in the foregoing paragraph, for example, involved family members and adults as collaborators in the production process. As Benfield explains, "We think of this as an alternative to traditional schooling. It builds human relationships by incorporating life experiences that form an alternative." This focus on human relationships does not begin and end with a given production. Video Machete serves as a locus for community relationships that go beyond the videos. Ramiro Rodriguez, a media producer who was involved in their first collaboration with Youth Struggling for Survival, wrote material for more recent Video Machete productions while awaiting trial in prison.[28]

Since the group's first collaboration with Youth Struggling for Survival, Video Machete has maintained an involvement with issues related to gangs through a series of projects and workshops. This sort of sustained workshop focus provides depth and meaning to their media productions, shifting the role of technical skills and the tapes themselves to the background. Concerns about reception are of great significance

Teen mother in *Self-Protection:*
Teen Moms Expand Their Options
(Sara Safford and Alex Juhasz, 1989).

for workshop participants struggling to shift views on a topic that has affected and continues to affect siblings, friends, and families.

Video Machete includes postproduction experience as a central component of its pedagogical approach. Young producers participate in public forums that accompany the distribution of their tapes and presentation of their media projects in exhibitions. In 1996 members of Video Machete created a sculptural installation at the New Museum of Contemporary Art in New York City that incorporated their videotapes on youth and gangs. The group builds on the reactions that their tapes generate, adding new levels to its projects. For example, a speak-out with youth and representatives of the Chicago police force has developed into an ongoing video dialogue between the two groups. This positioning of production experience within a larger process of communication and public discourse is in fact characteristic of the work of many of the groups that have pioneered production-based media pedagogy including EVC, Rise and Shine, and others.

I will conclude this chapter with an account from my own experience in a youth media production project. In 1989 I worked with Alex Juhasz, Sara Safford, and choreographer Mark Truitte on the production of *Self-Protection*, a videotape sponsored by a public health organization and written and performed by a group of Latina and African American teen mothers in a GED and job training program.[29] This project differs from the ones described earlier in that it featured the strategy of media appropriation. Rap is a form that subverted musical codes by building the idea of appropriating and altering text into the form itself. In *Self-Protection*, Public Enemy's music was a convenient springboard for a statement about the experience of teen parenting. Participants rewrote the lyrics to the popular rap song "Self Destruction," recasting the message to confront the demeaning experience of public-assistance bureaucracies. As one student put it, "They try to tell you what position you're in, and talk down to you in a degrading fashion, when you know what it's like because you're in that position." The students' version of the rap advocates resistance to institutional racism and negative views of teen mothers. These women present themselves in the video as the proud and responsible parents that they are, advocating reproductive choice through condom use. The intended audience for this tape is their peers. The young women who participated frequently referred during scripting and production to the pedagogical impact they wanted their tape to have on the teenagers who would see it through educational media distribution networks. Unlike Fiske's Aboriginal youth, these teen moms were able to mobilize their own productive reading of a mass media text, going beyond the level of spectatorial fantasy to generate an alternative media product conveying their view to a (albeit limited) national audience of teens in similar social circumstances.

The GED program this tape was produced within had a clear vo-tech orientation. Each teen mother received training in a trade such as carpentry, electrical work, or plumbing. The video production component of the program, however, did not fall into the vo-tech model. It was specifically designed to foster discussion of social and emotional aspects of these women's experience. Production experience was bound so closely with discussion of overcoming social and institutional barriers that the vocational possibilities of video were never directly discussed.

The chapter epigraph quotes Raymond Williams on the need for a press owned by, and responsible to, its readers. I've provided an account of instances where video is "owned" by and responsible to its users, collaborative teams of teachers and students. My argument—and the examples of pedagogical reform I have described—shifts the terrain of the call for media intervention from the popular press to the classroom, and from the written word to the audiovisual medium of video. The projects I describe may not have the universally revolutionary impact Benjamin and Williams hoped for, but they nonetheless hold enormous potential for the future reform of education. This chapter has proposed that we rethink the place of production in relation to the strategies of critical textual reading and resistant spectatorship on the basis of some work carried out by video activists and educators. Whether the approach to media pedagogy they advocate will be successful depends in part on how visual media are incorporated into the curriculum in the next few decades. Whether video will become part of a new class-elevated vo-tech curriculum, or whether it will be implicated in a structural reform of the broader curriculum, depends on a number of factors. The question of media pedagogy's future is a crucial one as media, and visual culture generally, increasingly are the means through which we experience and interpret our world. Computer media and the impact of media convergence on the distinctions between text and image will play no small part in this cultural transformation.

In the following two chapters, I expand this discussion of media pedagogy and progressive curricular reform by focusing more closely on specific examples of video and computer media education. In chapter 3, my case in point is the Rainbow Curriculum. A guide produced by New York City public school personnel in 1992 to aid teachers in incorporating diversity and multiculturalism into the curriculum, the Rainbow Curriculum featured video as one pedagogical strategy. This curriculum and the videos linked to its principles were met by a conservative backlash. I trace the role of video in the Rainbow Curriculum and the debates that ensued from it, and I examine the intersections of progressive education and media education in this particular moment in media pedagogy's history.

CHAPTER THREE

Critical Pedagogy at the End of

the Rainbow Curriculum

Media Activism in the Sphere of Sex Ed

The 1992–1993 school year was a tumultuous one in New York City, not only for students and educators but also for media activists and community members concerned with the state of sex education in the schools. Just before the start of the school year—that is, during the summer, while teachers were away—the city's Central School Board instituted a ban on certain curricular materials. Placed off-limits were texts and videotapes dealing with HIV/AIDS that did not privilege abstinence as a means of HIV prevention. This measure, which came to be known as the gag rule, was taken in part to counter the anticipated release of a document that had long been in the works: a multicultural curricular development guideline under production by the Office of the Chancellor of New York City Public Schools. Called "Children of the Rainbow Curriculum," this guideline for the development of a first-grade multicultural curriculum was implemented in autumn 1992. Written to support the implementation of a culturally diverse curriculum, the guide included six pages that urged teachers to recognize and discuss diverse family structures, including households headed by gay parents, and to teach general recognition and acceptance of sexual diversity. These pages became the center of a national controversy. The guide was heartily slammed by conservative parents, religious organizations, and school board members who condemned the document on the basis of the section on gay parenting and sexuality. The attack, mounted primarily by vocal members of one district (in Queens), received an inordinate amount of media coverage. The guide was not ultimately revoked, but several local school boards refused to use it. The controversy had further repercussions in school board politics. In February 1993, following the guide's release, the central school board failed to renew the contract of Joseph Fernandez, the New York City Schools chancellor whose office produced it. The gag rule was revoked just days before the decision about Fernandez was announced, but the Rainbow Curriculum never got a foothold. Instead it became the target of conservative criticism in educational and religious institutions around the country.

The ingrained heteronormativity of U.S. educational institutions has made the issue of sexual identity a volatile component of multicultural educational reform programs.[1] In what follows, I will first lay out some of the background of the Rainbow Curriculum conflict. Then I will examine a shift in critical discourses about sexuality toward a position that posits same-sex desire as an integral part of all sexual identities rather than homosexual identity as biologically predetermined. I will focus on analyzing two tapes produced by gay advocacy and AIDS outreach groups—works that situate AIDS and sexual practices within a range of cultural identities. The first, *It Is What It Is* (Gregg Bordowitz/GMHC, 1992),[2] is taken up as an example of work developed by a nonprofit gay advocacy and HIV/AIDS support organization in direct dialogue with public school administrators.[3] The second tape, *AIDS, Not Us* (Sandra Elkin/HIV Center for Clinical and Behavioral Studies, 1989), is considered as an example of media produced by a nonprofit research organization concerned with AIDS prevention in inner-city communities. These tapes are examples of kinds of work that must have a place in future curricula. Educators faced with the challenge of the social, cultural, and life-sustaining needs of their student communities must confront the interrelationship of sexual and cultural identities—an intersection that was at the core of conflicts over the Rainbow Curriculum. I will conclude with a brief look back at the way gay sexuality has been handled in U.S. curricula, and an analysis of a videotape produced in response to the handling of gay sexuality in the British educational system.

The End of the Rainbow Curriculum 85

The Rainbow Curriculum is basically a systemwide reference manual for individual teachers' selective development of a broad multicultural first-grade curriculum. Addressed directly to teachers (and not students), the curriculum suggests ways of introducing students to thinking about a broad range of cultures, ethnicities, identities, and social practices. The stated aim of the text is to foster "respect and appreciation for diversity of lifestyles, cultures, and languages."[4] The project was motivated in part by the idea that instituting dialogue about cultural diversity at the earliest possible point in the educational process may help to circumvent the conditions that were contributing to the rise in bias incidents and community conflicts. During this period, gay bashing and police violence against blacks and Latinos were on the rise, and communities were dealing with intercultural conflicts escalating into violence (the Hasidic and African American conflicts in Bensonhurst and Crown Heights, New York, for example).

Controversy over the Rainbow Curriculum centers on some school board members' objections to the text's brief mention of diversity in sexual orientation. The passages in question are a few sentences that appear on 6 of the text's 443 pages. They include a section in which it is suggested that children should be taught to acknowledge the positive aspects of diverse types of households, a suggestion that follows a notation that family structures vary and "may include gay or lesbian parents" (145). Also in question was a section suggesting that educators should foster sensitivity to "differences in sexual orientation" to minimize stigmatization, ostracization, conflict, and loss of self-esteem. All of these, the curriculum points out, are known to be contributing factors in the high rates of homelessness and suicide among gay and lesbian teens (372, 399–400, 402–3). Fixating on these passages, several members of the New York City School Board and a few local community boards condemned the entire text, with one member characterizing it as "dangerously misleading lesbian/homosexual propaganda" that promotes ideas about sexuality that are "as big a lie as any concocted by Hitler or Stalin."[5]

At the height of the conflict over the Rainbow Curriculum, the Central School Board announced its decision to terminate Fernandez's contract. Ultimately, sensational misrepresentation of the contents and institutional role of the Rainbow Curriculum by members of the Central

School Board and vocal members of local school boards and the religious Right was the key factor in the chancellor's termination.[6]

The media has represented this controversy as a power struggle between Fernandez and certain school board members. However, this struggle is only one part of a larger national controversy about sexuality in school curricula. The controversy has included, for example, debates about guidelines for condom distribution in New York City high schools (included in the "HIV/AIDS Program Implementation Guidelines"),[7] and debates about the sanctioning of media and texts in HIV/AIDS curricula that address the real diversity of sexual practices among youth.[8] Historically, gay sexuality has been represented as abnormal or pathological within the institutions of mental health and education.[9] The rendering of gay and lesbian desire as illness has posed an immediate threat to the health and welfare of gay youth. New York City's Hetrick Martin Institute estimates that gay youths in the United States are two to three times more likely to attempt suicide than heterosexual young people; a quarter of gay youths are forced to leave home. The exceedingly high rate of suicide and homelessness among gay youths is attributable in no small part to the effects of institutional practices that ostracize, "correct," and punish an already marginalized youth population.[10] To counter these stigmatizing and pathologizing measures, some progressive educators asserted that homosexuality is an inherent condition, behaviorally in place before school age in certain individuals. Since the seventies, a behavioral model that naturalizes sexuality has been used to intervene in policies supporting the use of disciplinary or corrective measures taken against students identified as gay. Theorist Eve Kosofsky Sedgwick has described the situation as one in which the discourse of a naturalized gay identity has gained a privileged status through its effectiveness in countering supposedly therapeutic, corrective, and punitive practices aimed at eradicating "perverse" desires and practices.[11] She calls this approach "minoritizing" because it strategically defines homosexuality quantitatively (a group of individuals occupying biologically homosexual bodies) instead of qualitatively (a form of behavior that deviates from the heterosexual norm, yet a potentially significant aspect of sexual identity in all people) (41).

The minoritizing approach in education has presented an important counter to those who would appeal to the authority of the institutionalized discourses of medicine and science to grant heterosexuality a normative status. Minoritizing arguments have been used with some success to defend the gay educators' right to teach (because it is biologically inherent, homosexuality cannot be learned or contracted). Such arguments have also been used to protect lesbian, gay, and bisexual students from institutional attempts to change or discipline their desire (an inherent condition cannot be corrected). But these arguments have been less helpful in implementing a historical understanding of sexuality in all its cultural complexity, and in situating same-sex desire as an integral and positive part of *all* sexual identities. In opposition to minoritizing views, Sedgwick proposes a category of approaches to sexuality that she designates "universalizing views." These positions hold that same-sex desire is not a mode attached only to particular bodies or identities but informs a diverse range of sexual practices, including those designated heterosexual. Sedgwick concludes that in the context of Western discourses on sexuality, neither framework for understanding homosexuality is untainted by a pervasive and potentially eugenicist homophobia (40–44).

Advocates of gay-affirming education must come to terms with a critical dilemma ominously voiced in Sedgwick's assessment that "there currently exists no framework to talk about the origins or development of individual gay identity that is not already structured by an implicit, trans-individual Western project or fantasy of eradicating that identity" (41). A barely concealed subtext of the attack against the Rainbow Curriculum was conservative anxiety over the increased authority and legitimization of gay and gay-affirming organizations and educators in conjunction with the institution of HIV/AIDS curriculum. Critics of the Rainbow Curriculum responded to the new institutional status of educators and activists who, having been educated by their work and experience with a decade-long struggle against HIV/AIDS, had become leaders in producing youth-focused educational materials. These materials acknowledge and foreground the critical fact of diversity in sexuality and the culturally situated nature of sexuality. The discourses on sexuality represented in HIV/AIDS curricular material produced by activists and progressive organizations emphasize the fact that AIDS transmission occurs not on the basis of who you are (your sexual identity) but on the basis of what you do (how you practice whatever it is you practice). Behind this message are at least two conditions that conservatives would like to deny. First, AIDS education in the West during the 1980s and

1990s was most effectively managed by gay activists and organizations, because gay communities initially were hit the hardest. This placed gay men and others who have worked with AIDS organizations supported by the gay community in a position of expertise with regard to AIDS education not only for gay youth but also for all youth. Legislation aimed at gays and gay-affirming curriculum in education can thus be seen as a reaction to an increasingly visible presence of gay educators in the field owing in part to pedagogical qualifications linked to sexuality. Second, diverse modes of sexual practice have in common specific acts and methods (both gays and heterosexuals practice anal intercourse, for example), so it makes sense to educate all youth about a diverse range of safer-sex practices, regardless of their stated sexual orientation.

Organizations such as Gay Men's Health Crisis (GMHC) and the AIDS Coalition to Unleash Power (ACT UP) were among the first to recognize the need for HIV/AIDS education among youth. They produced media for school curricula that addresses not only the needs of gay students for information but the needs of students coming to terms with a range of sexual identities and practices (their own, their peers'). The media produced by these groups were part of the curricular material that supported the pedagogical strategies and approaches recommended by the Rainbow Curriculum—the pedagogy opposed by religious groups and conservative constituents within the school system.[12] Strikingly absent from most sex education curricula, homosexuality was raised as specter or stigma in contexts ranging from academics to sports to disciplinary harangues, not only among students but also between teachers and students in lunchrooms and schoolyards.

The GMHC audiovisual department was initiated when the organization hired videographer Jean Carlomusto as their audiovisual specialist in 1987. Her decision to set up an in-house video production facility suited an organization such as GMHC with an urgent need to get information out, in a time when little AIDS educational media had been produced that was specifically targeted to their constituencies. By the time the department was disbanded in 1999, it had produced well over fifty tapes for distribution. In addition, it produced numerous public service announcements and regularly scheduled shows for cable broadcast, which had a more limited shelf life.[13]

GMHC produced tapes targeted toward particular cultural groups. Of particular interest to my discussion is the GMHC production *It Is*

Still from *It Is What It Is*
(Greg Bordowitz, 1992).

What It Is (Gregg Bordowitz, 1992). Bordowitz created the video specifically for HIV/AIDS education in U.S. urban high schools. In a subtle variation on fictionalized documentary, the tape presents a multicultural gay, lesbian, bi-, and heterosexual peer group of teens performing scripted and improvised roles as gay, lesbian, bi-, and heterosexual characters who do not necessarily correspond to the actors' own sexual identities. The group selected is a virtual urban peer group that models youth community for its target viewing audiences, urban classrooms of teenagers. The actors hailed from various schools in New York City, including the High School of Performing Arts, and were identified through a casting call and auditions. As in some of the videos discussed in previous chapters, the production of the tape was an educational process in itself for the teen actors. In this chapter, I will be focusing more directly on the final tape and its address to its target audience rather than its production process. In both aspects of the tape, the peer education process is at work. My concern here will be the peer education model as technique and as object of reflexive parody. As in advertisements that reflexively acknowledge the consumer's awareness of the ad's techniques of media seduction, *It Is What It Is* makes the buy-in that is so essential to the success of the peer education message the object of subtle, reflexive humor.

The three vignette sections that make up the bulk of *It Is What It Is* are performed in campy, parodic styles. Skits based on real-life circumstances like coming out to family or making decisions about what to do during a steamy moment on a date are performed in stilted and reflexive performances. The exaggerated manner of the performances evokes Brechtian distanciation, a technique meant to cultivate in the viewer an awareness of the performed nature of the sequence, to foster a self-consciously didactic and ironic relationship between performer

Still from *It Is What It Is*
(Greg Bordowitz, 1992).

and viewer. In one of these skits, two characters perform the roles of a straight couple on a date. The status of this sequence as parody is made clear by the young man's silly "conservative" tie, the silly naïveté of their lovemaking. What most ensures our lack of emotional buy-in to, or identification with, the scene, though, is the fact that we had already been led to believe, through character monologues (which will be discussed shortly), that at least one of these "straight" characters is in fact gay. Further circumventing our identification with the scene is the intrusion of a third character, acting as the voice of safer-sex reason, who is abruptly cut into the sequence. This narrator explicitly plays the role of pedagogue, speaking the part of sex educator. She directly addresses both the couple and the camera and audience in a voice whose didactic tone adds to the hilarity of her appearance on the scene just as the couple faces the decision whether to have intercourse. Here the peer education model comes into play in a way that makes it the object of humor without stripping it of its effectiveness. The very idea of one's friends appearing on the mental scene with the right advice about safer-sex practice during the most intimate moments of a date places a humorous spin on the process of internalizing the peer educator as superego and voice of one's own conscience. It suggests the idea that sex may be intimate, but it is what it is, and we all face these moments. One's personal decisions can thus be informed by a peer-group response embodied in the imagined witness whose function is to instruct and to bring an internalized sense of collective authority to this personal scene.

As in the *Brothers* interactive dating game described in chapter 4, the didactic process and the internalization of the teacherly voice are made the objects of humor in *It Is What It Is*. The appearance of the safer-sex diva, a drag queen who pops onto the screen during the most intimate moments of *Brothers,* is funny because incongruous with the implied privacy of the moment. The idea that a safer-sex instructor should pop into one's mind to correct the course of action at the moments of most heated passion is of course preposterous, not to say infantilizing. But to embody the pedagogical voice in one's peer, or to parody the role of authority, is to defuse the disciplinary function of this scene, or at least to make self-discipline reciprocally peer based and fun. This reflexive humor defuses the potential offense of having a voice of authority rear a predictably straight, adult, or male head at this private moment. In both cases, the teacherly superego is not only an age group peer but also aberrantly female. In the case of *Brothers*, the diva is a drag queen, a feminized figure. In *It Is What It Is*, the voice of authority is a woman and, notably, a lesbian. These choices are worth commenting on because they subvert the stereotype of the teacher as authoritarian man or straight woman. Authority is internalized in the form of a figure whose status vis-à-vis power is both off center and in defiance of codes of authenticity.

Intercut with the dramatic-instructive vignettes that make up most of *It Is What It Is* is a series of direct-address monologues, confessionals, and testimonial personal narratives spoken by individual members of the cast. These sequences serve an important function in the tape relative to questions of what constitutes one's true identity. At first these sequences appear to function as foils, their realism heightening the parodic nature of the dramatic vignettes. Performers work within the codes of realism, exposing their true selves in these candid interviews. Their confrontational, "straight-talk" approach inspires confidence in them, as real people who can tell it like it is about identity and sex. These teens are truly in touch with themselves. But as the monologues unfold, the codes of realism are disrupted. One character lets us know that he will not be revealing his sexual identity as we might have expected—a statement that prevents us from giving credence to later apparent evidence of his sexuality. Another speaker contradicts our appearance-based expectations about her sexual identity and hints that what she or he is saying may in fact be scripted (which is in fact the case), and we are given information that suggests a sexual identity for her that is ambiguous and mutable. As a teen with sexual desires for women, this femme-looking young woman explains, she flirted with the boys all the more vigorously to contradict any evidence of her true feelings. But we still cannot be sure that her confession is not just another moment in the script meant to short-circuit any conclusion we think we have come to about the characters' identity. Assumptions about identity based on appearances and behavior are repeatedly revealed to be unreliable in the tape as in real life; the testimonials reveal themselves to be no less performed than the dramatic skits—a fact that would come out in postscreening discussion should any viewer have missed the point. As the codes of realism are exposed as just another set of narrative conventions, the viewer is disabused of his or her assumptions about fixed sexual and cultural identities. The "we" (the teen peer group audience) implied in the tape's address comes away from *It Is What It Is* with no real knowledge about who is who and what is what, not only for these particular individuals but for "ourselves," our peers. Rather, the message is that sexual identity, like video itself, is performed and mutable. It is what it is.

I want to reframe this discussion in the more general terrain of media pedagogy and the Rainbow Curriculum controversy. Bordowitz's use of reflexive dialogue reminds viewers that this is not straightforward documentary but a hybrid and ambiguous form that questions the claims to truth implicit in most educational and documentary media. This strategy fosters a productive ambiguity between the performed identities and the lived sexualities and HIV status of the performers. This ambiguity allows the tape to negotiate two contradictory positions associated with minoritizing and universalizing positions: on the one hand, the tape provides positive models of gay identity; on the other hand, it allows for identification across sexual identities, and the realization that identities can be complex and shifting. One youth asserts, invoking the 1970s developmental and minoritizing view, "Researchers have found [that gay] feelings are either set at birth, or at the very latest within the first year or two of life." Another states that "[being gay] is not a choice." The minoritizing position is reinforced at these moments by the affirmative association of same-sex desire with gay identity. However, it is also contradicted by the obvious fact that these identities are being performed and enjoyed by the actors. This is followed by a reflexive diegetic indication that two unidentified nongay actors are playing parts of gay youths. This hint in the script problematizes the viewing game of categorizing cultural signifiers (clothing, body type) according to sexual identity while also suggesting a subtext of relationships that are not acted out: closeted hetero- and homosexual relationships. The very title of the tape suggests a minoritizing argument that relieves gay youth of guilt and responsibility for same-sex desire: sexuality is what it is; you are what you are. This message is combined with more universalizing social-constructionist positions that posit same-sex desire in terms of a whole range of cultural practices (family relationships, friendship, cultural and gender identity).

Behind the apparent provision of role models for a range of sexualities are less explicit, more complicated models of identification in which straight and gay youths perform other identities and thereby encourage viewers to "perform," and identify and empathize with, people of other sexualities. The unfixing of fixed sexual identities is underlined in the safer-sex section of the tape, where the entire cast lines up to pass a kiss from one to the other and back again. This game, which is meant to illustrate that HIV is not transmitted through kissing, also serves to defuse anxieties around same-sex and straight-gay physical contact and pleasure.

In the school context, Bordowitz's tape is remarkable especially for its use of universalizing strategies to frame sexuality in terms that affirm gay desire. Traditionally, administrative support for sex education and alternative family curriculum has been carried out through negative mandates concerning the purported need to "control" perceived problems and behaviors around sexuality. More often, the curricular message is that we need to "control" teen pregnancy or HIV transmission or curb homophobia in the classroom to curtail students' loss of self-esteem and to curb suicide among gay youth. These can, of course, be productive approaches, but the emphasis is on control and prohibition. Many of the institutionally endorsed sex education curricula have tended to target adolescent women, a population almost invariably presented as victims to heterosexual male youths. Sexuality is most often addressed in terms of the mechanics of procreative biology. Gay sexuality is most often presented as a danger to mental health, in the few cases where it is considered at all. As a result of this collectively prohibitive emphasis on control, desire—and particularly the desires of straight women and gay, lesbian, and bisexual youth—disappears from the sex ed picture. As education theorist Michelle Fine has noted, sex education that avoids a discourse of desire further marginalizes students whose desire is already typically denied:

> The absence of a discourse of desire, combined with a lack of analysis of the language of victimization, may actually retard the develop-

ment of sexual subjectivity and responsibility in students. The most "at risk" of victimization through pregnancy, disease, violence, or harassment—all female students, low income females in particular, and non-heterosexual males—are those most likely to be victimized by the absence of critical conversation in public schools.[14]

An implicit message of *It Is What It Is* is that it is impossible to address sexual desire without addressing the real diversity of practices through which it is expressed in youth culture. This is a point that was taken up by Fernandez's staff in developing the HIV/AIDS curriculum, which, for example, suggested the discussion of anal and oral sex among other practices with fourth and fifth grade students.[15] Fernandez's office seemed to be acknowledging what AIDS organizations and activists have been saying all along: You can't expect to educate students about how to avoid transmission if you don't explain how it occurs, and how to prevent it. Realistically, this means moving beyond a biologistic approach that names the danger of exchanging bodily fluids to one that names specific practices associated with desire. *It Is What It Is* does exactly this by first validating desire and then discussing at length both the mechanics and the social and emotional aspects of dealing with a range of sexual feelings through practices regarded as safer.

It Is What It Is was among the first curricular aids officially produced to speak to high school students about sexual diversity, desire, and safer-sex practices. Completed just before the Rainbow Curriculum was distributed, the tape was released at precisely the time that a major capitulation to conservative demands took place within the New York City school board. In the summer of 1992, the school board ruled that educators addressing the issue of HIV/AIDS in the classroom must sign an oath requiring that "substantially more time and attention be devoted to abstinence than to other methods of prevention [of HIV infection]."[16] This ruling applied not only to teachers' speech but also to media used in the classroom. Because *It Is What It Is* did not advocate abstinence quantitatively more than other safer-sex practices, it was officially barred from classroom use. In previous stages, the "HIV/AIDS Program Implementation Guidelines" had instituted progressive developments such as the approval of condom distribution and the teaching of needle cleaning and practicing safer anal and oral sex. But modification of these guidelines in 1992 brought some serious pedagogical restrictions, such as the elimination of the subjects of anal and oral sex in elementary school curriculum, and the institution of this "oath of abstinence" across the curriculum. According to later drafts of the guidelines, all educators who taught HIV/AIDS prevention had to take a standardized teacher training course and follow restrictive official mandates regarding the teaching of safer-sex practices. Much of the information provided by the teacher training program was useful, and guidelines would have been helpful in ensuring accurate information and enforcing the need for confidentiality with regard to student HIV infection. However, teachers already beleaguered by institutional demands were often unable to take the course and were thus not allowed to address the issue of AIDS without repercussions. System-wide attention to the issue led to an increase in surveillance of individual teachers' classroom activities. The situation escalated to the point that the New York Civil Liberties Union filed a suit against the board on behalf of teachers, claiming that the guidelines "violate teachers' freedom of expression in the classroom."[17]

Videotapes, pamphlets, and instructional materials produced by social service organizations had been the main source of up-to-date and frank information that was not available in commercially produced textbooks. With the gag rule in place, these had to be approved by a review committee at the Central School Board to verify that they met abstinence-centered requirements. This resulted in the effective censorship of It Is What It Is, despite the chancellor's office's support for the project throughout its production. Despite this mandate not to show the tape, educators willing to risk challenging the board's mandates continued to screen the tape in many New York City classrooms.

AIDS, Not Us (1989), a tape produced by Sandra Elkin for the HIV Center for Clinical and Behavioral Studies in New York City, also contributed to a pedagogical discourse about desire and sexual diversity in public classrooms.[18] This tape was not, however, subject to the same degree of school board censorship as It Is What It Is. This is not because the school board gave the tape its stamp of approval. The HIV Center kept a low profile with respect to larger school board and administrative controversies. As a result, the tape was able to be widely distributed throughout New York City public schools while the gag rule was in effect, even though it did not come close to meeting abstinence-priority regulations. Many educational health care and correctional facilities received the tape through the New York State Department of Health. The success of the tape in reaching an inner-city public school audience and other education venues can be attributed in part to the producer's ability to enlist the support and input of a range of community organizations and cultural producers working in the margins of the school system.

Music for *AIDS, Not Us* was written and performed by rap stars Heavy D and the Boyz, and a first-person voice-over narration is spoken by a teen character within the narrative. The video's locus of authority is located, like that of *It Is What It Is*, within urban youth culture itself—a factor that likely is responsible for the tape's relative popularity among HIV educational videos for youth.[19] But the tape's position on sexuality and desire raises some other possible reasons for its relatively successful distribution during the period of the oath of abstinence.

AIDS, Not Us provides safer-sex information through a dramatic narrative about a posse of five teenage African American and Latino boys. AIDS is presented among crime, drugs, and drug-related violence as one of several life-threatening conditions of inner-city life. It was produced in 1989, a year in which educational authorities were just beginning to recognize the need to dispel the myth that AIDS is a gay disease. The video takes a step toward countering associations of AIDS with homosexuality while still acknowledging the presence of gay youth in urban youth communities. As in *It Is What It Is*, the peer education model comes into play. A young gay man—a teen named Chris who is *not* HIV positive—serves as the tape's didactic voice of authority. A peer of the video's target audience, this young man has information about safer sex that is useful not only to gay youth but also to his straight friends. His sexuality is revealed late in the tape, in a twist that undercuts any appearance-based assumptions viewers might have made about it. This pedagogical thread is not the only, or the central, narrative. A range of possible sexual scenarios is presented, and we are given the story of one character's idolized brother, who we learn has been infected with HIV through needle use. *AIDS, Not Us* does consistently invoke the work of gay individuals in establishing educational networks, whether the address is to gay or straight viewers. Chris, the narrator, is confronted by Miguel, his closest friend in the posse. Miguel accuses Chris of associating with "a faggot." When Chris responds by coming out to him, Miguel becomes violent. Later the two manage to mend their friendship when Miguel decides to accept his friend's sexuality—"even if [he] may never understand it." Chris attempts to educate Miguel on modes

Still from *AIDS, Not Us*
(Sandra Elkin, 1989).

of transmission, but we learn that his attempts to dispel the "AIDS, not me" lie are lost on his friend. The tape closes with the postscript "Chris won a basketball scholarship to college and went on to medical school. Miguel attended trade school until he became ill. He died of AIDS in his twenties."

Because *AIDS, Not Us* represents straight relationships in greater depth than *It Is What It Is,* the tape was more likely to be accepted among public school authorities. But the tape hardly valorizes the behaviors of its straight characters. Miguel's unwillingness to limit his partners is associated with his unwillingness to use condoms. This macho attitude, and his promiscuity, are punished by death. This is a departure from the punishing of promiscuous gay men in the many AIDS education stories that played on that more prevalent stereotype. We can see how an abstinence-minded reviewer might approve of this narrative turn. Although the subject of abstinence is never broached in the tape, the gay-sex narrative of Chris, as well as the straight-sex narratives of his friends, are all framed to imply that monogamy, combined with condom use, is the way to go. *It Is What It Is,* a tape that takes no single stand on monogamy versus promiscuity but advocates a range of sexual choices and experiences even within straight culture, was less likely than *AIDS, Not Us* to be accepted even in more liberal public school classrooms.

The positions taken up by these tapes, as different as they are, are representative of strategies for advocating a pedagogy of sexual diversity that has been informed by a dynamic and adversarial relation to those of conservative constituents within the politics of education. Opposition to gay rights in U.S. education has a long legislative history. In 1978, freshly inspired by Anita Bryant's successful campaign to challenge gay rights legislation in Florida, California state senator John Briggs authored an initiative for a similar referendum in his own state. Proposition 6, as it was called, would have required the firing of any school employee who was held to be "advocating, soliciting, imposing, encouraging or promoting private or public homosexual activity directed at or likely to come to the attention of schoolchildren and/or other employees."[20] The idea behind this legislation was that gays may be tolerated so long as they remain closeted—an implicit proviso that became confused by the legislation's inevitable blurring of distinctions between what constitutes "public" and "private" behavior. To be openly gay and a teacher was to be selling one's sexual identity to one's students.

This legislation prompted the question among some conservatives: From the standpoint of this legislation, is public display of any form of intimacy with a person of the same sex a pedagogical performance insofar as it "teaches" sexual behavior? What the Briggs initiative implied was that any public signifying of, or participation in, gay culture (within or outside the classroom, explicitly sexual or not) constituted pedagogical "advocacy," "solicitation," or even "imposition" of gay culture in the classroom and beyond.

Until three months before Proposition 6 was voted on, polls indicated that the Briggs initiative would pass. The press billed it as a done deal. Thanks to gay activists' and advocates' vocal opposition, Proposition 6 was ultimately defeated. But this was a partial victory at best, not only because the margin of defeat was frail and indicated that there was still strong support of homophobic legislation, but also because the entire contest placed in question the rights of gay educators to be openly gay. Certain arguments against the legislation embodied a different manifestation of homophobia that would have to be confronted in the years after 1978. This position is voiced in the following passage from the speech of then-governor Ronald Reagan—a single speech to which Briggs himself attributed the defeat of his bill. Reagan espouses the minoritizing position in his argument that "[Proposition 6 presents] the potential for real mischief. . . . Innocent lives could be ruined. . . . Whatever else it is, homosexuality is not a contagious disease like measles. Prevailing scientific opinion is that an individual's sexuality is determined at a very early age and that a child's teachers do not really influence this."[21]

Readers should not mistake this passage as condoning gay culture. In her historical account of gay-related educational law, lawyer and education theorist Karen Harbeck notes that the potentially ruined innocent lives Reagan refers to in this speech were not the lives of gay educators but those of educators presumed to be straight. Under Proposition 6, one could be railroaded out of the profession on the basis of a possible "mistaken" interpretation of behavior. The seeming defense of gay educators in this passage illuminates the complexities to be negotiated in the post–Briggs initiative struggle with discourses of sexuality in educational institutions. Reagan's partial exoneration of gay sexuality ("whatever else it is, homosexuality is not . . .") does little to hide the fact that he is disappointed in medical science's inability to control, or "correct," homosexual desire and behavior. Sedgwick notes that the American Psychiatric Association declassified homosexuality as a disease in 1973, only to reclassify the transgression of heterosexual norms in youth as Gender Identity Disorder of Childhood.[22] Following these shifts in medical terminology, Reagan and others may not have regarded homosexuality as a contagious disease, but they certainly viewed it as a disorder.

Reagan's apparent defense of gay educators makes it clear that in 1978, popular debates had not even begun to address the issue of the need for including material on gay identity and culture in curricula. Political opposition to the Briggs initiative was formed on the basis of a problematic view that homosexuality is innate and not culturally informed after an early developmental stage, and therefore homosexual behavior can be neither "caught" nor "taught" in the classroom. Reagan did contest the idea that gay educators are implicitly involved in recruitment to gay culture, but he sidestepped the volatile anxiety resonating in the Briggs initiative around the unstable, ambiguous nature of cultural signs associated with all sexual identities. In other words, what the proposition made clear is the unsettling fact that sexual identity is not clear or fixed.

This anxiety persists. In 2000 educator David Halperin was taken to task by the American Family Association and a member of the University of Michigan Board of Regents for offering a course titled "How to Be Gay: Male Homosexuality and Initiation," his critics claiming that he was trying to recruit students to homosexuality. The course, to be taught at the University of Michigan at Ann Arbor in fall 2000, considered the role that initiation plays in the formation of gay identity. In response to the accusations, Halperin states, "If I had the magical power to turn heterosexuals into homosexuals, I wouldn't be wasting my time teaching at a university. I'd be engaging in world domination."[23]

The belief that homosexuality is taught and can be learned in schools raises interesting questions about the perceived relationship of pedagogy to desire. A decade after the Briggs initiative failed, England saw the passage of a similar proposition, titled Section 28. Just as Proposition 6 had attempted to snuff out perceived classroom "advocacy" of homosexuality, so Section 28 prohibited the "promotion" of homosexuality. The 1988 British act states that "a local authority shall not (a) intentionally promote homosexuality or publish material with the intent of promoting homosexuality; [or] (b) promote the teaching in any maintained school of the acceptability of homosexuality as a pretended family relationship."[24] As with the Briggs initiative, Proposition 28 highlighted a broad cultural anxiety about homosexuality as something explicitly and problematically linked to schooling. A behavior that is not only passively "picked up," homosexuality threatens to be actively promulgated in the power dynamic of schooling. Schooling itself, by implication, is clearly identified as a sexualized dynamic in this public prohibition.

Cultural critic Simon Watney follows the train of this argument when he suggests that the term "promotion" was simply a euphemism for "seduction." According to Watney, Section 28 gave voice to conservative fears of their own vulnerability, and that of heterosexuals generally, to homosexual desire. It bespoke fantasies that a gay educator might be so powerfully seductive that students would be recruited into gay culture through his or her presence alone. On the one hand, these fantasies provide an overtly sexualized script for the barely veiled narratives of sexual desire that for centuries have informed popular representations of the pedagogical power relation (which for centuries had been represented in the figures of men and boys, as women were excluded from education). On the other hand, they fuel the statistically disproved, yet tenaciously persistent, identification of pederasty with gay male educators. The degree to which these fantasies are based on repression, desire, and denial is the subject of Stuart Marshall's satirical video *Pedagogue*, a tape that was produced in 1988 in direct response to the passage of Section 28.[25]

Using the conventions of the mock documentary, or "mockumentary," this ten-minute video centers on a scripted and staged interview with an art school professor, Neil Bartlett. The male interviewer never appears on camera but is present through voice-over. This disembodied examiner interrogates Bartlett with questions ranging from the mundane (What's your favorite color?) to the demand for confession (Are you a homosexual?). In an interesting twist, answers to questions that are not "loaded" are coded as possible "clues" to sexual identity, and responses to overt questions are stonewalled. Bartlett names the feminine-coded pink as his favorite color but responds to the question about his sexuality by making the assertion—twice and vehemently—that he is "absolutely not" a homosexual.[26] As Bartlett's talking head spouts disdain for liberal educational values, the examiner lowers his camera, as if against his will, to investigate more erotogenic areas of Bartlett's body. This strategy is open to various simultaneous readings. We might imagine the presumably straight interviewer is responding to the lure that the homosexual's very presence poses to the straight man, in the logic of Section 28. Or we might imagine that the interviewer is reading for appearances that belie speech, as if the body will silently exude the sexual identity that Bartlett is so vehemently disavowing on the sound track. The camera momentarily holds on an exposed bit of chest hair framed by Bartlett's open black leather jacket; on safety pin jewelry (inscribed with the word "care") hanging from the leather jacket's breast pocket— a zipper pocket, of course; and finally on the crotch of Bartlett's snug jeans. The evidence of homosexuality is unmistakable; the lure of and to homosexuality that Bartlett's very body presents is rendered clear.

The camera's fascination with Bartlett's body and its gay-coded accoutrements articulates the conservative fantasy/fear that is so unconvincingly disavowed in the speech that Bartlett mouths: that the very presence of the gay educator holds the pleasurable threat of seduction, "promotion," and recruitment into homosexuality, even for die-hard straights. Espousing ideals about proper dress and "old-fashioned" educational standards like paternalistic authority and disciplinary standards, Bartlett makes overt the link between conservative, neo-Victorian disciplinary practices and their simultaneous repression and production of the "deviant" sexual scenarios stereotypical of gay culture. He effectively reveals the institutionalization of deviance and its suppression as productive of meaning in the mainstream pedagogical discourse that supports Britain's Section 28 and the broader repressive culture of late-twentieth-century Britain.

Marshall's short tape concludes with absurd testimony by a number of Bartlett's students. They describe the infectious nature of their

Neil Bartlett in *Pedagogue*
(Stuart Marshall, 1988).

teacher's gayness. These young men and women confess that up until the arrival of professor Bartlett, they had been enjoying perfectly normal heterosexual lives, until Bartlett's presence made them suddenly aware that they themselves are gay. The simple presence of Bartlett for just a day unleashes an epidemic of homosexual desire that infects not only these students but also their parents, roommates, and pets. Like HIV, gayness threatens to infect everybody through sheer bodily proximity.

Pedagogue, in its send-up of the gay infection hypothesis, can be read as echoing the sentiment behind Reagan's argument against the Briggs initiative: one does not "catch" homosexuality by way of contact with gay teachers. But paradoxically, the conservative fear mocked by Marshall—the idea that sexuality is coded even in seemingly neutral areas of identity and culture (in color preference, for example), and can be acquired—acknowledges to some degree the social-constructionist position. But there is some tension in this critique. Another possible reading of *Pedagogue* is that the figure of the "straight" pedagogue in fact exudes a relationship of sexualized power that is not in the control of the speaker. The pedagogue is a figure in the pedagogical relation who verbally denies what his body nonetheless speaks and his behavior so insistently demands. The first reading seems partly congruent with a gay-affirming curriculum like that represented in the controversial six pages of the New York City public school system's Rainbow document. Reagan's argument that homosexuality is behaviorally in place after a certain age (and is therefore unlearnable at school) is one counter to the incredibly retrograde discourse of Section 28. But this dissociation of sexuality from pedagogy, as it is evoked implicitly and in a different way by *Pedagogue,* leaves unconsidered the issue of the cultural practices of homosexuality vis-à-vis other areas of ideology, culture, and desire. What the Rainbow Curriculum implies is that homosexuality is consti-

The End of the Rainbow Curriculum 103

tuted within a complex of ideologies. It is articulated through cultural practices both inside and outside of gay culture—and is lived by gays *and others* through cultural elements that can (and must) be "taught" through gay-inclusive and gay-affirming curricula. As Watney has noted, antigay educational laws like Section 28 "paradoxically . . . draw attention to the fact that fundamental definitions of sexual identity and sexual morality are historically [that is, ideologically] contingent and by no means 'natural.' "[27]

In their push to counter homophobic laws like Section 28, pro-gay legislators, educators, and activists have sometimes recalled developmental models of identity as fixed, models that circumvent the plausibility of contamination-by-education theories. But this strategy leaves unexamined dominant assumptions about the mechanisms through which gay, straight, and other cultural practices are in fact learned and lived. The Rainbow Curriculum, by focusing in its controversial six pages precisely on gay culture as it is lived in and through other cultural institutions (like the family), began to problematize institutionally the nexus of ideology, cultural practice, and education. It is this nexus that is at the heart of both Section 28 and the Briggs initiative. The Rainbow Curriculum represents a broader institutional shift in the United States from the question of *who may teach* to the question of *what is taught*— that is, from the right of gay educators to teach to the institution of gay-inclusive material across the curriculum.

Generally, the conservative legislative backlash of the late twentieth century represented in Proposition 6 and opposition to the Rainbow Curriculum can be seen as a response to visible, institutionalized shifts in educational policy toward support for gay teachers and curriculum.[28] Whereas in the 1970s antigay measures within education were largely directed at individual teachers identified as gay, by the late 1990s conservative forces more frequently focused their attack on gay-inclusive and safer-sex curricula. Harbeck hypothesizes that gay educators' legal and financial backing from teachers' unions across the nation during the seventies is one explanation for the diminished frequency of conservative legal attacks on individual teachers.[29] But the nexus of the battle has shifted to the curricular terrain, which is being structurally transformed (though only in some places and in small degrees) to include material on gay culture, history, and sexuality. The struggle between New York City school chancellor Joseph Fernandez and opposing school board members over the Rainbow Curriculum was just one highly publicized moment in this shift. An equally critical intervention has come in the form of curricular media produced by educators who work at the margins of the school system, such as Bordowitz and Elkin. As would be expected, their inroads were compromised by the necessary mechanism of institutionalization.

Student Involvement in Media about Sexuality

Organizations devoted to youth-produced classroom media have taken a leadership role in developing a new model for peer-based sex education. In the following chapter, I discuss the work of a number of organizations including Rise and Shine and the Educational Video Center (EVC) at length. In Rise and Shine's narrative production *Blind Alley*, a young man who participates in a gay-bashing incident learns a hard lesson about his own sexual anxieties.[30] The victim of the bashing turns out to be a close friend of the young woman with whom he wants to get involved. The tape underscores the elusive nature of the boundaries that divide heterosexual and gay cultural realms. EVC's *Free to Be Me* is a student-produced documentary that includes candid interviews with lesbian and gay youth relating stories about confusion, fear, relief, and pride associated with coming out.[31] Through the process of peer education, these tapes allow students to occupy roles of pedagogical authority. Clearly this sort of pedagogy doesn't happen spontaneously, especially with respect to fighting homophobia—an issue that is more often vehemently silenced. Support for this type of production has come from organizations such as the Hetrick Martin Institute, a social service organization for gay youth that runs the Harvey Milk High School in New York City. The institute conducts workshops on homophobia and other issues in high schools throughout the city. Students from Rise and Shine and EVC participated in workshops run by the Hetrick Martin Institute before producing these tapes, and institute staff and Harvey Milk graduates worked with both Bordowitz and Elkin on their tapes as well. Clearly interorganizational support is critical not only for the circulation of these tapes but for their production.

In the aftermath of the Rainbow Curriculum controversy, this network across progressive education, social services, and media activism was critical to the life of production and distribution of the kind of tapes discussed in this chapter. The controversy had important ramifications nationally not only for educators but for media activists. The "Program Implementation Guidelines" for mandated HIV/AIDS education instituted in 1992 placed limits on what could be taught in the classroom, putting progressive educators under surveillance and creating official channels for the censorship of intrainstitutional media production as well as teachers' classroom media choices.

The problem at the beginning of the twenty-first century is how to counter these institutional blockades while finding ways to make tapes that challenge curricular mandates from the margins. This project may require working with youth from sites outside the public school system. Media organizations such as GMHC, the Educational Video Center, and Rise and Shine have played a leadership role in this movement. In the following chapter, I consider in greater detail the work of groups that have marginal or partial relationships to the school system to show what happens when youth media education moves outside the schools proper.

CHAPTER FOUR

Peer Education and Interactivity

Youth Cultures and New Media

Technologies in Schools and Beyond

The academic analysis of youth media has focused primarily on young people as consumers, overlooking the extent to which they are also producers of media texts and cultures. Examples of youth media production include Internet countercultures and the revival in the 1990s of the trend from the 1960s of self-publishing magazines, called zines. A quick glance through *Factsheet 5*, the alternative publication that reviews independent magazines, gives a sense of the growth of youth-produced print media and their related countercultures. This chapter focuses on a range of new youth media, from video to digital multimedia. I begin with in-school peer education participatory video projects like those described in chapters 2 and 3 and move on to discuss interactive computer projects produced by and for youth through nonprofit organizations working in conjunction with, or with funding from, federal, state, and municipal government agencies. I conclude by discussing educational computer programs designed for communities outside schools, to demonstrate the impact of the peer education model beyond the education system proper, in areas including public health and social welfare.[1]

This chapter demonstrates, by way of case analyses, some of the arguments developed elsewhere in this book. I expand on chapter 2's discussion about participatory or peer education and new media in progressive education. I also develop an argument that is implicit in earlier chapters: that alternative work with new media in education does not take place outside institutional boundaries but is always institutionally situated. But this does not mean that such work is complicit with institutional policies. Many of the organizations engaged in youth video production exploit their marginal or ambiguous relationship to institutions such as schools, government programs, and other official channels through which education is officially conducted. The projects described hereafter were made with institutional support, not in the independent sector strictly speaking. In some cases, their producers exploited the contradictions among their various funders, sponsors, and institutional connections, evading strict oversight and long-held policies in the process. These projects invoke the discussion in chapter 1 about the ambiguous relationships among the government, schools, and other educational entities. This kind of interinstitutional relationship has become more typical of education from the late twentieth century onward.

The programs described in the second half of this chapter were initiated from outside schools proper, even if they were ultimately conducted in schools or with students. These programs have something in common with the museum education programs described in the next chapter, in that their ties to institutions are multiple and ambiguous. As chapter 5 will make clear, museums and other institutions took up the explicit mission to educate that had previously been associated more strictly with schools. The projects and programs described here will demonstrate that the pedagogical mission to educate was not developed in education proper and then passed down to educational programs in health care, social welfare, entertainment, or high culture. Pedagogical projects and philosophies were developed and shared across the boundaries of these institutions, blurring distinctions and objectives. The mission to heal and the mission to educate were seen as interlocking in the era of public health's expansion. The mission to entertain has always been linked to the mission to educate. The linking of public education to media technologies made communications an essential aspect of pedagogy. Channel One, a closed-circuit network that broadcasts educational programs in conjunction with advertising in schools, is a perfect example of this kind of institutional blurring of boundaries.[2]

Finally, this chapter extends the discussion in the previous chapter about sexuality education by focusing on peer education projects that deal, for the most part, with issues of sexuality and gender—topics often glossed over or reduced to neutral terms in conventional schooling. Media education has helped to reform curricula in areas such as sexuality and diversity training, transforming (or taking these issues out of) the health and social studies curriculum and opening them up to subjective discussion and issues relevant to the real lives of young people.

This chapter also introduces some new themes. I emphasize the degree to which youth can have agency within institutional settings such as schools, health education facilities, and media industries. I further propose that young people working in new and hybrid media forms are not just creating isolated works of personal expression. They are forging media for a more collective and public voice for youth cultures. These are more optimistic and perhaps utopian claims than those made in previous chapters. I temper these assertions, however, with a perspective expressed elsewhere in this book: the voice of new youth media is institutionally situated and is thus subject to the same forces of the market as adult media production. Media projects by youth in the classroom or in youth-oriented programs are not exempt from economic and social forces outside the classroom. Indeed, this is one of the interesting aspects of youth media—the potential to circulate beyond the classroom, inflecting media markets targeted toward youth consumers with youth-produced texts. I consider a number of cases in which projects in education move outside and beyond the world of the school proper. The cross-disciplinary movement of pedagogical projects and missions is discussed throughout the chapters that follow, as well.

With the focus on new technologies in the 1990s to the present, video has faded into the background. In chapter 2, I discussed a number of programs using video, not computer-based media. I continue this focus here by considering some videos produced by young people in conjunction with schools, social service agencies, and nonprofit arts organizations. I begin with a discussion of this work because it provides important insight into the newer and more prominent computer-based instructional technology work. The principles of video pedagogy already laid out more fully in chapter 2 deserve a brief review. Since the late 1970s, political art groups and activists in the field of education have developed programs in which low-cost video technology is made available to public schools in low-income communities to encourage students to engage more actively in the educational process and to address issues in their lives. These initiatives followed the somewhat earlier movement to make low-cost consumer video technology available to community organizations as tools for consciousness-raising and activism. The general idea behind media education is that television holds potential for young people beyond their passive consumption of generic programs. The medium can support self-expression and empowerment; moreover, production can be a useful therapeutic tool for kids in crisis. Media production has been used therapeutically in fields including abuse counseling, drug counseling, and dropout prevention programs. Although video produced in these venues is usually poorly distributed, it often reaches its target audience and serves its purpose quite effectively. Programs engaging in this kind of production are places where young people gain access to skills while also finding a venue for expression about personal and political issues proscribed by institutions of education and social welfare. Sexuality and abuse, for example, are themes that frequently appear in tapes produced by youth in "therapeutic" media production programs. Tapes about these issues are sometimes the first projects in which students begin to think through social issues such as gender and power in an organized fashion, and in a way that allows them to draw on their learning to manage their life experiences.

In the 1990s, progressive approaches to education found fertile ground in programs devoted to bringing media production into the schools. These programs have tended to involve collaboration among nonprofit arts and youth service organizations whose political sensibilities (e.g., a commitment to work on gender issues) might not otherwise pass muster under school board review. As newer technologies become available to youth in the educational system and at home, the production became a more viable possibility for a broader range of young people.

I encountered the work discussed in this chapter through professional experience in primary and museum education, so a biographical note is in order. My contact with the organizations and producers discussed, and indeed my means of acquiring this video and computer-based work for assessment, came largely through my involvement in primary school video education. In the late 1980s, I taught video and art at the Bank Street School, a progressive private school on Manhattan's Upper East Side. I subsequently helped to found and taught at the Lower East Side

School, a bilingual alternative public school in one of New York City's poorest Latino communities. In the mid-1990s, I was curator of education at the New Museum of Contemporary Art. This position gave me the chance to gather some of the youth-produced media projects I had followed through the informal national network of youth-produced media educators that had formed among those of us working at the intersections of progressive education, art, and media. In 1995 this material became the basis for *alt.youth.media,* an exhibition whose title references the "alt," or alternative category, of on-line newsgroups devoted to subcultural themes. The idea was to bring together a wide range of youth media to demonstrate the current and historical importance of production in the formation of new modes of citizenship and political engagement among contemporary youth in the United States. The diverse perspectives of the works in *alt.youth.media* challenged and redefined images of youth prevalent in mainstream media. They articulated in a nuanced way the diverse aesthetic and political sensibilities of young people in contemporary media cultures.

In this chapter, I will focus on videotapes, interactive computer and CD-ROM projects, and an e-zine (a Web-based alternative magazine), many of which were included in *alt.youth.media.* All projects considered in this chapter deal with youth sexuality. They are examples of collaborations in which young people worked with public schools, social service agencies, academic institutions, and nonprofit arts organizations. My interest is to demonstrate the benefits of interinstitutional collaboration.

The projects came about through programs engaged in two general areas of pedagogical philosophy: peer education and media-based learning. I will briefly provide background on these two concepts. Peer education has been a central component of critical pedagogy and liberal education reform initiatives since the 1960s. This approach is based on the view that the educational process, and young people's sense of political engagement and power, is enriched when young people assume pedagogical roles among their peers. The roles of teacher and student are interlocking. The model of learning by rote from the teacher as master of the discipline is replaced by a process that emphasizes the development of the students' own collective and individual critical thinking skills and rhetorical skills of discussion, group collaboration, and debate. Those embracing this approach use techniques that foster student-to-student exchange and group activities. Interactivity, a term with strong currency in computer discourse, has had an important place in peer education, where the emphasis is on encouraging peer interaction on interpersonal and group levels.

Sexuality education has a privileged place in the history of peer education. Sexuality has long been part of the curriculum (through health education, for example), but the peer education model has in many cases opened up dialogue about sexuality to include discussion about taboo issues such as sexual practice among youth, family life, and experiences of physical or sexual abuse. These issues may be taken up in more conventional health education curricula, but not with the same degree of emphasis on personal practice, experience, and working through personal issues. The philosophy of peer education fosters the kind of forum where kids talk to kids. Ideally, peer education provides a safe community and develops a useful vocabulary in which youths can publicly articulate and analyze their life experiences. By creating this kind of forum, peer education sometimes cultivates a setting where students deal openly for the first time with hidden issues in their lives such as physical or sexual abuse.

Media-based learning had a politically dubious beginning in fifties government- and foundation-sponsored attempts to reduce labor costs and generate new markets for technology (and other goods and services) by establishing networked classrooms. This continued with programs such as Whittle's Channel One, a secondary school educational package of the 1980s and 1990s that involved the mandatory screening of commercials for items like sneakers and candy bars in order to gain access to the educational programming and technologies offered by the company for free.[3] But more progressive models of media-based education have sprung up alongside this approach. Programs like the New York–based nonprofit arts education entity Rise and Shine, discussed briefly in chapter 2, sponsor public-school residencies and after-school programs where youths participate in poetry and video workshops geared toward creating videos through which students work out complex personal experiences that previously were unarticulated in their lives. In these tapes, peer education comes into play insofar as creating the videotape is a therapeutic and group-interactive experience: the process of production becomes a means of working through personal issues in peer group settings, and students learn leadership and skills for working in groups in the process. The peer education model also comes into play later, when the completed tape is used in classes and peer support groups as a means of generating discussion. In a sense, the media education ethos represented in these kinds of tapes draws directly from theories of peer education, bringing together technological and sociological definitions of interactivity in a setting that is broadly therapeutic. In the remainder of this chapter, I discuss video projects produced with these approaches—peer education and media-based learning—tacitly in place.

Video as Therapy

Kept Quiet (1995), a tape about sexual abuse produced by a group of seven students at the Manual Arts High School in South Central Los Angeles, is a good example of a number of issues I've raised thus far concerning peer and media-based education. The project began with video artist Julia Meltzer, who was brought to Manual Arts as an artist in residence through a government humanities grant. Meltzer was assigned to a studio arts course dedicated to the project of designing and producing banners for school functions. She immediately shifted the focus of the course to video production. The mixed-gender class was divided to form production teams, which Meltzer met with individually. Meltzer's strategy was to meet with each group for only a portion of their class meetings, providing guidance in the areas of video technique and group process, leaving each group alone for periods of time to talk and to develop projects on their own. One group, composed of seven young women, settled on virginity and celibacy as the topic of the video they wanted to produce. However, as Meltzer began to encourage this group to discuss these issues, a more compelling subtext emerged. Several of the women in the group used this forum to talk about their sexual abuse. For some of them, this was the first time they had spoken openly about these experiences.[4]

Meltzer encouraged the group to shift their topic to sexual abuse. The tape that resulted took the form of two vignettes dramatizing the experiences of two members of the group. The first vignette recounts in first-person voice-over a girl's experience of sexual abuse by her mother's friend. The second reconstructs a case of date rape. For the women in the group who had experienced abuse, the video production was the basis for a therapeutic process that was spontaneous, peer based, and effective. For the other women in the group, the group discussions and the tape's production taught them how to support their peers as they worked through the trauma of their experiences. The course as a whole gave the group a forum through which to develop and articulate a sexual politics of their own, and how to negotiate issues such as consent and power.

Kept Quiet is essentially autobiographical and testimonial. To a certain degree, the women spontaneously drew on the conventions of reality television, a genre popularized in the early 1990s. In reality television, real-life crimes or crises and their resolutions are reenacted in dramatic narratives, often accompanied by voice-over narration by the triumphant survivor of the crisis or the victim of the crime. This format is exactly replicated in *Kept Quiet*: the two crises depicted in the vignettes are dramatically reenacted on the image track while first-person voice-over narration by the women whose stories are being told recounts the incidents. Replicating a convention often seen in reality television, the vignettes are shot primarily (though not entirely) from the point of view of the perpetrator, creating temporal and subjective tension with the narration spoken in voice-over by the victim after the fact. Anna Williams describes these conventions as they are used in reality television episodes about domestic violence in particular.[5] As is so often the case in the shows Williams describes, in *Kept Quiet* we never actually see the abuser. His presence is indicated by his shadow, by the camera point of view, and by the responses of the victim, who is played by a member of the production group (though not the woman whose story is told).

The conventions of reality television that so clearly influenced the students in their choice of dramatic structure converge with those of therapeutic role-playing: the tape became a means of working through trauma by reenactment. The two women whose stories are told were able to perform experiences that might have been too difficult for them to describe publicly (in the space of the larger class group, for example, or before the eyes of the teacher). These experiences became accessible through the distancing device of the quasi-fictional formula of dramatic reenactment. Not only did this process help these two women in their process of recovery; it helped their peers to articulate their own similar experiences, as well as to speak out about these issues as they concerned all members of the class, male and female.

The proposition that video can serve a therapeutic function has been made in reference to popular television by Mimi White, who describes reality television as part of a broader televisual therapeutic ethos. She explains that by getting to tell his or her story on television, the confessional subject experiences the processes of repetition and recovery.[6] Perhaps the most crucial contribution of autobiographical tapes like *Kept Quiet* is precisely this therapeutic potential to aid recovery. However, *Kept Quiet* does veer from the conventions of confessional television in at least one important way. Tapes such as this are not intended for a wide audience. The peer group is a space of relative, if not absolute, privacy. Reality television differs in that it facilitates the process of recovery by engaging the confessional subject in public celebrity. White explains of these subjects that "their stories are told on national television, and they get to participate as actresses and expert witnesses. In such instances, the successful therapeutic trajectory is signified by the patient's accession to celebrity status via an appearance on television."[7]

Kept Quiet is part of a broad group of more personal video projects in which public celebrity does not always or necessarily come into play, particularly not as a springboard to cure. I will return to this issue of public display near the end of my discussion of the tape. For the moment, I would like to extend the discussion of therapy in the production process itself. There is also a history to the idea of video production, the less public side of video, as therapy. Video has proven to be well suited to various local amateur contexts where the medium is used to foster self-analysis and interpersonal relationship building, enhancing reflexive insight into the dynamics of a group and its distinct identity. As video historian Janine Marchessault explains, "From 1969 onward, video became the choice technology for participatory practice. Not only was it cost-effective, but it could, ostensibly, provide an automatic—instantaneous and simultaneous—record, a mirror machine that needed no operator."[8]

Home video is the most obvious example of this use of video as "mirror machine." Other examples of participatory video practice include teacher training, ethnographic documentation, group therapy (particularly where role-playing is recorded and analyzed), and playback in sports and performing arts training. In some of these examples (sports, teacher training), the medium is simply a means of displaying—and thereby mechanically correcting or refining by way of rote repetition—physical and auditory performance. But in many cases, performance, observation, discussion, and repetition or correction of performance are all integral to establishing various therapeutic processes for group members: catharsis, projection, transference, and ego development are just a few of the psychic processes that can be effected through this use of video.

In these applications, public display is limited to a relatively small group. The video functions somewhat paradoxically as a means of establishing the group as a private space of therapeutic community interaction. Through videos like these, intended as they are for local use only, groups can safely articulate a collective story or set of stories for their own internal consumption and analysis. In this sense, video can be a catalyst not only for the honing of physical and auditory performance but for identity formation, crisis intervention, and community building. The therapeutic process is enacted through the production experience itself, and not solely through the catharsis of performance displayed.

From this perspective, the success of *Kept Quiet* hinges in part on how well the tape fostered social interaction and articulation among members of the production group during the making of the tape, and not at the moments of performance and exhibition. This point echoes chapter 2, in which I argue that production, so often neglected in favor of consumption in the cultural analysis of media education, can play a crucial role in students' education and personal development. To evaluate the success of the tape on this scale, it is necessary to return to the issue of peer education. By all accounts (those of Meltzer and the group members), the tape's production process provided an unprecedented forum for articulation and working through of previously unarticulated trauma, as well as the development of a collective and informed sexual politics. These goals were largely achieved in the process of working on the tape. What came after—displaying the tape to the class and other classes, and the discussions that ensued—was supplementary to these effects, which were already evident during the course of the production process.

This success is largely due to Meltzer's investment in the peer education model. She insisted that students take charge of all aspects of production rather than allowing them to perform for her in front of the camera, as participants in reality television do for their producers and crew. By placing the students themselves in the position of producer, Meltzer complicated the "patient" or "victim" orientation that White describes in her account of reality television "confessors." Students were given the authority not only to speak their experiences but to craft their own images in the course of that "confession." This greater degree of control allowed for a less passive orientation to emerge and shifted catharsis from scripting and performance, distributing it across the entire experience (which included planning, shooting, and editing the tape). The women who produced *Kept Quiet* scripted the points of view of their abusers, the course of events, and other aspects of the episode. "Confessors" featured in reality television episodes rarely have this degree of direct input on, much less control over, production. Meltzer further empowered the students as a group by encouraging peer-supported dialogue during the process of scripting and production. When she did participate in student discussions, Meltzer's role was that of discussion facilitator, not leader. The great degree of trust she exhibited regarding the students' authority about their own sexual experiences facilitated both a working through of trauma at the individual level and the emergence of a collective sexual politics unencumbered by censorial oversight.

Meltzer's status as a partial outsider to the school system was essential to the project's success. Through her status as a visitor, and therefore as a marginal member of school staff, she was able to bring in a progressive educational program that would otherwise not have gotten a foothold in the more conservative climate of the public school system in which she worked. All of these factors contributed to the project's success as a therapeutic experience.

At this point, I would like to return to the issue of public display. The tape was eventually shown not only to the class but also to the entire school. This moment in its process was anticipated with some unease by all of the members of the group, and particularly the women whose stories were told. Privacy was essential to the project from the beginning to the end of its production. If not for this sense of privacy and discretion, the women could not have used the project to speak out about their experiences. Not surprisingly, some members of the group initially resisted having the tape shown publicly. Throughout the production process, the girls struggled to ensure their anonymity. For example, names and locations of the events depicted were changed, and they did not reveal whether the narrators were telling their own stories or those of other members of the group. The issues they addressed remained secret outside the group until the moment of the class screening. Even the girls' parents never learned about the project's content, though the tape was eventually included in a public screening for the assembled school as part of a larger video program (and so parents may have learned about the tape's focus later).

Meltzer claims that the public screening benefited the women in the group. In fact, she continues to exhibit the tape with the students' consent. The *alt.youth.media* exhibition was one site where the tape was shown. The women's consent can be read as an indication of their view that they benefit from the tape's public exhibition. I want to shift the focus from the producers' therapeutic benefits, however, to that of the potential benefits available to other young people through exhibition of personal tapes like this one.

Therapeutic Mirroring

From the perspective of a youth audience, viewing a tape like *Kept Quiet* is different from the experience of watching a network television after-school special about the same topic (sexual abuse and date rape). It is impossible to watch *Kept Quiet* without being made aware that this is a youth production, and moreover that this tape was made by the very women who experienced the abuse it documents. The tape itself makes these facts inescapably clear. The conditions of production, and the information that we hear about the production personnel themselves, are woven into the text, so that the dramatic narrative cannot be experienced without knowledge of these conditions. In this sense, videos like *Kept Quiet* share some qualities with the youth-oriented reality television series *The Real World* (a series, incidentally, that is directly indebted to the genres of community-based, participatory, and personal video). Aired on MTV since 1992, *The Real World* follows selected performers who are filmed in the course of real-life activities performed spontaneously with a group of peers assembled according to the episode's thematic blueprint of a journey, with minimal scripting and direction. *Kept Quiet* does not share with *The Real World* this commitment to spontaneity and filming life as it happens. But the two programs do share the message to their targeted youth audiences that the events depicted come directly from the lives of real young people, whether scripted or not; that these are documents of the real experiences of one's peers, whether their depiction is "acted" or not. It can be argued that the performers in the documentary *Real World* "act" their parts no more spontaneously than performers in a dramatic narrative. Nonetheless, "liveness," performed or not, remains a crucial point of distinction between these programs. Conventions that suggest that both tell the "real" stories of young people like themselves allow youth viewers a kind of identification and empathy that is simply not available in the viewing of the more conventionally dramatized after-school educational programs offered by other networks. Spontaneity, the lack of an intermediary adult gaze, and the technical and linguistic signifiers of off-the-cuff or low-tech production all contribute to the viewer's experience of a real world, however contrived these effects may in fact be.

The lore of participatory production is extended through extra-textual data that come to the fore not only in the video itself, self-referentially, but in the exhibition setting. Program notes provide the facts surrounding the production, feeding a sense that this is a truly intertextual experience in which the video bleeds into the real world, and vice versa. The presence of the producers themselves (or representatives like Meltzer) at screenings can also add to the sense that the video is a slice of a real-life experience that permeates the here and now. A therapeutic "mirroring" effect of the production process, then, is textually extended to youth viewers in the exhibition stage, carrying therapeutic peer education over from the "real" group into a larger arena where identification allows young viewers to imagine themselves as part of this process of belonging, articulation, and self-analysis. The process comes full circle when tapes like *Kept Quiet* are used in peer education settings such as classrooms and therapy sessions to forge a sense of community, to model and prompt mirrored confessional behavior, and to articulate and draw out previously unspoken traumas.

Situating Video Therapeutics outside the Classroom

The therapeutic potential of video has been exploited more directly and self-consciously by Rise and Shine, a New York City–based after-school video education program discussed briefly in chapter 3.[9] Established in 1985, Rise and Shine grew out of a program in which video artists and poets were paid to work in residencies with students in public schools.

Over the years, Rise and Shine has shifted its work to an out-of-school facility where groups of students work collaboratively on productions during three terms per year, sometimes for school credit. Rise and Shine is, on one level, a dropout prevention program. Students tagged "in danger of dropping out" are more likely than their peers to be experiencing crises at home or outside school. The term "crisis" can imply lack of parental guidance, economic hardship, involvement in drugs or crime, or any number of circumstances.

In the case of the program in which *Kept Quiet* was produced, the artist in residence had to negotiate the policies and politics of the school, a process that restricted everything from shooting location to content. To a somewhat limited degree, Rise and Shine has been able to achieve greater autonomy from the schools, thanks to the organization's acquisition of more stable funding, equipment, and production space. The institutional autonomy of Rise and Shine is beneficial to students, allowing them a degree of creative autonomy not attainable in most public school settings.

Rise and Shine is a nonprofit organization that employs the students as well as the teachers who participate in its projects. Adult artists and poets employed by the program work after school and on weekends with about forty students per semester. Production groups of five to ten students are organized to work together on a project. Significantly, students are paid for the after-school work that they do: they receive a stipend for working on their productions, and in return, they must do community service that takes the form of presenting finished tapes to audiences through social service agencies and schools. Some of these students have gone on to become the paid employees who run Rise and Shine's workshops.[10]

Rise and Shine has been particularly successful in using poetry writing and performance-based exercises to develop complex portrayals of young peoples' experiences. Executive director Laura Vural notes how these exercises allow students to articulate experiences that are underrepresented or misrepresented in the mainstream media. After working in journal- and poetry-writing workshops, students are invited to perform their poetry for members of the group. These performances become the basis for discussions about the issues enacted in them. This use of performance as a means of generating group discussion is not unlike the use of role-playing exercises in psychological and social service counseling settings—in AIDS support groups or addiction support groups, for example.

The work of writing and performance is relatively introspective. Students are then led into a second phase, during which they discuss and research the issues about which they wrote and performed. Rise and Shine staff members direct students to find out more about the characters and themes they wrote about by interviewing others who have had similar experiences. The research and interviews become the basis for a video script. In some cases, this research takes the form of documentary video footage that is eventually used in a final video production. Inter-institutional collaboration becomes important in this phase of the program: Vural and her staff teach students to support their productions by reaching out to a range of personal contacts and social service agencies.

A good example of this approach is Rise and Shine's *Stolen Innocence* (1995), a tape that combines dramatic narrative with documentary-style interviews, many of which are shot using techniques to obscure the identities of the speakers. In the opening sequence, a teenage girl agrees to a blind date with a cousin of her friend. The date goes sour when the teenage boy ignores her resistance to his sexual advances. This narrative sequence is gradually interrupted by a montage of television and film images of rape and violent sex, accompanied by voice-over descriptions of women's experiences with rape and sexual violence.

Stolen Innocence maintains its original basis in confessional journal writing and poetry, also bringing in perspectives from people interviewed during the fieldwork stage of the production process. However, a number of other Rise and Shine projects venture further from role-playing, confessional, and documentary techniques to incorporate a pastiche of styles, in some cases producing a much more complex take on issues of sexuality and violence. A good example is *Mending Wounds* (1994), a tape about a young woman named Jennai who comes to terms with her own sexuality in relation to her mother's lesbianism and her father's contempt for, and violence toward, his ex-wife and daughter. The tape intercuts montage sequences inspired by experimental documentary and poetry with soap-opera-inspired vignettes. We follow Jennai's process of asserting her difference from her mother's lesbianism by sleeping with many men; she eventually becomes pregnant. Her condition prompts her to run away to her father for support. However, her father receives the news of her pregnancy with anger, striking her and accusing her of being just like her mother. Jennai comes to terms with the identities of all involved, including herself—but only after her despondent mother commits suicide by a drug overdose.

The therapeutic functions of youth production and the peer education model are well represented in the making of *Mending Wounds*. The tape is based on the experience of one of its producers, a young woman who began to become conscious of her feelings about her own and her parents' sexuality, and her father's violence, only through the process of journal and poetry writing and video production. Like White's reality television confessors, Jennai used the tape to bring these issues to a public and a collective level, outside the perimeters of the school system, as a means of mending the wounds from her childhood traumas. This making public of the tape took place even before its screening, during the production phase. For example, members of the production group interviewed a range of gay and lesbian youths to help Jennai and themselves better understand the issues at stake in the experience Jennai wanted to narrate. Young people they spoke to were members of YELL, a queer youth branch of ACT UP (AIDS Coalition to Unleash Power); staff at the Hetrick Martin Institute, a gay and lesbian youth services organization; and students at the institute's Harvey Milk High School for gay and lesbian youth. The interviews were not used in the tape but instead helped Jennai and her group to better understand and work through issues surrounding her family life and her sexuality.

In the production of *Stolen Innocence* and *Mending Wounds*, Rise and Shine was able to offer youth in crisis a social space apart from the institutional framework of the school system. By offering a semiautonomous space, by promoting peer education, and by encouraging student interaction with public and private organizations beyond the usual scope of young people, Rise and Shine fostered the development of a youth counterculture with respect to issues of sexuality, violence, family, and death. Young people who participate in Rise and Shine projects come away with a sense of agency and knowledge beyond what they might have gained in a school setting where media texts are viewed and discussed but not produced, and where the peer education model is not in place. Finally, they come away with a sense that their creativity and self-awareness can benefit others—and that they can be compensated for providing this benefit.

At this point it becomes necessary to clarify the argument I make in this section about institutions. I include this discussion about Rise and Shine to make it clear that I do not uphold the utopian position that countercultures exist only outside the boundaries of institutions such as schools. My position is that youth countercultures depend on institutional support for their means of production, whether that means is a building in which to meet, or access to, and training in, media technologies. Clearly, youth cultures like rap are supported by commercial entities like the music industry. However, it is important to see how micropractices and subcultures also emerge at the intersections of more mundane kinds of institutional settings. Youth media groups that work between and at the margins of institutions such as schools, social service agencies, and government-funded nonprofits are able to get away with a bit more precisely because they are not beholden to a single set of regulations or policies. The regulatory mechanisms monitoring the work of entities such as Rise and Shine are somewhat less operable because of the organization's slippery position between funders and schools, and between young people and broader sectors of the communities in which youths live. So these marginal institutions are crucial to the promotion of peer education, as well as to the introduction of new technologies and new approaches, because they are less constrained by conventional or historical educational practices. Unlike schools in the New York City public system, for example, Rise and Shine does not have to contend with internal opposition to visual media, or fear of losing classical educational values. The organization simply was not founded on these principles. Rather, the peer education model is the foundation on which programs such as Rise and Shine were built, with the goal of fostering not only therapeutic process but community interaction as the heart of the educational process.

No single medium has been lauded more widely for its potential to facilitate community interaction and participatory education than the computer. As noted in chapter 1, the claims made for televisual education in the fifties were echoed in 1990s rhetoric about digital media education. In the following section, I turn to cases in which computer programs join videos and television broadcasts in the quest for therapeutic, peer-based, and interactive educational production projects. I would like to emphasize here that by describing videos and then computer programs, I do not mean to imply that the latter replace the former as the peer-educational medium of choice. Rather, computer programs join television and video in the multimedia classroom of the twenty-first century.

Peer Education Meets Computer Interactivity

Earlier I noted that the term "interactivity," so central to debates about computer-mediated education, has had long-standing significance in discussions about alternative learning models. In the projects I have discussed, the term refers to the fostering of social interaction among group participants. Media technology is a corollary to the social interactive process. In discussions about computer technology, interactivity most often refers to the range of user options: the addition of multiple hyperlinks and multiple-choice selections within a text, for example. In this section, I consider two projects in which the social definition of interactivity is more fully realized within the terms of technological interactivity familiar to computer discourse. The first, titled *Sex Get Serious* (1993), is also an example of a successful peer education program supported by a collaboration among social service agencies, arts organizations, and schools.[11]

Sex Get Serious was produced by urban youth working with Jubilee Arts, a nonprofit arts organization based in Birmingham, England. Jubilee started out in the 1970s primarily as a theater arts group involved in developing peer education programs with teens. Situated in the demographically diverse and working-class Sandwell area of Birmingham, Jubilee has a production facility where it holds workshops with a range of community and school groups. Over the years, Jubilee has expanded and shifted its emphasis to include print and electronic media productions. Some of the group's earlier projects include a poster series produced in collaboration with the Sandwell Area Rape Crisis Center, a community documentation photo display coordinated by members of an Asian welfare center, and a commemorative tea service and desktop-published book about the Tipton community produced with the Tipton Youth Forum. *Sex Get Serious*, Jubilee's first large-scale computer project, is an interactive sex-education computer program designed for use by teenagers in schools, youth clubs, public health clinics, and informal educational settings. The primary financial and institutional sponsor for the program was the Sandwell Area Health Authority, a public health agency within England's socialized medicine system.

The program was produced through a peer education scheme: groups of teenagers worked on segments of the project through a series of classroom and after-school production workshops. Segments of the interactive project were produced over the course of a few years by different groups of young people, so the program encompasses a range of styles and perspectives. The peer education model comes into play here in an interesting way: each group coming in to work on the project would view the previously produced segments, playing off of the ideas and issues raised in them to create their own segment.

As in Rise and Shine productions, *Sex Get Serious* is informed by a range of "authorities" on health and sexuality beyond the Sandwell clinic. The young people who worked on the project conducted research at HIV/AIDS service organizations, in libraries, and in addiction and sexual counseling agencies. But they also drew on teen magazines, their friends, acquaintances at youth clubs, their families, and popular music to generate a kind of archive of viewpoints about safe sex, pleasure, and knowledge. Program segments encompass these perspectives along with the more conventional institutional viewpoints on these issues, and all are subject to intensive interactive interrogation in a program that effectively generates a new kind of educational text.

The design of *Sex Get Serious* is a direct outcome of the production process. Just as the process allowed different groups of young people to produce segments reflecting different perspectives on sexuality, so the design of the interface invites participation by youths with a range of cultural interests. This is most evident in the spatial metaphor that is used to organize the program. At the start, users are invited to take a trip through Kooltown, a fictional urban setting where users might enter a nightclub, a newsstand, a health center, a youth club, or a home. Within these various spaces, one can choose to listen to music, view television clips, view posters close-up, flip through a family photo album, or listen to testimony of people living with HIV or friends in a nightclub talking about sex. There is the opportunity to select a kind of social engagement suited to one's specific interests. For example, within the youth club, girls might choose to enter the FAB Room—a room where "Females Answer Back" to male-dominated discourse on sex. Here users listen to women vocalists and rappers who expound on women's views of relationships and safe sex.

Sex Get Serious is startlingly well produced for a student-produced

Bus stop from *Sex Get Serious* CD-ROM (Jubilee Arts, 1993).

program of its period. Its high production values reflect the more positive climate of government support for media arts education that existed in Britain in the eighties and early nineties. Jubilee Arts successfully engaged the support of local government health and education authorities whose agendas were, in turn, addressed in the student's productions for the project.

Sex Get Serious was a big success with youth users, inspiring Jubilee's technical consultant, a design group called ARTEC, to embark on a more elaborate interactive software project with funding from the East London and City Health Promotion Services. Published on CD-ROM, *Think Positive* is mainly targeted to schools where it will be used by eleven to sixteen year olds. *Think Positive* is staged in two spaces: a virtual café, a social space made up of a number of connected rooms populated by hip characters and high-tech cursor-activated objects; and a comic book world that can be entered either by following or assuming the identity of a particular character. To get into the café, users log in with a door person by providing a name or pseudonym, age, and gender. This information determines some of the characteristics of the "help" facility, such as the gender of the narrative voice. There are five areas within the café: the Holodeck (a science fiction name appropriated from the tele-

Females Answer Back in the Video Room from *Sex Get Serious* CD-ROM (Jubilee Arts, 1993).

vision series *Star Trek: The Next Generation*), the Chill Out Room, a reference room, a mezzanine, and a reception area. The Holodeck is a cyberspace zone where users can access the Metamedia audiomobile (a safer-sex sound bite device), VideoPositive (a place to experience audio-visual media about HIV transmission), and areas for one-on-one discussion with an adviser. The Chill Out Room is a space for interactive music jam sessions, with songs about HIV issues, and the option of hearing solos from particular musicians in the room. Aspects of the dialogue and events throughout the program are keyed to the actual time of day or season. Each time a user logs on, the events are different, and if a user visits the café repeatedly, the characters become more chummy, recalling past interactions.

Ro Rai, coordinator of ARTEC's multimedia workshop, notes that the design team adapted the idea of the navigable environment from some of the most engaging commercial entertainment products then available in the United Kingdom (such as *Virtual Night Club* by Trip Media). "The real challenge," he explains, "was to make contacts and understand the actual context in which this sort of project can be used." [12] ARTEC worked with youth at several schools, getting feedback on current CDi (CD-ROM interactive), CD-ROM, and laser disc products as well as HIV/AIDS pamphlets and videotapes. *Think Positive*'s design was based in part on the aspects of programs the students liked. For example, many students felt it was important to be able to specify their gender, sexuality, and race and wanted to be able to specify and express aspects of their particular communities and subcultures as well. These views are accommodated, for example, in the narratives of the comic books, which are about youths whose personalities reflect a range of sexualities, cultures, and personal tastes. Entwined plots bring up critical issues that youth users might face in daily life, allowing them to negotiate actions and solutions by taking on the points of view of a variety of characters and a variety of circumstances.

The British health authorities were not alone in recognizing the possibilities of reaching youths with new media in the early 1990s. In the United States, the New York State Department of Health commissioned several HIV/AIDS interactive projects during this decade. These included the interactive dating game called *Life Challenge,* a kiosk that traveled to sites that service sexually active adolescents, and a slick HyperCard stack called *CondomSense* that was distributed for free for Mac and IBM platforms. In the next section, I focus on a San Francisco–based program that, like *Think Positive* and *Sex Get Serious,* was designed to function as a sex-educational "game." However, this project, titled the *Brothers Dating Game,* is geared to a range of age groups within the category of gay black men. This project demonstrates how the conjuncture of peer education, media interactivity, and therapeutics converge not only in youth education but in broader institutional settings, including public health and social welfare, where the target audience is adults.

The Brothers Dating Game:
Peer Education and Interactivity in Adult Sex Education

The user of the computer interactive *Brothers Dating Game* (1993) is confronted with a provocative invitation: "Touch any man on the right to turn him on," reads the game's first menu option. To the right of the text appear wallet-sized portraits of four African American men, potential dream dates who come alive, speak, and engage in dialogue with users at the touch of the screen. This is no ordinary arcade game, but a program created by and for gay, bisexual, and transgendered African

American men and intended to generate dialogue about safer-sex practices—a laser disc and computer interface designed to be installed in freestanding kiosks in gay bars and in clinics, to be accessed at no cost to the user.

Brothers was a collaborative project of the Interact Program of the Bay Area Video Coalition (BAVC) and the Brothers Network, a service organization within the National Task Force on AIDS Prevention that focuses on HIV/AIDS prevention, treatment advocacy, and counseling among transgendered, bisexual, and gay black men. The program is one of several interactive software projects for adults produced through collaborations among independent producers, media arts organizations, and AIDS advocacy groups. Video is a familiar mode of safer-sex education and media activism among nonprofits, in part because it is relatively cheap and standardized and can be broadly distributed. In the 1980s, some advocacy groups, like the Gay Men's Health Crisis (GMHC) of New York, created in-house audiovisual departments devoted mainly to video production and distribution. Interactive software products such as *Brothers*, however, are largely unfamiliar items in the HIV/AIDS nonprofit media context. Requiring expensive production facilities and specialized playback platforms, programs like this were viable only among institutions and businesses that could afford to install special multimedia stations. Why then did nonprofit media and HIV/AIDS advocacy organizations pursue interactive multimedia production in the 1990s?

Interactive programs like *Brothers*, along with other programs such as Canadian First Nation producer Russell Wallace's *AIDS and the Native Community*, serve a particular need that can't be adequately met by video alone. In most cases, AIDS videos are presented to audiences in workshops, groups, and classrooms and are often followed by peer- or counselor-led discussions. Interactive computer programs can offer a very different kind of viewing experience, one that potentially engages its audience in more casual, less structured settings, effectively reaching people who may not choose to read a pamphlet, attend a video screening, rent a tape, or participate in a workshop. The interlocutors and community a computer program invokes are virtual, not actual. Installed in kiosks, interactive software can have an ambient public presence. Furthermore, these programs can be designed to incorporate multiple narratives, characters, or kinds of information, which users can selectively choose from to cut right to their particular interests and needs.

Interactives engage viewers in an exchange that has the potential to be more to the point and more intimate than a video screening. Media producers and HIV/AIDS service organizations are recognizing that despite their current high production costs and the technical obstacles to distribution, AIDS software programs are useful venues for media outreach, communication, activism, and education.

Many commercial interactive software releases in CD-ROM and laser disc formats have been little more than translations of existing educational materials (textbooks or reference materials, for example) into digital format. These programs may provide convenient features like random-access indexing through a computer word search, or in-text digitized video clips. The conception of interactivity they offer, though, too often remains entrenched in models of rote learning where "choice" becomes simply a matter of choosing the right answer, deciding among limited options, or being able to leave a comment on a message board. AIDS computer media by independents have so far not fallen into the trap of representing computer menu selections and user message boards as necessarily more engaging or more interactive modes. The three safer-sex and AIDS programs I will be considering rework and transform the conventions of interactivity that we find in commercial software programs. They offer experiences that are engaging and informative not because they offer more choice or more viewer control but because they offer a pleasurable fantasy of interaction and a kind of virtual intimacy. These programs demonstrate a sensibility that runs counter to popularized high-tech fantasies of disembodied "electronic communities." Instead they present a model of interactivity based on production by and for particular communities.

Prior to the BAVC/Brothers Network collaboration on *Brothers* in 1993, a study was released by the University of California that had great bearing on thinking about the pedagogical approaches behind safer-sex education programs.[13] This study, based on a sample of approximately one thousand self-identified gay, bisexual, and transgendered black men, showed that knowledge about risk doesn't translate into safer-sex practices. Although 97 percent of the men knew how the HIV virus is transmitted, only half reported consistently observing safer-sex practices. When BAVC and the Brothers Network (a subsidiary of the National Task Force on AIDS Prevention) set out to produce an educational program, their aim was not to teach facts but to promote compliance. They created a fictional and entertaining—and hence presumably more comfortable—environment that invites users to creatively devise, enact, and rehearse safer sexual behavior. The Brothers Network members acted as content experts, and BAVC's Interact Program provided a team of ten interns to help design the interface. In this project, we see a strategy discussed earlier with reference to Meltzer's peer education video work: role-playing as a therapeutic means of changing behavior. The idea was to translate role-playing games that had proved effective in risk-reduction workshops into scripted narratives with the potential for multiple pathways of user interaction. Video could provide for role-playing a mirror and model for behavioral rights and wrongs. So too could a computer program make available model performances of behaviors familiar to members of the group, enforcing a sense of community while also allowing the community's members to debate the consequences of the modeled behavior and allowing them to talk through possible alternative actions.

Brothers began as a prototype laser disc called *Hot, Horny, and Healthy*. The project, in its final form, invites participants to engage in simulated encounters with a range of fictional characters. These characters are scripted to express a diversity of sexual preferences and perspectives on safer sex. Their dialogue is highly nuanced and, like any "real" person, each character may express ambiguous or inconsistent views in the course of a conversation. By scripting in nuance and ambiguity, the producers of *Brothers* avoid stereotyping and didacticism. As Tony Glover, director of the Brothers Network, notes, "Each of the characters in the *Brothers Interactive Dating Game* are well-rounded and developed with different psychological motivations in mind."[14] For example, Jelousy, a transgendered character, makes statements about safer sex that are not programmatic but embody ambiguity and emotion. She says that she never has unsafe sex—"except when tempted by the heat of the moment." Certainly, Jelousy's position is no model for safer-sex practice. However, if users bring out her impulsive side, a safer-sex diva crashes the encounter to offer commentary, words of caution, and suggestions for the user to take responsibility for safer sex.

The interactive component of *Brothers* is not limited to the one-on-one encounter between an individual user and the character(s) chosen on the touch screen. But the safer-sex diva is not the only third party in the game. Set up in public spaces such as bars, the game invites joking and

Jelousy in the *Brothers Dating Game* (Bay Area Video Coalition and the Brothers Network, 1993).

casual conversations about the issues it raises. The task force hoped the arcade game would function like its role-playing workshops, initiating open discussion about topics that viewers usually negotiate in private. In other words, the organization sees the interactive as a means of encouraging peer education interactions among adults in the public spaces of bars and clubs.

Only one *Brothers* kiosk was produced, but it was very popular in the various sites where it was installed. BAVC and the Brothers Network targeted gay clubs, bars, and organizations frequented by gay black men as the first user sites for the project. Interestingly, the kiosk was also placed on temporary exhibition at the Exploratorium in San Francisco, where it drew long lines of curious adolescents. The task force aimed to produce kiosks for other U.S. cities. They also aimed to make specially designed kiosks to be installed in public spaces (for example, along San Francisco's Castro), much like bank machines. These erotic ATMs would be set up in various cities around the nation to display different narrowcast programs designed to suit the targeted community. Narratives and characters would be designed to correspond with the interests and tastes of gay men living in particular geographic areas and socializing in specific gay subcultures.

The *Brothers* project demonstrates how peer education and media education, joined through the concept of interactivity, have migrated out of school-based settings and back into public space, where government and private entities forge unusual partnerships to fulfill the mission of educating the public. *Brothers* joined "serious" public health education with sheer entertainment—role-playing "games"—to put its agenda into effect.

I conclude this chapter by turning to a project that does not explicitly purport to teach but instead brings issues of gender and sexuality that are quite "serious" into the realm of entertainment proper. I discuss *gURL*, one of many World Wide Web–based projects that derive from the culture of zines, or alternative self-published magazines. This project brings us back to youth culture.

gURL

gURL is the brainchild of Ester Drill and Rebecca Odes. It was started while they were students at New York University in early 1996. The women had been friends since nursery school.[15] Drill and Odes see *gURL* as an alternative to the commercial magazines marketed to teen girls. It is an on-line space that provides information of interest to this group and allows for forms of exchange unavailable in the mainstream media. "Girls lack representations of options available to them," Drill and Odes explain.[16] Without setting out to do so, Drill and Odes perfectly carry forward the peer education model as well as the agenda of participatory media education more self-consciously promulgated in some of the other media texts I have described in this and previous chapters.

Drill and Odes designed their e-zine, or electronic magazine, much like a paper magazine, with thematic areas that feature changing content from month to month. In its early years, the zine had a staff of nine young women who worked on a volunteer basis. Although it has grown into a larger and more professional organization, it has not lost its close involvement with its core constituency. Material is gathered through e-mail correspondence and through work that their staff writes and designs with teens. They also publish projects that teens contribute on a

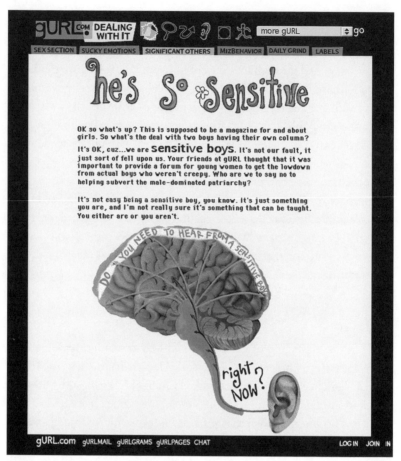

A column from the *gURL* e-zine.

solicited and unsolicited basis. *gURL* includes areas devoted to fashion, beauty, and self-image, life choices and careers, relationships and sexuality—topics common to teen and women's magazines. But unlike more traditional publications, *gURL* emphasizes options underrepresented in the mainstream (nonmonogamy, keeping body hair, alternative career options).

Some of the most successful components of the project are those designed as thematic areas for user interaction and dialogue. It is here that *gURL* most closely mirrors the open conversation of paper zines and alternative newsgroups. *gURL* embraces the multimedia capabilities of the Web while maintaining multiple access levels. The real draw of these areas, like the personals column in a daily newspaper, is the way

The Hairstories Repository from the *gURL* e-zine.

they frame direct user communication, or peer-to-peer dialogue. For example, one issue of *gURL* invites readers to share narratives about body hair, asking girls where they have it and how they cope with or cultivate it. Focus points like this on the personal and the everyday make *gURL* an important place for readers to share stories and concerns that have no other venues and would otherwise remain in privacy.

The project presents a compelling example of the pedagogical potential of network technology, at least within the current economy of its dissemination. *gURL* is a model for non-site-based education projects. Staff members build on the array of existing projects and organizations engaging young women. The success of *gURL* is based on pinpointing strategic social networks as much as digital ones. Leveraging the simultaneous anonymity and intimacy of the Net, the e-zine engages a targeted youth community in dialogue about personal politics. The scope of the project seems expansive considering that the zine began with a small staff and overhead. Few video-based media education projects can claim the same level of impact. Unlike their peers in print and video, independents like Drill and Odes are able to maintain production standards that are the envy of corporate counterparts. Their distribution is not limited by the cost of a print run or dubbing.

Like many forms of alternative media, *gURL* got its start through the direct or indirect support of institutions that assert little control over the e-zine's content. As noted earlier, its first issues were edited and produced by students at an academic institution. It was a challenge for the collaborative producers to maintain autonomous control over content of the zine while also making it a viable economic entity, especially after they graduated from school and lost access to institutional facilities. *gURL*'s growing constituency of readers caught the notice of several publishers and other corporate entities, and Drill and Odes were offered corporate backing. In the end, they expanded the e-zine into a broader content portal that offers member benefits such chat areas, the *gURL* palace (a visual-based chat), posting boards, pen pal lists and home page hosting, and e-mail accounts. Their corporate choice was not a communications entity but a youth clothing corporation. *gURL* is now published by Delias Interactive, a teen clothing and fashion retailer. The site has few links to the company and maintains autonomous control over content, but the connection nonetheless evokes the corporate mergers among product manufacturers and communications companies in the 1990s. By the end of the decade, the project continued to play the same educational and activist role it played earlier, despite its rapid growth and transition to the commercial sector. The economics of the Web are so young and volatile that the future direction of such a project is necessarily unclear. Nonetheless *gURL*'s ability to maintain its critical edge and sustain a dedicated constituency seems to provide some basis for optimism about alternative educational practices on-line despite the rapid commercialization of the Web.

Conclusion

I've argued that the media education projects discussed in this chapter provide young people with access to production technologies as part of a broader agenda of facilitating the expression of personal and political issues that have limited outlet in other areas of their lives. The artists, activists, and educators who facilitate these projects take advantage of their relatively autonomous position at the intersection of larger institutions to support the development of youth media countercultures. The production process, when combined with the peer education model, functions as therapy for youth in crisis, allowing them to work through memories of traumatic or painful experiences, and encouraging them form collective politics of resistance. In discussing *Kept Quiet*, the video testimonial about sexual abuse, I mentioned that the producers were reticent to exhibit their tape publicly because they wanted to protect the anonymity of the women whose stories it tells. In all cases, these projects are narrowcast productions geared to specific communities of viewers and users. A question emerges for art and media curators and scholars: What is the value of these tapes for audiences not directly engaged in issues of youth sexuality and domestic abuse? How does one best present youth-produced tapes or computer programs to adult audiences whose members have little or no knowledge about the pedagogical strategies behind these projects, much less the politics of youth culture within which these tapes circulate? These questions bring me back to the issue of exhibition and audience that I will examine more closely in the following chapter, which is devoted to education and museum exhibition. It is clear from the mainstream media that youth culture (in the form of rap, rave, music television, and fashion) has become a major commodity in the adult consumer marketplace. One of the minor goals of the *alt.youth.media* exhibition was to generate support for this kind of production during a period when public funding for nonprofit arts ventures is in jeopardy. In a sense, one of the functions of the *alt.youth.media* exhibition was to generate broader range of distribution venues in the public sector. The following chapter will examine some of the historical and contemporary policies and practices in place in the art museum and exhibitions context that preclude a focus on the sort of communities addressed in this chapter. Diversity, as I will show, is managed in such a way as to preclude questions of youth authorship or participatory production, for example.

There are three more points to be made about the work in the *alt. youth.media* exhibition before moving on to a closer examination of museum education and its technologies and practices. First, the work I have just described clearly counters most representations of youth culture that circulate in mainstream media. These projects collectively offer to adult audiences a view of youth culture that demonstrates the varieties of emotional, political, and aesthetic agency that can be enacted by young people engaged in media culture. Historically, one of the problems inherent in theorizing youth culture has been the predominant viewpoint that youths occupy a status of dependency and need. These projects suggest the degree to which youths have the capacity for political agency not only on behalf of themselves and their peers but also in the resolution of social problems that extend to intergenerational groups such as families, classrooms, and communities.

Second, these projects demonstrate that young people working in new and hybrid media forms are not just creating isolated works of personal expression but are forging a public space to collectively address "adult" issues such as family, sexuality, rape, domestic abuse, and suicide. These works simultaneously engage and resist the institutional and political forces young people confront in everyday life. Taken as a whole, this work represents an emergent and distinct youth cultural aesthetic embodied by an original vision and style, irony, political savvy, and an immediate sense of young people's urges to carve out independent spaces for exchanging ideas, images, and information.

Finally, the role of institutionally based peer education and participatory media projects cannot be underestimated in the facilitation of these agendas. Youth media exist not in vague subcultural margins but in the transitional spaces between changing institutional forms and media. *alt.youth.media,* mounted as it was in an alternative museum space, broke many of the institutional rules of art museum exhibition in showing youth-produced work, popular forms such as zines, and new media forms.[17] It challenged art critical distinctions between work produced inside and outside of academic settings.

In part 2, "Visual Pedagogy beyond Schools," I shift my focus to the dispersal of pedagogical techniques to sites outside formal educational institutions. Some of the work addressed in this and previous chapters (the *Brothers* project, for example) moved in this direction. I open this next set of chapters with a more concerted examination of the museum setting and the technologies through which it more conventionally puts into effect its exhibition practices.

PART TWO

Visual Pedagogy beyond Schools

CHAPTER FIVE

Museum Pedagogy

The Blockbuster Exhibition

as Educational Technology

The emergence of the museum coincided with the rise of the modern Western nation-state. The ordering of bodies and things in the colonial period was well served by the museum, an institution devoted to collection and display. Its collections provided a perfect resource for the education of Western subjects in the relative value and meaning of artworks and artifacts, both Western and colonial. This chapter considers the fundamental place of pedagogy in the twentieth-century museum. This institution is the perfect primer for explaining the historical connection between visual modes of knowledge in Western science and social science, on the one hand, and political rule, on the other. As an institution of the state, the colonial museum collected and gave meaning to both the material spoils of colonial conquests and the discourses that surrounded those conquests. Today's museum, in its multiple functions as edifying tool, warden of national patrimony, and legitimator of elite and mundane forms of knowledge and treasure, lays claim to a complicated and paradoxical set of missions. Not the least of these is the mission to educate its public. The contemporary museum bears the legacy of having the mission to educate at its core; this is played out through the institution's own pedagogical techniques and technologies.

Influenced by the writings of Michel Foucault and Louis Althusser, critical theorists since the 1970s have become more cognizant of the work of institutions such as the hospital, the school, and the prison in the discipline and regimentation of modern culture. More recently, art historians and cultural studies scholars have analyzed the institutional function of the museum. James Clifford, Carol Duncan, Alan Wallach, Douglas Crimp, and Tony Bennett, among others, inaugurated a dialogue about the work of the contemporary museum as an institution that organizes knowledge, class structure, and cultural difference as it regulates the microeconomies of Western markets for art and artifact.[1] Bennett emphasizes the historical place of the museum in the formation of the modern European nation-state:

> Museums, galleries, and more intermittently, exhibitions played a pivotal role in the formation of the modern state and are fundamental to its conception as, among other things, a set of educative and civilizing agencies. Since the late nineteenth century, they have been ranked highly in the funding priorities of all the developed nation-states and have proved remarkably influential cultural technologies in the degree to which they have recruited the interest and participation of their citizenries.[2]

Bennett emphasizes the historical role of the museum in the formation of the nation-state (a point that is also made by Carol Duncan and Alan Wallach). It is the role of the museum as an "educative and civilizing agency" not in turn-of-the-century Europe but in contemporary culture in the United States that interests me in this chapter. Bennett's examples are taken from the museum in an earlier period, but his analysis of the museum as an ideological agent of education and civilization will play an important role in my discussion of the institutional power of the contemporary museum, especially as embodied in developments such as blockbuster exhibitions and the overall reorganization of museological strategies of using educational technologies.

Pierre Bourdieu, Duncan, and others have argued that the contemporary museum unifies the upper and middle classes around an elite culture, excluding the dominant (popular) cultures of the working class.[3]

Bourdieu takes up this system of class distinction specifically in the museum's conjunction with institutions of education such as the school system (for example, he analyzes museum attendance according to levels of education). For Bourdieu, the contemporary museum's main educative purpose is to set up categories of class distinction based on access to (or education in) a particular set of aesthetics and tastes coded as elite.[4]

Bourdieu's formulation emphasizes the contemporary public museum's ability to maintain the exclusionary function inherited from its royal origins. But however well the late capitalist museum maintains its function in the reproduction of upper- and middle-class taste, the transformation of many museums into public institutions around the turn of the century nonetheless entailed the formation of cultural programs meant to encourage the education of a broader audience. (This is particularly true in the case of U.S. museums.) As Bennett points out, the nineteenth-century museum was more generally an institution for organizing working-class people around nonthreatening cultural practices. The twentieth-century museum culture explored by Bourdieu and others does function on some level to exclude the working class in order to reproduce racial and sexual difference, as well as class distinction. But the dynamic described by Bennett nonetheless remains an important pedagogical agenda of the contemporary museum. "Education of the general public" continues to be a critical disciplining mode, especially when it becomes a subtle and implicit agenda in museum policies and structure.

Implicit Educational Agendas

According to Bourdieu and Jean-Claude Passeron, it is precisely because the museum does not have explicit, structured programs for the transmission of knowledge that it epitomizes late capitalist institutional pedagogy:

> The museum, which delimits its public and legitimates their social standing simply by the effect of its "level of transmission," i.e. by the sheer fact of presupposing possession of the cultural code required for decoding the objects displayed, may be seen as the limiting case toward which tends all PW [pedagogical work] founded on the implicit prerequisite of possession of the conditions of its productivity.[5]

The museum's educational policies are implicit but central to its structure. Indeed, the museum is an exemplar of the performance of pedagogical work in an institution that is not explicitly devoted to education. This is especially true in the United States. It is no coincidence that in this country the opening of museums to the general public coincided with the institution of public and eventually mandatory schooling. Indeed, in the United States, education was a major motivating factor in the development of the public museum and has remained a core, though in many cases understated, element of museum policy. The 1870 charter of New York's Metropolitan Museum of Art states this agenda outright. This document claims that the museum would serve the purpose "of establishing and maintaining in said city a museum and library of art, of encouraging and developing the study of fine arts, and the application of arts to manufacture and practical life, of advancing general knowledge of kindred subjects, and, to that end, of furnishing popular instruction and . . . *it shall be classified as an educational institution.*"[6]

Since the late nineteenth century, the orientation of the museum toward pedagogical work has been asserted repeatedly by U.S. museum boards and educational organizations alike. In a text that perfectly illustrates Bourdieu's theory of distinction, Molly Harrison, the author of a 1960 UNESCO publication on education in museums, asserts that museums are, "by definition, custodians of quality." However, she ultimately argues that museums have moved toward, rather than away from, the agenda of educating a wider public:

> The broadening concept of the museum's responsibility first came to include people who, if not initially interested, were potentially so. . . .
> They were a passive audience, but one easily captured and not actively hostile. But it is only recently that the idea has taken root that the museum has an obligation to the whole community, regardless of age, or type, or intellectual capacity.[7]

Harrison sees the museum as a progressive pedagogical form—indeed, as a potential site of the "integration of a world suffering from division."[8] She notes the disproportionately high attendance of upperclass, educated visitors from more prosperous countries at the Museo Nacional de Antropología in Mexico City and the Gemeentemuseum in the Hague. However, she emphasizes that museum studies indicate the insufficiency of limited policies like free admission to attract a more diverse group of visitors. Her analysis makes it clear that if a more diverse audience is desired, the museum would need to make structural changes in its pedagogical strategies. This is indicative of a larger effort to diversify museum audiences beyond the ranks of middle- to upper-class and educated groups through new popular modes of audience address and entertainment.

A curator by profession, Harrison speaks from a position within museum administration; her statement can be taken as an advertisement for the good intentions of museums, and not a theory of the museum's actual social function. But her agenda—the move toward a more class-diversified audience—is reiterated throughout postwar texts on museum policy and practice. Blockbuster exhibits, instituted in the late 1970s, are exemplary cases of subsequent strategies to organize the entire museum as a venue for educating large sectors of the public. They constitute one important development in the populist educational agenda described by Harrison more than forty years ago.

The Blockbuster Exhibition:
A New Mode of Exhibition Spectatorship

Large-scale exhibitions of the past two decades, including the Museum of Modern Art's Picasso retrospective (1980), the Metropolitan Museum of Art's Tutankhamen exhibit (1976–79), and the Metropolitan's showcasing of the traveling Van Gogh retrospective (1984), have demonstrated the ability of U.S. museums to draw unprecedented numbers into their galleries. These exhibits provide the closest contemporary analogy to the great exhibitions of the nineteenth century that, according to Bennett, signified the development of "a technology of vision that served not to atomize and disperse the crowd but to regulate it."[9] Organizers of each of these major contemporary exhibits extensively remapped museum space, transformed entrance procedures, and created a new mode of exhibition spectatorship to manage the large crowds they anticipated. They installed information tents outside museum buildings, instituted electronic off-site advance ticket sales, offered taped "self-guided" tours, installed museum shop booths at key points within the galleries, and, finally, tightened security, training new, temporary guards hired specifically for each of these shows.

Drawing from Bennett's analysis of the nineteenth-century museum, I

Crowds wait in line to view
the Picasso Retrospective at
MOMA in New York, 1980
(© 2002 The Museum of
Modern Art, New York).

take as my case study the 1980 MOMA Picasso retrospective. My vantage
point on this exhibition is not only that of art and media critic but also
that of museum guard. My information about the exhibition is drawn
in part from my experience as one of numerous temporary guards hired
by MOMA to help manage the greatly expanded attendance generated by
this exhibition. This experience gave me the unique ability to hear the
inside story on mechanisms of crowd control and public relations, and to
experience what it was like to be a cog in the management of this major
art and media event. I observed for the duration of this exhibition the
viewing practices of the crush of people that streamed past the artworks,
many with headphones in place. I will be recounting my observations of
this exhibition to consider some of the strategies used in it and similar
exhibitions toward organizing the museum as a new kind of pedagogical
space—a space deploying a new kind of educational technology geared
toward entertaining and educating a nonelite public.

In earlier chapters focusing on schools, I touched on the connection between entertainment and education. The mission to reach a mass
public with the blockbuster exhibition required a marketing and de-

sign approach more akin to the style of mass entertainment institutions like the cinema than to the more staid school or museum. The term "blockbuster" evokes the phenomenon of the blockbuster hit—the movies families flock to see in droves during peak leisure seasons, like summer and the winter holidays. The blockbuster exhibition parallels the blockbuster movie in its appeal to a mass audience, its sense of being *the* thing to do for leisure during that period of time across a broad sector of the national public. In terms of markets, both forms generate commodity tie-ins (commercial goods spun off from the art of film) and earn the title "blockbuster" by the overall marketing and financial success of the event.[10]

What distinguishes the blockbuster exhibition from the blockbuster movie, of course, is the overt goal of the former to educate its public. Most blockbuster movies make no pretensions to education. One of the unique features of the blockbuster exhibition is its aim of marketing a high-art and -culture experience to a sector of the public that may never have entered a museum of art, but would certainly be familiar with the behavioral codes of movie and television viewing. One might unfairly characterize this as sugarcoating high-culture education for the masses, but I am hardly concerned about the blockbuster exhibition's appropriation of entertainment for education. What interests me is the successful integration of high art with "low" forms of cultural consumption, and the success of this new form of museum pedagogy for the masses.

Bennett suggests that nineteenth-century exhibition structures were designed to "render the crowd visible to itself."[11] The very experience of entering blockbuster exhibitions of the 1970s and 1980s produced this experience of reflexive crowd gazing. But the architecture of these exhibition entryways also generated in visitors an experience of themselves that was more intimate and interactive while instituting an unprecedented degree of control through spatial regulation—that is, crowd control. Many of the museums built in the nineteenth century greet their visitors with grand entranceways and sweeping center staircases, features originally designed to provide a sense of scale that is both grand and imposing. Entering through any one of multiple doors, the visitor is dwarfed and swallowed up by a cavernous lobby in which a crowd mills about in various directions, some individuals forming lines for tickets in a spot that seems almost random in its placement.

The blockbuster exhibition called for a space that would be both less

Merchandise sold as spin-offs from the 1978 King Tutankhamen Exhibit at the Metropolitan Museum of Art, New York (John Sotomayor/NYT Pictures).

intimidating to the general public, and more controlling of the movements of a public uneducated in proper museum conduct. Even MOMA's smaller modern lobby entrance could not provide this desired experience for the Picasso retrospective. The museum opted instead for a more pedestrian approach. Visitors were directed to enter the exhibition literally through the back door, through a passageway that led them through a small-scale garden at the back of the building. Similarly, the Metropolitan used a small lower-level entrance for its Van Gogh retrospective as well as for other large exhibits. King Tut exhibit viewers used the museum's main entrance but were immediately channeled through a second narrow internal entrance. This entry theatrically evoked passage into the tomb while also circumventing the viewer's potentially alienating experience of the imposing palatial scale of the classical museum entry and its confusing lack of clear directives for entry to exhibitions.

In addition to fostering a more hospitable and directive greeting to those unused to the grand experience of museum going, replacing multiple-doored lobby entrances with smaller single passageways funneled people into neat, and always long, lines up to the exhibition's starting point. These queues provided the crowd with a congenial contemporary group experience, not unlike that of waiting in lines at the movie theater, bank, or grocery store. Not coincidentally, these are places where the length of the line and the duration of the wait are sometimes measures of the worth of the commodity or service received at the end. The Picasso exhibition was the first exhibition for which advance tickets were sold that specified not only the date but also the hour the bearer could enter the exhibition. This allowed MOMA to move many more people through the galleries, upward of seven thousand.[12] The value of the experience was heightened by the fact that advance sales of the ticket had generated a demand that could not be filled during weekends and peak vacation days.

One outcome of the sold-out phenomenon was the inevitable presence of people hawking tickets outside the entryway, as if Picasso were a rock star or opera star. Conversations I overheard in my capacity as guard suggested that this was not the art public so at home in this museum. A good percentage of the group had never been to MOMA, had never experienced a fine-art exhibition, and knew little about Picasso and his work beyond his reputation as one of the masters of modern art. They were there to learn. Whole families came out for the event, and they traveled from afar on the basis of its reputation as a must-have cultural experience. The tenor of the crowd was at once carnivalesque and reverent, an odd mix of circus and religious worship.

Visitors' first experience from inside the museum itself, then, was that of a member of a carefully regimented crowd. Cordons ensured that the crowd did not disperse and mill to people watch in the style afforded by the open museum lobby. Rather, the pre-exhibition experience was limited to interaction with those who happened to be closest in line. These randomly formed groups typically remained somewhat stable for the duration of the exhibition, for the line did not disperse with admission to the exhibition. Visitors were channeled into a gallery and directed by signage and guards to move forward through the exhibition along a pathway clearly marked by more cordons and posts strung mazelike along the walls of a series of galleries. The artworks were positioned in a line on the wall or at freestanding stations, at a distance beyond the cordons that would ensure their visibility while also placing them safely out of the reach of the novice visitor unfamiliar with the cardinal rule, no touching the art. To further ensure an orderly march of the shoulder-to-shoulder crowd pressing through the exhibition, guards were positioned at transit points (the end of a set of cordons, a gallery door). We were instructed to serve as crowd facilitators, guiding the flow of traffic and preventing visitors from breaking the flow by returning to rooms they had already passed through, and encouraging the breakup of bottlenecks around works featured on the audiotape. Like hawkers at a market, guards called out the correct direction of traffic flow at frequent and regular intervals, ensuring that everyone who passed from one station to the next would stay on course. The regularity of the hawking was such that guards had to be rotated to preserve their voices.

Regulation of crowds through cordons and guard facilitation ensured that viewers remained with the cohort they had entered with, potentially building a community feel into what could otherwise have become an anonymous milling mass—except that members of this cohort were hardly encouraged to speak once inside the galleries. The sheer volume of people made noise control essential. On entering the exhibition, visitors were offered their first of many purchase options: a self-guided tour on audiocassette, with headphones for a private listening experience. This tour option minimized the noise level by enveloping individual visitors in their own private audiovisual space in the crowd. It also served the pedagogical purpose of acquainting visitors with basic knowledge about the artist and the work. Perhaps most importantly, the tape reinforced the linearity of the exhibition already instituted by the cordons and guard guidance. The audio flow of information corresponded exactly to the ordering of artworks throughout the galleries, requiring the listener to move along at a fixed pace to keep in sync with the tape. Only key artworks were addressed, so that most people using the audio tours skipped quickly past paintings in between. Everyone renting the headset could be counted on to move through the exhibition at the same pace, allowing the museum to anticipate how many people it could accommodate each day and ensuring a predictable rate of turnover for those managing the crowd at the entryway.

The pedagogical strategy relied on a degree of regimentation untypical of museum going. That job fell not to museum education personnel per se but to the guards. Their role as disciplinarians cum pedagogues is worth elaborating. Security guards served as traffic cops, keeping the crowd flowing and preventing visitors from retracing their steps. But however restrictive this experience proved to be for visitors, it was also directive and reassuring. What the museum took away in terms of freedom of movement, it gave back in the form of organized information

Shoppers at Bloomingdale's examine King Tutankhamen Wedgwood pieces (Marilynn K. Yee/NYT Pictures).

and accessibility of data. Visitors who had never experienced a museum could feel safe that they would not violate its codes of behavior. They would get the most out of the experience even without knowing the rules. Large thematic typeset plates with informational text and close-up reproductions of some of the works of art supplemented the audio narrative and ensured that those who passed up the headsets would get another chance to purchase them, without having to fight traffic to return to the starting point. For those who opted out of the audio experience, the guards' directives ensured passage by placards in the correct sequence, guaranteeing the accrual of the right information in the right order.

Comparison to the blockbuster movie also deserves elaboration. Like the blockbuster movie, the blockbuster exhibition is both narrative and audiovisual. It immerses the viewer in a linear narrative whose flow is beyond his or her control. Also like the blockbuster movie, the exhibition form immerses each participant who chooses to use headsets in the paradoxical conditions of entering a private audiovisual world in a space that is both public and crowded. But the parallel is broken on grounds of pedagogy. The line, the construction of the exhibition as a narrative that is physically moved through, and the function of the guards to regulate that passage are all pedagogical techniques not found in the cinema.

The visitor's embodied performance in the pedagogical process in the blockbuster exhibition is far more overt and disciplined than his or her "passive" consumption of a movie from a seat in a theater. Moreover, the outcomes differ. Blockbuster exhibition visitors walk away with cultural enrichment and information. It satisfies not because it entertains but because it entertains to educate. This is not to say that movies do not educate. Insofar as they inculcate their viewers in the ideology they embody, movies most certainly serve an educative function. But it is much more subtly enacted by comparison. What makes the exhibition model interesting is that viewers knowingly enter into a passive and guided experience of inculcation, and they apparently enjoy it rather than finding it didactic or boring. They pay to have the experience, and they come in droves. The same can hardly be said about optional adult-education programs.

The overtly pedagogical strategies of the blockbuster did not entirely replace the contemplative and unstructured viewing relations found in more traditional exhibitions. Elite modes of knowledge are used in both. The pedagogical model of the blockbuster remains steeped in the traditions of literacy and literary or historical narrative. Indeed, the blockbuster admirably fulfills the conditions of the more traditional pedagogical mission of the museum. Rather than leaving conventional forms of knowledge about art (textbooks, for example) to the libraries and classrooms, the blockbuster incorporates into the exhibition itself the very texts and histories from outside the museum that inform and give value to art. These texts and the artworks themselves are presented as a package deal. The work is framed as one aspect of a mélange of aesthetic, informational, and consumer options through which we experience art.

The Picasso exhibition was not only about Picasso and his work. It was also an introduction to the world of modern art for the mass public. Picasso, the chosen representative of Western modern art in this instance, opened the door to a world previously inhabited by a cultural elite. As William Rubin stated in his introduction to the exhibition catalog, "Picasso's oeuvre, in its multiplicity of styles, variety, and inventiveness epitomizes twentieth century art as a whole." [13] In a sense, one could say that the Picasso exhibition signaled a shift in art museum practices from the elite approach to education typical of the modern period that Picasso himself represents. The exhibition in its very style opened the door to a postmodern approach to museum pedagogy, an approach that made art education a consumer experience available through various modes of consumption and commodity forms. These forms included the service of the exhibition itself as consumable education. Many viewers walked away with nothing more than their ticket stub. But it also offered a number of more conventional consumer options through which the visitor could make the work his or her own. Satellite museum store kiosks were positioned at key points in the exhibition, allowing visitors to select from coffee table books, posters, and other items bearing reproductions of Picasso's work and the logo of the exhibition. The blockbuster phenomenon brought us innovative variations on the commodity tie-in concept, with satchels and silk scarves bearing reproductions of great works of art joining the standard fare of T-shirts and postcards. To bear a King Tut satchel was to signify belonging in the new mass culture of high art.

Duncan and Alan Wallach, who analyze a broader period than Bennett does, describe how U.S. art museum spaces and rituals of the late nineteenth century were transformed in the middle of the twentieth century to conform to changes in the idealized citizen-state relationship. They formulate an image of the museum as an institution in ongoing flux, responding to changes in the dominant interpretations of citizenship—a process that, Duncan emphasizes, is a dynamic struggle over identity. Modern art museums characteristic of the mid–twentieth century ritualize the ideology of individualism and subjective freedom dominant in late capitalism. In their analysis of MOMA, the building's entranceway is emblematic of a pervasive ideology of free choice: "The ground floor is an open, light-filled space. You feel you can go wherever you wish. There are no architectural imperatives like those of the Metropolitan, with its grand stairway and succession of great halls. On MOMA's ground floor you experience a heightened sense of individual free choice—a major theme of the building as a whole." [14]

Duncan and Wallach's analysis of MOMA's interior galleries reveals the linear orientation of the museum, albeit a line that is interrupted by spatial cul-de-sacs and detours. This prescribed route directs and confines the viewer, but the narrative it implies is disrupted. Irregular labyrinthine turns and a lack of markers or signage make it a hard narrative to follow. These conditions ensure the disorientation of the uninitiated viewer. The modern art museum remains a sanctified repository of high culture and a space of privileged access.

In blockbuster exhibitions, the linearity of the exhibition—and knowledge about it—is obvious and easily followed. This orientation suggests changes in the relationship of the public and the private within the museum. Blockbuster exhibitions restructure museum space for a citizenry accustomed to an increasingly stratified semipublic sphere. Whereas previous implementations of the museum as repository of high culture served to delineate differences between those inside and those outside, the blockbuster exhibit affords multiple viewing positions and different modes of organizing, as well as degrees of ownership of, cultural artifacts. The blockbuster exhibition is set up so that social distinctions and hierarchies can be maintained within the same space as the cultural archive.

Changes initiated by early blockbuster exhibits have been incorporated more generally into museum design and renovation since the 1980s. For example, in the renovation of MOMA directly after the Picasso show, and in numerous other modern art museums, larger galleries located near building entrances were devoted to temporary and traveling exhibitions, and permanent collections were moved to less-trafficked spaces. Significantly, the new design of the Modern included escalators between floors to ensure the fluid flow of large numbers of visitors during crowded periods. This department-store-like approach to circulation was mirrored in the design of other museums designed or renovated in the following decades. Appeals to more popular taste were also seen in terms of exhibition content in the 1990s. This was reflected in more frequent inclusion of popular cultural artifacts and an emphasis on viewer interactivity (as in the *High and Low: Modern Art, Popular Culture* exhibition at MOMA in 1990, or the *Art Mall* exhibition at the New Museum of Contemporary Art in 1992).

Museums have broadened their audiences by instituting changes such as these, but they have also alienated many of the museum's traditional supporters. Not surprisingly, the democratization of museums has been subject to criticism from a range of perspectives, aesthetic to political. The blockbuster phenomenon in particular has been criticized by some conservative art critics for displeasing, if not threatening to displace, the elite audience unaccustomed to crowds and regimented viewing. Some of the criticisms of the new museum practices, interestingly, are grounded in a discussion of the museum's historical mission to educate. Mark Lilla's 1992 essay "The Museum in the City" is a good example of this. Lilla sees the popularization of museums as the result of a misguided attempt to fulfill the museum's charter to educate. New exhibition strategies and "architectural concessions to new visitors," he argues, signal a decline in standards of excellence. Lilla laments that the American museum is "at sea without an anchor of clearly articulated principles."[15] Lilla accuses museum administrators of being in a state of confusion. His description of the state of affairs, however, presents some unsettling contradictions of its own. Arguing for a civic basis of the museum's educational function, he teams conservative and leftist ideologies as well as commercial interests as demons of the new museum. What seems to elude Lilla is that the museum's popularization is not a response to increased governmental control or the influence of the liberal Left but a shift of cultural power into the hands of an economic elite that is not necessarily a cultural elite. The historical mission to educate the public dovetails with a contemporary imperative to sell the museum to the public.

Lilla asserts that the museum has lost sight of its original civic mission. A more apt assessment is that the museum is belatedly adjusting to the civic codes initiated by other institutions of contemporary society. Like the public school, the museum has begun to acknowledge diversity by accommodating a range of disciplining pedagogical models and regimenting modes of address. The corporation, with its strategies for managing diversity, is a useful model for understanding the new organization of the museum. The corporation parallels the museum in its existence as an institution built on globalization, and moreover, it has increasingly become a key player in the museum world. Corporate leaders sit on museum boards of directors, shaping the pedagogical function of the museum so that it speaks to corporate interests. Corporations have increasingly taken up the role of institutional manager of the museum, guiding its structure, growth, and public image. The blockbuster exhibition itself is in part the product of corporate sponsorship, and many such exhibitions have noticeably been shaped by corporate representatives.

Corporate Hierarchies: A New "Pluralist" Model for the Museum?

The growing prominence of corporate sponsorship and control of blockbuster exhibits goes hand in hand with a new paternalistic pedagogy. Building on Bourdieu's theories of cultural capital, Paul DiMaggio and

Michael Useem describe a change in control over museums from the cultural elite to the corporate elite. They describe both the influence of external corporate sponsors and the museum's adoption of conventional commercial management practices, listing six components in the reorganization of museum control: "a shift in board composition; a change in board priorities; increasing importance of professional managers; increased reliance on marketing and public subsidy; expansion and consequent de-emphasis of exclusiveness and screening role; heightened concern with content and emphasis on legitimating role."[16]

DiMaggio and Useem's thesis of a shift of control from a cultural elite to a corporate elite is convincing, in part because it is supported by substantial quantitative data. They argue that the traditional elite control of high culture is oriented toward what they call a screening function. A concept similar to Bourdieu's term "distinction," screening function refers to the screening or regulation of access to cultural capital as a means of reinscribing class hierarchy. For DiMaggio and Useem, the screening function of the museum is gradually replaced by what they call a legitimation function. This is the use of high culture to legitimate corporate identity among a range of public subjects who may or may not make use of the museum, but who understand this association as a mark of prestige.

The notion of a screening function reflects Bourdieu's thesis that the symbolic function of elite control of cultural capital ensures class solidarity and privilege. In Bourdieu's scheme, the cultural meanings in relations of pedagogic power are ultimately arbitrary.[17] In any given situation, cultural meanings are socially and historically determined. Bourdieu's lack of attention to specific cultural content in pedagogical power relations, however, tends to level the field of cultural signifying practices in his analysis. This amounts to an overgeneralization of symbolic power. DiMaggio and Useem repeat this tendency in their discussion of the traditional elite control and use of high culture as a device for screening out lower-class audiences: "For the screening role, the content of high culture is less important than the fact that it can be monopolized by upper and upper-middle class status groups."[18]

DiMaggio and Useem suggest that exclusive networks of transmission of taste and cultural knowledge within family and peer groups are the central means by which traditional elite power is consolidated. This amounts to a simplified economy of cultural haves and cultural have-nots. Cultural knowledge is an empty commodity form, but clearly the specific content of high-cultural discourse, the narrative spun around cultural treasures, has played a significant role in regulating access to artifacts and institutions. In fact, the transmission of dominant cultural values across economic and social groups has played a key role in filtering out lower-class groups from institutions such as museums.

But the mechanism of screening cannot be reduced to the regulation of knowledge; it is not lack of knowledge that screens out certain groups from the museum. Rather, the screening function itself instructs—that is, it performs the pedagogical work—of instituting difference. In many cases, disenfranchised audiences are not unable to access cultural values, but rather they experience the discourse of the museum as instruction in the facts of one's own reputed difference, inferiority, or ignorance. Minimal attendance at museums by certain groups can thus be understood as resistance to a knowledge that has already been thoroughly inculcated in members of these groups elsewhere. Michelle Wallace points to the role of visual culture, as opposed to music, in the production of American racist discourse:

> If the positive scene of instruction between Africans and Europeans in the U.S. is located in what is now triumphantly called the tradition of Afro-American music, the negative scene of instruction is in its visual tradition. . . . As even the smallest child seems to instinctively understand, institutionalized education has always been, first and foremost, a means of transmitting social values, not power or knowledge.[19]

If as DiMaggio and Useem propose, the legitimation function is the key motivation for museum-sponsor relationships, it does not necessarily follow that museums abandon the role of mediating—or, as Wallace points out, of teaching or transmitting—the structure of cultural distinction. The broadening of audiences through blockbuster and postblockbuster shows seems to attest to the diminishing of the screening function of the museum; however, cultural stratification is maintained inside the museum's galleries in this new, more overtly pedagogical mode of transmitting social values.

But is it not only the disenfranchised who are the target of the museum's new pedagogical work. As suggested earlier, corporate involvement has led to the image of the corporation as educator and benefactor, and their targeted audience is not only audiences previously excluded from the museum because of class or cultural identity. Corporate employees who gain museum privileges as job perks make up one potential audience. They fit awkwardly in the scheme of difference promoted in standard museum pedagogy. During MOMA's Picasso exhibition, card-carrying employees were conferred a new kind of distinction. In full view of less privileged visitors, employees of corporate sponsors—people all along the rungs of the corporate ladder and class scheme—were privileged recipients of reduced admission fees and preferred access to admissions scheduling. At higher rungs of the corporate ladder, parties were thrown for executives and their business associates in the museum's galleries at night and on days when the museum was closed to the public. In the case of the corporate museum goer, social distinction has little to do with class-based status, art historical knowledge, acquired taste, or cultural capital, and everything to do with a professional-familial link to patronage. Not surprisingly, the blockbuster's literacy-based pedagogical strategies pander to this group of museum goers and hence encourage continued corporate sponsorship as much as they service a working-class audience. Both audiences are equally presumed to be uneducated in the discourse of elite art forms.

Beyond architectural concessions and new marketing strategies, the new organization of the museum has reformulated the relation of Western high cultures to non-Western cultures. Throughout the greater part of the twentieth century, exhibitions featuring modern and contemporary Western art distinguished this work from the traditions of antiquity and non-Western cultures by emphasizing the abstract notion of individual genius or creativity. Modernist works were displayed apart from those of earlier periods, and an almost ritualistic organization of works according to a self-referential narrative of modern art history supplanted any broader historical or cultural context. Most often works were grouped in galleries or exhibits featuring individual great artists.[20] A curatorial trend of the 1980s and 1990s broke with this approach, emphasizing the work of art in the community rather than the individual artist and the hermeneutics of art movements. These exhibitions seemed to speak across cultures and bridge cultural divides as if, without bridging, these divides would threaten to undermine democracy. A case in point is MOMA's 1984 exhibition *"Primitivism" in 20th Century Art: Affinities of the Tribal and the Modern*. This exhibition exuded an explicitly pedagogical, even didactic, form of conservative multiculturalism. It was indicative of a 1990s postcolonial approach to museum education in which acquisition and tourism were regarded as an acknowledgment of diversity.

In the several years that separate the Picasso retrospective and the primitivism exhibition, curator William Rubin, who curated both exhibitions, shifted his thesis dramatically in keeping with this understanding of diversity. In 1980 Rubin portrayed Picasso as having been heavily influenced by the "primitive" art of Africa. By 1984 Rubin had changed his account to argue that the work of Picasso's Western contemporaries and African "primitive" artists shared a common formal aesthetic. "Shared" is the term he intended: the aesthetic was not borrowed or taken but uniformly shared.[21] Hal Foster suggests that the new framework for understanding primitivism put forth by the primitivism exhibition reasserts the colonial extraction of non-Western cultural objects by appropriating them into the Western artistic tradition.[22] Rubin's fiction of a shared aesthetic for Eastern and Western art forms is repeated in the museum's larger attempt to flatten real political, cultural, and economic differences to make a pluralist audience address. Just as class interests and discourses are flattened in the museum's corporate educative model, so national and cultural differences are flattened in the museum's appeal to a global model suggested, not surprisingly, by the corporate multinational.

Mandatory public schooling (and later desegregation) necessitated tracking mechanisms and other means of gauging and regulating distinction from inside the institution. Similarly, the democratization of the museum necessitated new categories of classification within its walls. Twentieth-century museums approached the status of egalitarian institutions of democratic education. However, the democracy at work in them was that of a global economy that necessarily incorporated the microeconomies of art and artifact trade and consumption. The 1980s and 1990s saw a transformation of U.S. museum pedagogy, bringing the museum closer to the explicitly educative agenda posed in nineteenth-century founding charters. The techniques of this pedagogical mission's enactment during these decades must be seen in the context of the multinational corporation, a corporation that was (and continues to be) a profoundly globalizing pedagogue within the museum. Philip Morris, Inc., overtly articulated its own diverse and global vision in its sponsorship of

MOMA's primitivism exhibit: "The idea of interchange between cultures is something we understand: We deal with people of all backgrounds in the United States and 170 other countries and territories."[23]

Simply put, the multinational corporation has gained a strong foothold in museum pedagogy because it has a strong economic foothold in a vast spectrum of cultures and economies. The role of the multinational corporation as chief pedagogue in cultural globalization as well as economic globalization rests on an established connection between visual modes of knowledge in Western science and social science, on the one hand, and political rule, on the other. The history of institutions of instructional display in the West—institutions that have become the object of corporate philanthropy—is closely tied to pedagogical projects directed at colonial and neocolonial subjects. The next chapter further considers this local-global connection through an examination of the legacy of colonial uses of instructional media in postliberation West African cinema.

CHAPTER SIX

A Pedagogical Cinema

Development Theory, Colonialism,

and Postliberation African Film

The problem of colonization did not only concern the overseas countries. The process of decolonization—which is in any case far from complete in those countries—is also under way at home, in our schools, in female demands for equality, in the education of small children and in many other fields. . . . If certain cultures prove capable of destroying others . . . the destructive forces brought forth by these cultures also act internally.—Octave Mannoni, *Psychoanalysis and the Decolonization of the Mind*

In chapter 1, I considered the Ford Foundation's development of educational television "at home" and in U.S. overseas "possessions." I discussed how the media strategies developed to educate the Samoan populace intersected in overt ways with media education projects launched by the Ford Foundation during the same period in low-income urban schools on the U.S. mainland. The Ford project is an example of precisely the interrelated local and global "destructive forces" of colonialism that Mannoni describes in this chapter's epigraph. The project of educational media colonization in Samoa was clearly under way "at home," in our schools, and so forth. However, as many other examples of educational media strategies considered in this book demonstrate, disciplinary pedagogical techniques such as those used in Samoa have in some instances been marshaled and reconfigured for the task of resistance to centralized pedagogical authority "at home."

In this chapter, I extend the discussion of local and global media pedagogy to consider French colonial authorities' uses of the cinema as a tool to educate and inculcate West African subjects. I also consider the transformation of French colonial pedagogical media strategies by postliberation West African directors. French colonial rule was internalized by African subjects through distinctly pedagogical techniques. Instructional films and documentaries were primers in this process. These films were used in ways that tied in explicitly to theories of education and child development current in Europe and the United States during this period—a conjuncture that parallels, in many ways, the overlapping projects of the Ford Foundation. But the situation differs in a crucial way from that of Samoa: In West Africa, we see the emergence of a "pedagogical" cinema of liberation during decolonization—a West African–produced cinema that both draws from and undercuts the modes of visual pedagogy or media education that we see in French media produced for West African audiences before 1960. In Samoa, there is no evidence of this kind of appropriation or resistance.

In an indirect way, the critical approach to pedagogical authority I have employed throughout previous chapters has a basis in the anthropological study of French colonial subjects in Africa. Pierre Bourdieu's critical theories of pedagogical strategies, for example, can be traced to his early training as an anthropologist in French colonial Algeria.[1] In *Algeria 1960*, Bourdieu criticizes the essentialist ethnographic bias in anthropological literature on colonial development projects. He argues that these texts give limited consideration to colonial subjects' agency under colonization. He cites the central role of the "ensemble of formal and diffuse mechanisms of education" that allowed Algerian peasants to adapt to French colonial authorities' attempts to make them proletarians. Importantly, Bourdieu seeks to identify how Algerians acquired agency through strategic uses of French colonial pedagogical techniques in acts of internal resistance.[2]

Bourdieu's later work does not refer to colonial or neocolonial relationships; his focus shifts to French institutions. However, he does apply the lessons he learned about Algerian subjectivity and agency under colonialism to his later analyses. As I show in chapters 2 and 3, Bourdieu's later writing influenced work by Giroux and others on the transversal, transinstitutional nature of pedagogical practices. In a sense, then, this chapter takes later applications of the work of Bourdieu back to the West African colonial context out of which his foundational ideas about pedagogy emerged.

The reader might look askance at the focus on French colonialism and West African film, and not some more obvious example of media pedagogy. Film was used extensively as a pedagogical tool by British, German, and Belgian, as well as French, authorities in colonial Africa. But it was the former French colonies that produced some of the most politically influential films (and filmmakers) after liberation. This was due in part to the fact that the revolutionary governments of these newly formed nations gave high priority to the subsidy of films that took up the issue of local and national politics with the explicit agenda of community education.[3] Further, the French colonial system schooled the authors of negritude, a generation of revolutionary thinkers who were crucially cognizant of the central place of pedagogy in colonial power and in their own resistance to neocolonialism. In other words, the legacy of French pedagogical authority could not be erased; rather, it grounded a revolutionary discourse in which pedagogical techniques were strategically reconfigured, and a revolutionary form of media education was reformed.

This point is demonstrated in the following anecdote related in an interview with Senegalese filmmaker Ousmane Sembéne. In his successful career as a novelist and in his earliest films, Sembéne worked most often in French, the language and cultural conventions he was taught in the colonial educational system in Senegal. Sembéne recalls that using the colonial tongue seemed appropriate at the time: French "was a fact of life." However, when he began to show his films in Senegal, peasant audiences criticized his language choice, identifying it as emblematic of an internalized Eurocentrism. "The peasants were quick to point out to me that I was the one who was alienated," he explains. "They would have preferred the film in their own language, without the French."[4]

Sembéne's story speaks to relations of pedagogical authority. It illustrates the broader struggle over language, colonialism, and pedagogy that has marked West African cinema since its inception. Like Jean Rouch, the French anthropologist and documentary filmmaker who taught many now well-known African filmmakers during the years of liberation, Sembéne viewed film as a pedagogically useful medium. However, Sembéne and other postliberation directors radically reconceived the didactic role of the cinema. Films could teach Western audiences about the damaging effects of colonialism; moreover, they could demonstrate to Africans strategies of political resistance against imperialism. As Françoise Pfaff explains, Sembéne turned from writing to film precisely because he saw the latter as a more viable medium for reaching audiences in Africa across divergent language groups and among nonliterate people.[5] But Sembéne's anecdote also suggests that the cinema served another, perhaps more important, political function. In postliberation Africa, the cinema, an institution historically and currently reliant on Western industry and conventions, had become a critical site of contestation over language and pedagogical authority. To understand Sembéne's own pedagogical strategy in telling this anecdote, it is important to note that cinematic pedagogy and linguistic imperialism were not new issues for him during the period in question. Even before this exchange with a peasant audience, he had produced a film that raised exactly those questions of language and authority posed by his Senegalese critics. French voice-over dominates the sound track of his 1966 *La Noire de* . . . (Black Girl), a film in which the narrative centers precisely on the linguistic and cultural isolation of the film's displaced Senegalese protagonist. Her interior monologue is represented in French, though we know that she cannot speak French well, during her isolating experience as a maid in a French household. The film can be seen as a pedagogical vehicle through which the filmmaker teaches his audience about the profoundly debasing effects of colonial servitude combined with enforced isolation from one's own country, language, and culture. But Sembéne's anecdote also tacitly demonstrates how the audience can also play the role of pedagogue, teaching the filmmaker a lesson about cultural imperialism. Sembéne's film was introduced to Africa by the West as a means of "educating" African colonial subjects to the ways of assimilation, and it was appropriated for countercolonial political "education" in antiassimilation and in the retention of cultural forms. But it is also a critical site of a more complex contestation over agency, authority, and pedagogical form in postliberation colonialism.

In Africa, a pedagogical tradition of cinema is in part artifactual of overt colonial disciplinary practices (practices in which the cinema "taught" language and values). But this same tradition has been an important means of intervention in the current dismantling and reconfiguring of colonialist cultural forms. In this chapter, I examine what I will call a pedagogical mode of West African cinema. Relying on analyses of colonialism by Johannes Fabian, Pierre Erny, Ashis Nandy, and Edward Said, I consider how Western theories of Third World development intersected with Western theories of pedagogy and child development. I also show that indigenous filmmaking in West Africa has appropriated and transformed these same developmental and pedagogical theories. Drawing on the writings of Manthia Diawara, Roy Armes and Lizbeth Malkmus, Françoise Pfaff, and L. S. Senghor, I consider the legacy of this colonial pedagogical tradition in many of the postliberation films of the 1970s and 1980s produced by African filmmakers. My analysis centers on the textual and structural place of pedagogy in Sembéne's *Emitai* (1971) and *Camp de Thiaroye* (1988), and in Burkina Faso filmmaker Gaston Kaboré's *Wênd Kûuni* (1982). These films engage the colonial legacy of filmic didacticism, critiquing and dismantling it through textual allegory while also appropriating and subverting its conventions for local struggles and broader oppositional and cultural politics.

Colonial Development and Development Theory

Paternalistic programs of education and development in colonial and postliberation Africa drew on social science theories that derived not only from fields devoted to the study of "other" cultures (anthropology) but from apparently unrelated fields, specifically, child psychology—a field that takes as its object the Western child. Overt links forged between anthropology and pedagogical theory, and between the colonial subject and the Western child, indicate that the terms "paternalism" and "infantilization" were not simply convenient analogies for colonialist techniques of social management. They were also methods institutionalized in emergent paradigms of pedagogy in the West during precisely the same period (as indicated in my study of the Ford Foundation projects in the United States and Samoa). These methods were employed not only inside but also beyond educational contexts such as schools. In the following, I consider the intersections between anthropological developmental theories and theories of child development. Not coincidentally, visual representation figures centrally in both of these social science areas. Pedagogical theories of visual representation informed a broadly conceived colonial "educational" system that embraced the cinema as a pedagogical medium uniquely suited to the management of African subjects.

In his well-known critique of anthropology, Johannes Fabian suggests that a focus on visual representation is common among the various forms of domination that contributed to the maintenance of Western imperialism. He describes early anthropology as a set of practices that presented "knowledge through visual and spatial images, maps, diagrams, trees, and tables."[6] The practices of collection and display of photographs and artifacts taken by colonizers and missionaries became the basis for a body of work produced by eighteenth- and nineteenth-century anthropologists, many of whom never left Europe. This emphasis on visual methodology was reinforced in the instructive manuals on fieldwork written by twentieth-century anthropologists such as Marcell Mauss.[7] A contradiction emerges in this focus on visual media. Although the field favored using visual modes in the representation of its own data, anthropologists nonetheless considered the visual forms used in the cultures they studied to be indicative of "lower" cognitive ability. Furthermore, as Fabian shows, social scientists made explicit connections between the designation of "lower" cultures and "lower" developmental stages of Western subjects—that is, between subjects of colonialism and children, in part on the basis of these groups' reliance on visual modes of representation.

> It is commonly believed that the visual-spatial is more germane to the infantile and adolescent mind than to the mature intelligence. Whether such is indeed the case may be for the psychologist to decide. However it is easy to see how arguing from ontogenetic to phylogenetic visualism may turn pedagogical principles into political programs.[8]

As the final sentence makes clear, Fabian centers his critique not on the West's devaluing of visual systems in its textual hierarchy but on the West's deft linking of individual development and development of the species—an association that grounds a broad social science program that is profoundly paternalistic and pedagogical. If some sectors of the species are "developmentally lagging," they must be raised and schooled even if they are adults.

The critique of this view has a history in the critique of Darwinian evolution for its inherent support of a racialist social program.[9] Perhaps equally crucial, though, is the way that this slippage between individual and societal development encourages a blurring of boundaries between individual cognitive development and technological development, giving a biological cast to political and cultural decisions. For example, a country's political decision to "develop" (i.e., to industrialize with the help of the West, to support the introduction of Western industrial and cultural institutions like the cinema) becomes the cognitively advanced, "intelligent" decision. This recasting of ethnographic evolutionism in the formulation of a discourse of national development within the realm of Western political diplomacy became the paradigmatic response to the impending dissolution of direct colonial rule in the post–World War II era. Arturo Escobar provides an insightful account of the emergence of political discourse on development as a "powerful mechanism for the production and management of the Third World" by the West.[10]

The specific place that anthropology afforded visual culture within the narrative hierarchy of social and technological development was linked to the central role literacy had attained as a a marker of class distinction in the West, and as a marker of difference between colonizers and colonial subjects. Colonial anthropologists regarded visual representation as a "lower" discursive mode privileged among nonliterate African cultures. But visualism—the commandeering and regimenting of visual culture in the diagrams, maps, texts, and museum displays described by Fabian—was also the late-nineteenth-century anthropologist's favored means of studying and monitoring colonial subjects. Film historian Fatimah Tobing Rony clearly ties anthropology's visual discourse of racial evolution to the emergence of cinema as a means of ethnographic classification and surveillance in her analysis of the chronophotographic typologies of human gesture produced by French ethnographer Félix-Louis Regnault.[11] These two contradictory tendencies—to designate a "lower" culture as visual, and to privilege the visual as means of monitoring that culture—converge in the decision to use visual media as a means of disciplining and schooling colonial subjects.

Fabian states that visualism forms a juncture between the various forms of domination that crisscross modern Western empire. He is referring to the pervasive use of visual systems to observe and to educate.[12]

> The hegemony of the visual as a mode of knowing may thus directly be linked to the political hegemony of an age group, a class, or one society over another. The ruler's subject and the scientist's object have in the case of anthropology (but also in the case of sociology and psychology) an intertwined history.[13]

Fabian draws a connection between various implementations of visual modes of knowing within Western science and political domination. In short, he suggests that science is one means by which colonial rule has been established and maintained. Through the combined social science discourses of anthropology, sociology, and psychology, a pedagogical principle was formulated as a mechanism for maintaining imperial power relations. This principle was based on the conception of visual cultures and cognitive modes as "inferior" or "subservient" *and* as sites for control and correction via visual aids.

Fabian's discussion of the visual and developmental models of colonial anthropology encompasses a broad period of history. How was what Fabian calls anthropology's developmental "visual mode of knowing" enacted in liberation and postliberation Africa? As Fabian points out, anthropological theory drew on ontogenetic models to naturalize its own cultural hierarchies, and developmental and pedagogical theories have been important sources for these social science models.[14] The work of child psychologist Jean Piaget is a useful example of the specific theories that informed social science discourse on development during the first decades of African cinema. His theories intersect in explicit ways with writings on Third World development during the late 1950s and 1960s—the general period of African liberation struggles. Piaget openly draws on the stereotype of the colonial other as a mentally underdeveloped primitive to support his claims about the development of the Western child.[15] Indeed, Piaget regards the stereotypical view of "primitive" culture he presents as so universally accepted that he finds it unnecessary to indicate his sources. Non-Western peoples are excluded from Piaget's widely accepted developmental model by virtue of the fact that he regarded them as developmentally analogous to Western children. Not surprisingly, Piaget's model of a highly developed individual is a scientist—more specifically, an anthropologist. Moreover,

Piaget provides an explicit theoretical explanation of the relationship between visual representation and pedagogy that informs his own and anthropology's developmental theory. This explanation offers some insight into anthropology's pedagogical cinema and its legacy in liberation and postliberation Africa.[16]

Piaget uses the term "realism" to refer to what he sees as nascent conceptual schemata that inform children's concrete physical activity. For Piaget, realism has important ties to visual representation. It is a precursor to the more developmentally complex and abstract forms of scientific reasoning that he attributes to Western adults. Piaget's conception of realism can be traced directly back to the work of developmental psychologist Georges Henri Luquet. In 1895, coincidentally the year of cinema's first public screenings, Luquet used the term "intellectual realism" to describe what he saw as similarities between children's perception and drawings and those of "primitive peoples."[17] Perhaps not surprisingly, this nineteenth-century association is repeated by Piaget in 1965, a period marked by the ascendancy of African liberation struggles. That he perceived as identical the political management of African subjects and the pedagogical management of children is spelled out in clear terms in the following passage:

> Social constraint—and by this we mean any social relation into which there enters an element of authority and which is not like cooperation, the result of an interchange between equal individuals—has on the individual results that are analogous to those exercised by adult constraint of the child. Two phenomena, moreover, are really one and the same thing, and the adult who is under the dominion of unilateral respect for "Elders" and for tradition is really behaving like a child. It may even be maintained that the realism of primitive conceptions of crime and punishment is, in certain respects, an infantile reaction.[18]

Piaget attributes what he perceived as the prevalence of "developmentally lower" cognitive modes in "primitive" societies to traditional authority and indigenous rule. He thus deems this authority unhealthy, claiming that it stunts moral and cognitive development of the social group across generations: "One can . . . surmise that the outstanding features of 'primitive mentality' can be explained by the conjuncture of childish mentality with the effects of the constraint exercised by one generation upon the other. Primitive mentality would therefore be due to social constraint being refracted through the childish mind." [19] The perceived "childish mind" of African colonial subjects is attributed to traditional values and ancestral authority, a fact that is highly ironic, considering the infantilizing strategies of colonial paternalism. Piaget's logic becomes a rationale for the use of constraint by Western authorities advocating paternalistic decrees in the management of colonial subjects.[20] Piaget's theory thus lends itself to discussion of colonial endeavors during a period of struggle for independence, rationalizing both the imposition of Western pedagogical discipline in the colonial setting (in order to aid the future development of "primitive" peoples) and the maintenance of authoritarian rule in conjunction with national autonomy.

Piaget is only one example of a long and complex relationship between pedagogical methods exercised locally and at a distance. Ashis Nandy analyzes the parallel and interconstitutive relation between colonial rule and the changing Western conception of the child at the turn of the century:

> Colonialism dutifully picked up [social science's] ideas of growth and development and drew a new parallel between primitivism and childhood. Thus the theory of social progress was telescoped not merely into the individual's life cycle in Europe but also into the area of cultural differences in the colonies.[21]

Nandy's point is that there were no ahistorical notions of the child or of development that could be transposed simply onto colonial subjects. Rather, a modern conception of the child—its development and its management through pedagogical practices—emerged in conjunction with imperialist paternalism. Colonial administrators, aided by the classificatory work of anthropologists, developed mechanisms of discipline and indoctrination of colonial subjects; however, the same sort of research justified an elaborate system of discipline and education of Western children. As Guari Viswanathan has shown in her study of British colonial power and literacy, modern English studies originated in an educational system initially imposed on colonial subjects and only later imported into England's own schools.[22] The geopolitically broad project of pedagogical relations forms a complex relation between local and distant points in the imperial web.

In a discussion of the significance of Europe's colonial legacy to African independence movements and contemporary film production, Lizbeth Malkmus and Roy Armes note that the need for cultural and linguistic intermediaries between the metropolitan nation and colonized peoples led to the creation of educational institutions that taught European ideas.[23] These institutions were part of a broad colonial policy of cultural and technical-economic assimilation based on the intersecting paradigms of economic and psychological development theory. As Nandy and others have pointed out, theories of social and cognitive development served as the justification for the paternalistic control of African economy and culture.

Assimilation held out to African subjects the false promise that colonies would eventually achieve equal status with the paternal state. Assimilationist policy served to mitigate resistance, justifying colonial rule by presenting it as a temporary measure with a program to dismantle itself.[24] This paternalistic posture of colonial powers constituted an attempt to maintain rule by ideological means despite waning economic and military resources in Europe. French, British, German, and League of Nations policy reports from the period reveal a widespread effort to shore up failing colonial administrations through reform of pedagogical and cultural institutions in Africa.[25]

But assimilationist strategies were not entirely successful. Ideals of democracy and nationalism strongly embedded in the assimilationist pedagogy of European states clashed with the experience of the colonial student. Malkmus and Armes quote Alistair Horne's account of the colonial Algerian school experience as "an admirable breeding ground for revolutionary minds."[26] Along similar lines, Said suggests that although the liberation movements followed on the instruction in "colonial schools which taught generations of the native bourgeoisie important truths about history, science, culture,"[27] the indigenous elite also gained "a pronounced awareness of culture as imperialism, the reflexive moment of consciousness that enabled the newly independent citizen to assert the end of Europe's cultural claim to guide and/or instruct the non-European."[28] Said stresses the role of pedagogical autonomy as one of the goals of revolution. The very institutions of assimilationist education fostered resistance to European authority, carried out by means perhaps inspired by, but not wholly appropriating, European revolutionary models.

Colonial administrators' decision to implement developmental pedagogical models as part of assimilationist policy was prompted by a motivation essentially distinct from Western educational authorities' implementation of such models at home. Institution of assimilationist policy in the colonies, though purportedly aimed at bringing colonies to a status equal with that of European powers, was at the same time a means of maintaining their status as dependent. Colonial administrations were never fully committed to bringing "childlike" colonies into the fold of "adult" national power. Rather, they selectively imbued a colonial elite with the degree of European culture and authority needed to serve specific imperial interests such as administering and ruling other colonial subjects. Consequently, the limits of colonial assimilation were determined by the need for the establishment of an indigenous administrative authority. The radicalization of educated colonial elite within the assimilationist system was not, then, merely the effect of exposure to European revolutionary models but a confrontation with the hypocrisy of assimilationist policy itself.

Given the overtly pedagogical mission of colonial rule, it is not surprising that the history of Western-produced cinema directed at African audiences begins with the consciously didactic use of film by missionaries, colonial administrators, and anthropologists.[29] In his history of African cinema, Manthia Diawara points out that this project had contradictory implications for newly formed African nations and their subsequent film practices. We find didactic films that were clearly implicated in a colonialist pedagogical "civilizing mission," such as those produced by the British Bantu Educational Cinema Experiment (the 1935–1936 *Post Office, Savings Bank, Tax, Progress*) and the Congolese Center for Catholic Action Cinema (Father Van de Heuvel's 1940s animated series *Les palabres de mboloko* and Father Van Haelst's series of the late 1940s, *Matamata et Pilipili*). These films were designed as lessons to be learned easily by an indigenous viewer assumed to be developmentally immature, illiterate, and needful of instruction.

By insisting on visual form, colonizers (the French in particular) helped to institute a representational mode that would later prove useful to African filmmakers interested in using film in liberation struggles that spanned multiple language groups and included nonliterate communities. As with post–World War II U.S. and European independents, the relatively low-budget 16 mm filmmaking techniques provided missionaries with a media alternative that allowed a greater degree of economic

Postcard of the Committee of
African Cinematographers
"For the Defense and Promo-
tion of African Film."

POUR LA DÉFENSE ET LA PROMOTION DU FILM AFRICAIN

and technical independence from the European industry. For better or
worse, the didactic film of missionaries, anthropologists, and colonial
administrators was the first cinema shown in Africa to take into consideration the specificity of its audiences' languages and cultures.[30] These
circumstances contributed to the emergence of independent African film
production.

A Pedagogical Cinema

In following pages I draw on the foregoing discussion of colonialism,
development, and pedagogical theory to examine the appropriation and
contestation of the didactic film tradition in African-produced cinema.
My discussion focuses on three films: Sembéne's *Emitai* (1971) and
Camp de Thiaroye (1988) and Gaston Kaboré's *Wênd Kûuni* (1982). By
retelling the story of Africa's involvement in World War II, *Emitai* and
Camp de Thiaroye address the formation of national liberation struggles
through the confrontation with French pedagogical authority. Focusing
on the social dimensions of military confrontation, Sembéne provides a
history of resistance that is also a commentary on struggles against con-

tinued European cultural domination in postliberation Senegal. *Wênd Kûuni* is an example of how traditional narrative and cultural forms have been employed in Burkinabe cinema to negotiate and reclaim pedagogical authority. Stuart Hall argues that "we cannot and should not, for a moment, underestimate the importance of the act of imaginative re-discovery. 'Hidden histories' have played a crucial role in the emergence of some of the most important social movements of our time."[31] Sembéne and Kaboré demonstrate two qualitatively distinct practices of critically reconstructing histories. Reimagining past pedagogical relationships is central to both their projects.

Emitai and *Camp de Thiaroye:*
The Critique of Assimilationist Pedagogy

Sembéne's experience in the French colonial army during World War II no doubt exposed him to assimilationist policy and gave him first-hand insight on the apparent necessity of assimilation to the imperial military project. In *Emitai*, set in Senegal during World War II, Sembéne draws on this experience to show how the expedient implementation of assimilationist policy was carried out in a haphazard and even hysterical manner by the troubled French regime. Early in the film, a French officer assembles and instructs young men of a Diola village: "You have been volunteered. France is at war with Germany; Marshal Pétain is the chief of France. He is my father and yours. France does you a great honor. You will go to Dakar and then to France. On return you will have war stories to tell your children."

The officer conjures up the image of Pétain as collective father, ceremoniously implying the consummate assimilation of colonial subjects into the imperial culture. But in this instance, assimilation is invoked prematurely—that is, before any pedagogic approach has been applied to inculcate the would-be soldiers into the imperial fold. The oxymoronic notion of "being volunteered" underscores the hysterical illogic of French rule. Clearly the colonizers desire to have it both ways: the officer holds out the motivation of inclusion while refusing to grant colonial subjects self-determination. "Assimilation" appears as a flimsy justification for the forced conscription of the Diola.

The irony of this scene is underscored when in a later scene, posters of Pétain, a four-star marshal, are torn down and replaced with those of his successor de Gaulle, a two-star general. One conscripted Senegalese soldier responds with incredulity to the change in the designated rank of the figurehead of imperial leadership, marveling at the seemingly arbitrary nature of France's power structure. This brief sequence indicates that though able to force West African soldiers to fight for France, the French lacked a cohesive program for establishing and stabilizing their own authority. This point is reinforced again in a later scene in which the administration fails to convince the women of the village to give up their harvest of rice to feed French troops. Repeatedly facing such resistances to their various attempts to gain the Diola's compliance, the French administration is brought to a standstill.

Sembéne says that *Emitai* marks his own recognition of the need for a history of resistance. "For the struggle against neo-colonialism," he explains, "it is possible to reactualize all these scattered and little-known battles." [32] Notably, the battles whose memory Sembéne sees as essential to the struggle against postliberation domination have escaped recognition precisely because they were not merely countermilitary insurrections but also resistances to the very forms of authority that the forces of the colonial regime stood for. *Emitai* shows resistance to the prospect of assimilation by members of the various social groups that make up the village (the elders, the women, and the young men). The film is complemented by Sembéne's later *Camp de Thiaroye* (1988), a film in which resistance also ensues from within the ranks of conscripted troops on recognition of the hypocrisy and illogic of the assimilationist experience they have been through. In *Camp de Thiaroye* Sembéne illustrates the effects of "successful" assimilationist pedagogy to show how the French investment in "educating" colonial subjects proved to be deeply conflicted and disingenuous.

Camp de Thiaroye is a study in the subtle and complex interaction of a range of pedagogical forces. Based on a historical incident, the film depicts the gradual realization of the limits of assimilationist policies by a World War II battalion of Senegalese infantrymen undergoing repatriation after being drafted into battle for the French. Exposed to European culture and the ideology of First World struggles for democracy, the battalion is also subject on its return to opportunistic and often contradictory treatment by colonial authorities. In effect, the French officers attempt to reverse the process of assimilation to repatriate the soldiers to their colonial setting. Feeding them an inedible mush, ceremonially stripping them of their uniforms, and finally withholding their pay, the French officers infantilize and humiliate the Senegalese infantry-men. Ultimately the colonizers' desire to maintain a strict social and racial hierarchy overrides any notion of human development that in-forms assimilationist pedagogy. For the French administration, no mat-ter what degree of cultural assimilation colonial subjects achieve, they will always be children.

The success of assimilationist policy depended on the colonizer's ability to maintain for his subjects the illusion that attaining European status and power is possible. Sembéne's primary focus is colonial sub-jects who have achieved various levels of identification with European power within the military hierarchy. Through the character of Sergeant Major Diatta, the Senegalese drill sergeant whose command of both French and English and knowledge of classical music and jazz place him at the crossroads of contemporary European culture, Sembéne under-scores the relationship between cultural knowledge and power within the military hierarchy. Diatta is emblematic of the enforced limits of African subjects in France's paternalistic ranks. A modern Renaissance man, Diatta is a military anomaly. As an exemplary product of the heterogeneous pedagogical-disciplinary mechanisms of cultural, educa-tional, and military institutions, he occupies the pinnacle of the assimi-lationist hierarchy among colonized subjects. Yet although he is intel-lectually superior to his French commanding officers, he is continually placed in a lower military standing—a rank determined by racial hier-archies. The only authority he is allowed to exercise is among his fellow colonial subjects. His situation is replicated in society outside the camp. When he ventures into town, he is thrown out of local establishments and beaten and abducted by U.S. military police. His authority under-mined and eroded, Diatta is ultimately forced to confront his conflicted allegiances. In a move that recalls the third phase of Fanon's native intel-lectual, Diatta finally takes up the side of his countrymen—albeit too late to avoid their tragic massacre by the French.

Through the other infantrymen (who, as Malkmus and Armes note, bear nicknames evoking the administrative divisions of France's West African empire), Sembéne represents degrees of European loyalty and identification.[33] As the conscripted battalion members gradually come to recognize that they have lost their wartime status in the eyes of the French, they argue among themselves in pidgin French about how to re-spond. Pays (whose name phonetically approximates the French word

Senegalese infantry-
men confront French
officer in *Camp de
Thiaroye* (Ousmane
Sembéne, 1988).

for country), a mute infantryman who seems to suffer from shell shock,
is perhaps the character most symbolic of the pedagogical predicament
of the assimilated subject. Intent on wearing a Nazi helmet, Pays am-
bivalently identifies both with concentration camp victims and with
Nazi soldiers. His character embodies the tragic effects of Eurocolonial
pedagogy: the contradictions of assimilation internalized as psychosis.
In his schizoid identification with the colonizer, Pays is both the sub-
jugator and the subjugated. His condition represents the "colonized"
side of complicitous infantrymen like Diatta. Pays is at one moment
hyperconfident and the next terrified. Like Piaget's and Luquet's "primitive" subject, Pays is a childlike adult. But unlike Piaget's and Luquet's
"primitive" subject, his childlikeness affords him an incisive take on the
colonial experience: a recurrent hallucination is that he is still in a concentration camp—a delusion that, by the film's bitter end, proves more
accurate than the perceptions of his apparently more stable comrades.
His fears are realized when the men, who await payment and release,
are slaughtered and the camp burned by the French.

Camp de Thiaroye demonstrates the invocation and failure of assimilationist ideology across a diverse range of state and cultural institutions.
The intertwined projects of colonial military and pedagogical control
produce internal contradictions that are articulated through the experiences of soldiers in their treatment by American, French, and Senegalese figures of authority, in the transitory world of the camp and beyond. These contradictions eventually lead to the rupture in paternalistic
policy, unleashing a barbarous reaction, demonstrated in the film's dev-
astating conclusion. Faced with organized insurrection of the African
infantryman, the French military authorities dispense with them in a
massacre.

Emitai and *Camp de Thiaroye* are installments in a single sequential narrative, *Emitai* taking place during the height of World War II, and *Camp de Thiaroye* in the war's immediate aftermath. The films' historical settings are separated by only about one year, but the conflicts that form the core of each film's narrative are distinguishable less by time than by the political and cultural situations of the characters. The films enact distinct responses to assimilationist pedagogy by colonial subjects. *Emitai* shows the unfolding of resistance to incorporation in the European war effort by various groups within the traditional Diola village. The French fail to convince the Diola that incorporation into the French military campaign is in the villagers' best interest. The response of the commanding officer to the Diola people's refusal to support the French war is the response of a failed pedagogue who resorts to irrational techniques of discipline and punishment. *Camp de Thiaroye* shows the resistance of soldiers who, through their participation in the war, have already been assimilated to various degrees. A similar outcome follows the dutiful compliance of colonial subjects to the war effort. They have *learned too much* in their participation in the Western military enterprise and thus are perceived as threatening. In this case, the disingenuous nature of French assimilationist policy is evident not so much in the lack of investment in an effective pedagogy as in France's inability to deal with the outcome of its program. In the end, French authorities are unable to manage these newly educated colonial subjects. The Westernized African is, for the West, a threat that must be eradicated. In each film, the colonial subjects call the bluff of French assimilationist pedagogy.

Sembéne's depiction of the failure of Eurocolonial authority at two historical moments is articulated alongside a critique of pedagogical models from the past. The critical representation of traditional leadership in films such as *Emitai* and *Ceddo* (1976) clearly suggests that Sembéne views a return to precolonial African pedagogical authority as an untenable solution. Sembéne's critical relation to tradition is, however, never totalizing. For example, he incorporates in both films the pedagogical address of the griot in his historical narrative and editing style. His is a cautionary response to the uncritical embrace of the precolonial past (represented in negritude, for example). He says of *Emitai*, "I wanted to show . . . that the gods could no longer respond to the people's needs." [34] Traditional culture is depicted as it is lived and experienced within the colonial conflict, rather than as a pure precolonial past.

Sembéne is representative of a broader tendency in West African

cinema to take up modes of traditional authority, incorporating its pedagogical modes of address while mitigating reified notions of authenticity. Burkinabe filmmaker Gaston Kaboré presents an alternative approach to the critical appropriation of traditional culture. In *Wênd
Kûuni* (1982), Kaboré uses a precolonial oral narrative style to depict
change and conflict within African tradition. Kaboré's appropriation of
precolonial narratives undermines an essentialist conception of a reified
heritage, but precolonial narrative also serves as an allegory of colonial domination and liberation. In the following section, I suggest that
Kaboré's symbolic condensation of the overthrow of both traditional
and colonial authority within *Wênd Kûuni* points the way to an autonomous contemporary African cinematic aesthetic in which visual pedagogy is an important mode.

Wênd Kûuni and the Subversion of
Visual Pedagogical Relations

Diawara performs an extensive narrative analysis of *Wênd Kûuni* to
demonstrate a tendency within African cinema toward the appropriation of traditional narrative form for contemporary agendas. For Diawara, *Wênd Kûuni* is representative of works in which African filmmakers "use the material of oral literature to reflect the ideology of
the [present] time and not that of oral tradition."[35] This appropriation
of tradition is selective and transformative, rather than essentializing.
When filmmakers such as Kaboré restructure oral narratives, they "emphasize a notion of Senghorism . . . at the expense of historical authenticity."[36] Leopold S. Senghor, one of the founding theorists of negritude,
sought not simply to rid African culture of Western influences but to
assert African autonomy through the legitimation of tradition and its
integration with contemporary culture.[37] Diawara's invocation of Senghor is significant to my consideration of pedagogical authority within
African cinema. Senghor was one of many leaders of the early nationalist period who considered the formulation of a new pedagogy central to postliberation struggles.[38] The "Senghorism" of these filmmakers,
which Diawara describes as a subversion of traditional cultural forms
and symbols, is fundamentally associated with an appropriation of pedagogical authority from both traditional and Eurocolonial sources. Extending Diawara's analysis, I would argue that Kaboré appropriates and
transforms the structures not only of oral narratives but of traditional

Poster for *Wênd Kûuni*
(Gaston Kaboré, 1982).

pedagogical relations, reclaiming the modes of visual pedagogy designated "lower" by colonial anthropology to forge a new anticolonial filmic form.

As noted in the earlier discussion of Fabian, developmental models that served to legitimate Western authority situate literate culture historically after and hierarchically above coexistent oral and visual cultures. But the same practices of Western social science that produced these developmental models employed visual pedagogical methods and techniques to frame and control the cultures they studied. In *Wênd Kûuni*, Kaboré appropriates cinema for the tradition of oral and visual culture. Kaboré's emphasis on the oral as opposed to the visual properties of the filmic medium makes cinema the bearer of traditional pedagogical authority.

The title *Wênd Kûuni* (God's Gift) is taken from the name given in the film to the character of an orphaned boy by his adoptive parents after he is discovered in the woods—a scenario suggestive of European's paternal "discovery" of the primitive subject "in nature." The film's plot extends this allegory to the issue of language. The narrative centers on

Wênd Kûuni's loss and recovery of voice, a loss that results from a bout of amnesia apparently brought on by his abandonment. This loss and recovery of voice is clearly an allegory of the suppression of African oral culture during the period of colonial rule. Thus in *Wênd Kûuni* Kaboré draws on traditional oral forms and symbols to construct a narrative that engages critically with the cultural and political significance of orality.

The central role of the griot as community educator and historian reflects the great value placed on oral narrative as a transmitter of knowledge throughout African societies. *Wênd Kûuni* is both an instance of this crucial educational form and a narrative about its politics. Diawara performs a close analysis of the complex interplay of narrative and diegetic voices to suggest that "orality is the subject of the film because it incorporates an oral rendering of the tale which it later subverts." [39] In support of this idea, he points to the construction of an external voice early in the film. The film begins with diegetic dialogue, but speaking characters are obscured; they are presented in long shot, hidden in shadow, in profile, or with their backs to the camera. Often dialogue is in fact situated off-screen. As Diawara suggests, making voice external suggests the mediating authority of the storyteller or griot in traditional oral culture even before voice-over narration is actually introduced. When voice-over narration is eventually introduced, it is to "remind the spectator of his/her authority" (47).

This first introduction of voice-over narration is marked by a lapse in narrative continuity. The narrator-storyteller provides a belated introduction to the film that situates the narrative within a precolonial time—a point that is already evident. Kaboré's introduction of the griot's voice through this redundant passage signals the beginning of a shift in authority from the traditional forms of orality represented within the film to the cinema itself as modern medium of oral culture. As Diawara points out, shortly after this point, yet another narrative voice is constructed in the film (48). This is achieved through the more distinctly subjective diegetic dialogue of Pongneré, Wênd Kûuni's adoptive sister. She gradually becomes the dominant aural "point of view" through whom viewers are invited to experience the narrative.[40]

As Wênd Kûuni regains his voice, pedagogical authority is transferred from one generation to the next. At the same time, the formal structure of the film enacts a transfer of authority from the traditional storyteller to the cinematic griot. The structure of *Wênd Kûuni* effectively enacts the supplanting of oral narrative by filmic pedagogical authority. By the time Wênd Kûuni takes on the role of storyteller in the final sequences of the film, cinematic diegetic form has fully replaced the storytelling modes of narration. The film closes without a return of the framing external voice.

Kaboré figures cinema, a medium based in contemporary technology and a world economy, as the progeny of oral and visual culture. This appropriation of the visual technology of Western culture for an African pedagogical tradition subverts its implementation within the Western paternalistic pedagogical project. The cinema remains a pedagogical medium, but its narrow construction as an emblem of Western culture is challenged. In effect, Kaboré constructs an alternative and non-Western (pre)history for the cinema.

Also important is that youth takes on a particular allegorical significance in *Wênd Kûuni*. With children in lead roles, *Wênd Kûuni* presents an allegorical representation of the usurping of Eurocolonial authority that subverts Western notions of youth as ignorance. A corollary to this is the film's tacit representation of the transitory nature of adult and paternal pedagogical authority. *Wênd Kûuni* constructs a new notion of youth by drawing on two divergent sources. First, the film uses youth to symbolize the leadership of a generation of young, institutionally educated revolutionary leaders. Second, it draws on the pedagogical authority accorded to youth within their own age groups by some African cultures.[41]

Certainly, youth has figured as a symbol of revolutionary change throughout the history of modern liberation struggles. But in different contexts, this symbol takes on unique inflections. Comparing the revolutionary movements in the Old World and the Third World, Benedict Anderson notes that metaphors of age had a more literal basis in the latter-day colonial liberation struggles than in European revolutions. He points to education as the factor that brings about this distinction:

> Both in Europe and in the colonies "young" and "youth" signified dynamism, progress, self-sacrificing idealism and revolutionary will. But in Europe "young" had little in the way of definable sociological contours. . . . There was thus no necessary connection between language, age, class and status. In the colonies things were very different.

Youth meant, above all, the *first* generation in any significant numbers to have acquired a European education, marking them off linguistically and culturally from their parents' generation, as well from the vast bulk of their colonized agemates.[42]

Anderson's suggestion that the significance of youth as a defining characteristic of Third World liberation movements has direct bearing on representations of generational difference in Kaboré's film. This particular adult-child relation was not merely the archetypal tension created by the cyclic transfer of power from one generation to another—it was a transformed relation based on the imperial intervention of schooling in the traditional pedagogical transfer of authority. "In the colonies, then," Anderson states, "by 'Youth' we mean 'Schooled Youth.'"[43] Institutionalized schooling brought on a confusion between the paternal authority of the imperial state and local adult authority.

In *Wênd Kûuni*, this confusion of pedagogical authority is enacted through the intersection of literal history (precolonial narrative) and historical allegory (of colonization and liberation). This parallel representation of the transfer of pedagogical authority within traditional society and the resistance of the generation of liberation to colonial authority occurs within a space circumscribed by generational difference—a space defined by the distinct activities of children and of adults.

To understand the importance of this parallel, it is necessary to note the overdetermined nature of age solidarity in the colonial context. Anderson observes that the solidarity of age-mates was an effect of the transformative process of European education. But this formulation ignores factors that preexisted European influence. Senghor suggests that there was already an ingrained source of age solidarity within the pedagogical traditions of African cultures. He describes age fraternity as a historically maintained pedagogical mechanism of indoctrination into citizenship in many African societies. He argues that education and discipline within age groups ensured the cohesion of black African society.[44] Senghor supports this assertion through reference to the rituals and rites of passage that form significant components of traditional African pedagogies and that are often experienced by groups of peers who prepare for such experiences together.

Drawing on the writing of Senghor and others, Pierre Erny argues that within African tradition, it is possible to speak of "classes based on

Pongneré and Wênd Kûuni in
Wênd Kûuni (Gaston Kaboré, 1982).

age." He states that "within the society of children there is thus set up a
kind of mutual education which operates more or less outside the adult
world."[45] Kaboré represents this delineation of distinct spheres of pedagogical action in *Wênd Kûuni* by situating most of the significant narrative action in distinct adults' and children's spheres.[46] Toward the end of
the film, the most significant unfolding of the plot is represented within
the pedagogic arena of the society of children. Kaboré situates the viewer
among children, and within the experience of this pedagogy of age solidarity. Thus the transfer of voice from the external narrator or griot to
Wênd Kûuni and Pongneré by the end of the film evokes the transfer of
pedagogical authority to representatives within youth groups.

The film's allegorical structure superimposes the transgression of
rigid tradition and the overcoming of colonial oppression. This is indicated clearly by the final turn of events. The resistance of Timpoko, a
young unmarried women, to the village elders' attempt to marry her to
the elder Bila sets up a conflict over traditional rule. Timpoko's insinua-
tion that Old Bila is impotent symbolizes the viewpoint of youth that
traditional culture is inadequate. Timpoko's predicament and her resistance mirror the situation of Wênd Kûuni's mother, who, at the beginning of the film, was banished for refusing a similarly arranged marriage,
and subsequently perished. However, the tragic outcome is altered in
Timpoko's case. The older husband kills himself, leaving his resistant
bride to carry on. When Wênd Kûuni subsequently discovers the body
of Old Bila, he is jarred into recovering his memory and hence his voice.

The restoration of Wênd Kûuni's speech and memory after the death
of Old Bila is a condensed symbol of the overthrow of colonial and rigid
traditional authority. The allegorical representation of Africa's colonization and liberation, coupled with the literal narrative of precolonial

Poster for *Yaaba*
(Idrissa Ouedraogo, 1989).

history, suggests an appropriation of authority from two pedagogical regimes, both figured as past.

A generative ambiguity is created in the representation of a generational transition that functions simultaneously as a symbol of social transformation and as a component of traditional culture. By treating the situation of youth as object of both imperial and traditional discipline and authority, Kaboré avoids simplifying the conflict between tradition and modernization. The success of this strategy hinges on both the historical and the symbolic significance of youth in the intersecting areas of Eurocolonial and traditional African pedagogy.

Kaboré effectively resists the construction of an inferior infantile mentality within development theory by attributing to the characters of children authority and the ability to contest. The children in *Wênd Kûuni* actually take on pedagogic authority. The familial metaphor of "adult" colonizer and "child" colonized is subverted by playing out its obvious narrative consequences—the metaphor is embedded in an Oedipal narrative that serves to transform the colonialist myth of (arrested) development into a parable of resistance and appropriation of authority.

Poster for *Yeelen*
(Souleymane Cisse, 1987).

Conclusion

Although postliberation West African film was informed by the legacy of a colonialist pedagogical cinema, this pedagogical theory was transformed through strategic appropriation and allegorical critique. A number of questions remain unanswered here: To what degree does the slippage between theories of Western child development and Third World development continue in ongoing neocolonial endeavors? If contemporary West African films do problematize this slippage both in their structure and through narrative, what is being done in the film industry to address this paradigm in development policy? (The latter question is raised in light of African film's continuing reliance on French and U.S. funding.) Finally, given the centrality of pedagogical concerns in both colonial and African-produced film, is it feasible to consider African cinema apart from the related institutions of social science, education, and policy that continue to intersect and inform Africa's film culture? My discussion of postliberation films has focused primarily on textual evidence to support my thesis about pedagogy, but it is important to study audience and industry politics as areas also critically informed by the colonial pedagogical legacy described by Nandy, Senghor, Fabian, and others. As Sembéne seems to suggest in the anecdote cited at the beginning of the chapter, it is the African viewer who functions finally as the crucial figure of pedagogical authority in Africa's contemporary cinema.

CHAPTER SEVEN

Local Television and

Community Politics in Brazil

São Paulo's TV Anhembi

In 1992, at the ninth annual Videobrazil International Festival in São Paulo, Brazil, Jon Alpert, veteran U.S. video activist and cofounder of New York City's Downtown Community Television (DCTV), was interviewed by São Paulo's alternative television enterprise, TV Anhembi. Standing in front of the dazzling thirty-six-monitor video wall mounted to TV Anhembi's plush mobile production and exhibition unit, Alpert recalled that DCTV "started just like this, with a truck on the street. But instead of a hundred TV sets, we had only one and the power used to break all the time and we used to electrocute ourselves. But this is how we started—on the street."[1]

Formal and strategic similarities do exist between alternative TV enterprises separated by nearly two decades, substantial political and cultural differences, and vast geographic space. In this respect, DCTV is representative of numerous U.S. and Latin American media groups that were formed in the early 1970s and 1980s with the goal of using Portapak and new consumer video technology for community organizing.[2] Established in 1989 and disbanded in 1992, TV Anhembi sustained many of the defining agendas and practices initiated by these groups. Like earlier groups in the United States and Latin America, its advocacy and activist work centered on issues elided by network and public television. Also like these groups, TV Anhembi produced shows that featured current affairs and politics with the aim of fostering television countercultures or subcultures that would loosen the hold of mainstream television on public culture. Moreover, TV Anhembi used similar tactics for highlighting community participation and shifting TV viewing out of the private confines of the home.

But TV Anhembi's upscale technical apparatus and government support sets the group apart from previous examples of community media discussed in this book and elsewhere. The high-tech mobile unit against which Alpert was framed should alert viewers to the fact that TV Anhembi represents a new and significantly transformed relationship between alternative TV collectives and sources of power and finance. TV Anhembi's state-of-the-art technology and the scale and sophistication of its productions suggest they had more support than that received by U.S. alternative media groups in earlier decades.

What are the particular cultural and political circumstances that made TV Anhembi and its high-tech enterprise a possibility at precisely that historical place and moment? More than anything, its means of support and the mechanisms that brought about its formation were local products of a crisis of legitimacy within the Latin American cultural and political landscape of the late 1980s. The failure of established parties across the political spectrum to garner popular support was clearly registered in the success of São Paulo's nascent Workers' Party (Partido dos Trabalhadores) in the 1989 election, ushering in the mayoral administration of Luiza Erundina. TV Anhembi was quickly brought into being by this media-savvy left administration with the idea that community media were integral to the success of party politics, and party support was integral to the success of community agendas—a reciprocal situation that has few real parallels in the history of U.S. alternative television. As coordinating producer Almir Almas explains, TV Anhembi's goal was to educate people about the potential for engaging in community politics through television. By using alternative television strategies, he suggests, "people will learn to find their own solutions to the grave problems that afflict the city."[3] The situation Almas describes suggests that the São Paulo government aimed to use community media as a pedagogical tool to promote a more direct form of participatory politics rather

Expessáo, TV Anhembi's
mobile production and exhibition
van (TV Anhembi, 1992).

than to consolidate its authority over the community. This strategy was
in line with the broad-ranging attempts of the Partido dos Trabalhadores to reorient government toward the inclusion of local representatives
on neighborhood and special interest councils.

What, then, is the significance of this one example among the diverse
community media projects in Brazil's history? And what are the implications of this enterprise's short-lived history for media activism in Brazil and other contexts? TV Anhembi is an important case to consider
because it makes clear the complexity and specificity of relationships
that support various alternative television practices. In São Paulo as elsewhere, we saw alternative television ventures emerge out of sometimes
unlikely convergences of disparate community interests and broader institutional and governmental politics. We need to chronicle the specific
effects these unlikely media alliances have on programming, censorship,
technology access, funding, and so on. Moreover, it is important to consider how these projects and programs changed the meaning of terms
such as "community" and "alternative media"—terms that have been
overgeneralized. In the case of TV Anhembi, we see the emergence of a
new concept of community in which television plays an integral role, and
a new concept of alternative media as an entity that can be aligned with
state institutions (in this case, at the municipal level). The Erundina administration introduced some new ways of bringing together the apparently contradictory techniques and approaches of local video activists,
government agencies, and popular television. Although TV Anhembi
was short-lived, it stands as an example of some potentially viable alliances and strategies—and some of the potential risks—of state-subsidized alternative television production. The confluence of movement
strategies and government media initiatives can result in a somewhat

Almir Almas in front of
the Expessáo video wall
(TV Anhembi, 1992).

contradictory move toward both a more centralized, and a more hetero-
geneously community based, alternative television practice.

TV Anhembi's Local History

The formation and role of TV Anhembi was inextricably linked to the
political climate of São Paulo in 1989. The Erundina administration,
sensing the popular support it might generate with and through cultural
venues, established a dynamic network of city agencies and programs
devoted to the production of politically informed popular culture. This
was a kind of culture that spoke to the interests of local constituencies and communities, rather than to a broadly constituted mass public.
This apparatus was coordinated through a newly established city agency
nominally devoted to tourism (Anhembi Turismo e Eventos da Cidade
de São Paulo) and servicing a wider range of cultural forms, including TV Anhembi. Thus TV Anhembi came into being as a government-
backed alternative media production group and venue tailored to the
political agenda of the Erundina administration and to the local interests
of São Paulo communities.

But TV Anhembi's formation signals a development more far-
reaching than a single municipality's support of an agenda of decentral-
izing media knowledge and fostering atomized participatory democracy.
This seeming contradiction—state-run media joined with decentralized
media groups—was the by-product of a crisis in party politics throughout Brazil and other areas of Latin America in the 1980s. As Orlando
Fals Borda has explained, since the late 1970s, "the loss of legitimacy by
parties and governments has created a power gap, which [social] movements, in their expansive evolution, have been filling locally and region-

Television and Politics in Brazil 193

Spectators view a program about
street children (TV Anhembi, 1992).

ally in their own way."[4] By the late 1980s, the ascendant local movements began to form coalitions that were clear contenders for political
power. The Erundina administration in São Paulo was put into office
by building a form of party politics around a coalition of local movements. Once in power, Erundina's Workers' Party government made
various attempts to incorporate the diverse interests of its many constituents—by creating neighborhood councils and other community-focused
city agencies, and by adopting movement strategies designed specifically
for local organizing, such as using local community television to foster political participation. TV Anhembi was the product of media politics emerging from this confluence of movement strategies and a nascent
(and, as it turns out, short-lived) Workers' Party government.

In urban centers, an array of established local social movements and
organizations had come to pose popular alternatives to the party politics
apparatus that had risen up to challenge the military regime. This state
of affairs reflected a political crisis that was more broadly felt across the
continent. The political and economic upheaval from the mid-1960s onward in Latin America generally led to a situation in which many local
movements were able to thrive and numerous political parties founded
during this period were short-lived. Leaders of local social movements
gradually developed tactics to leverage their rooted local support against
elected officials, enabling them to sway policy decisions over specific
issues. In effect, these organizations used this local leverage to negotiate
for representatives within a myriad of community- and issue-oriented
city agencies created by politicians to mitigate their loss of centralized
power.[5]

In the 1990s, some urban Latin American grassroots organizations
joined forces. With this move toward coalitions and unification across

194   *Visual Pedagogy*

issues and constituencies, programs for change began to shift from framing initiatives as local concerns to representing them as broader issues. For example, the lack of a neighborhood day care facility might be cast in terms of the larger issue of child care policy vis-à-vis the status of women workers, drawing support from other neighborhoods and regions. It is not that politics became more universalized but that there was a shift toward the formation of strategic and delimited alliances across groups in the formation of coalitions that acknowledged, rather than subsumed, class, cultural, and regional differences.[6]

This tendency within the Latin American political arena had become particularly strong in São Paulo by 1989. Grassroots organizations had earned strong constituencies based on their mobilization around pressing local needs and had begun to see the benefits of alliances with other groups across the municipality. The formation of these alliances required that leaders negotiate unified political programs that went beyond the immediate and local agendas on which the popular support of each organization was based. São Paulo's newly elected Workers' Party government emerged precisely out of the success of this move toward coalition building and a broadening of agendas:

> The Workers' Party of Brazil (Partido dos Trabalhadores) . . . despite its name, is not, for any practical purposes, a party (at least not like the others are), a fact that its founders and directors admit. It is the outcome of an all-embracing process of organization involving sectors of workers, community and religious leaders, and organic intellectuals (including Paulo Freire, the educator) who drew up a common program of political, economic, social, and cultural action that went beyond the limits of associational or local concerns and now covers the whole of Brazilian society.[7]

The São Paulo Workers' Party, then, was the outcome of this heterogeneous mix of micro- and macropolitics. Its success in the 1989 election was a political coup unforeseen by most involved, including active party intellectuals such as Paulo Freire, the scholar and writer who served as the administration's secretary of education after playing a formative role in the evolution of the party.[8]

TV Anhembi was conceived as a semiautonomous project funded through the city's Office of Tourism and Events and was implemented almost immediately after Erundina took office. The administration drew staff for the project from alternative video groups that were affiliated with community organizations, from independent producers who worked within local social movements, and from progressive elements within the television industry. The group regimented a range of political and cultural institutions around agendas spanning local community and citywide concerns in a manner that mirrored the coalition-based formation of the Workers' Party itself. However, TV Anhembi's autonomy allowed it to address specific community interests without a program of explicit connection to the Workers' Party agenda. Indeed, the very structure of TV Anhembi reflected the uniquely interdependent but unified alliances that were the administration's trademark.

This principle is exemplified in TV Anhembi's programming. The group's primary production project was a series of closed-circuit, site-specific live video events entitled *Fala São Paulo* (Speak São Paulo). The series was uniform in format, yet it did not rely on thematic or narrative continuity between programs. It was important that individual programs could stand on their own, since the majority of audience members were unlikely to have attended shows produced in other neighborhoods. More importantly, though, this format enabled TV Anhembi to produce programs that played to specific issues of regional concern.[9] Thus although the show was centrally backed by the mayor's office and produced out of a relatively unified political agenda, it was able to take up disparate issues and represent a range of localized, and even competing or nonpartisan, points of view.

Episodes of *Fala São Paulo* were media events that took place four or more times each month. Programs were shot and closed-circuit simulcast (or screened with minimal delay to accommodate some mixing and special effects) in one of the squares, parks, or streets of the city. Audiences reflected the demographics of the particular neighborhood and varied in size from two hundred to nearly a thousand people. Although these programs were taped and archived for future screenings in venues ranging from organization meetings to broadcast television, their primary function was to facilitate local and site-specific exchange through the format of the on-site simulcast "town meeting." Programs were hosted live by media activists and well-known television personalities. These hosts took up a particular social or political issue such as poverty and homelessness among urban youth or the changing roles of women in the city, facilitating a dialogue among audience members and invited guests who included distinguished personalities, musicians, academics, experts in various fields, and government officials. Working from inside the mobile production van, TV Anhembi's crew pieced together live feed from cameras trained on the host, guests, and audience members with prerecorded video that included short tapes by community groups, clips from broadcast news, and footage TV Anhembi produced specifically for that show. This footage was juxtaposed with live feed to highlight or comment on the specific discussions taking place. Different parts of the program were then simultaneously screened on the different monitors that made up the van's video wall, resulting in a kind of mobile real-time/time-delay collage. Like town meetings, these shows were highly reflexive in the sense that cast and audience were composed of essentially the same people.

Although TV Anhembi's programs drew primarily on the scene at hand, popular media genres such as the variety show and the telenovela were also appropriated, along with news footage and other material, to tap into popular discourses and concerns that cut across cultural, gender, and class positions within and across groups. Brazilian alternative media throughout its history has appropriated popular genres for uses such as political parody, but TV Anhembi's link to city government provided professional equipment and technical expertise that allowed a more direct engagement with popular forms. TV Anhembi employed sympathetic talent from within the industry, effectively blurring the boundaries between community television and broadcast television, community members and popular figures.

The use of a popular television form such as the telenovela to foster public dialogue on issues of social relations is not groundbreaking in itself. As Nico Vink has shown, the mainstream telenovela had already been an important force in public discourse and social change.[10] What is important is the way in which TV Anhembi reversed familiar forms of viewer identification and combined them with community video forms to elicit a less conventional genre of public discussion and debate.

One successful example of TV Anhembi's use and transformation of popular media genres is an episode of *Fala São Paulo* titled "Women of São Paulo," an episode that happens to draw on the genre of the telenovela. "Women of São Paulo" begins with a vignette preproduced by TV Anhembi and featuring actress Acorda Raimudo, star of the popular telenovela *Alfredo Alves*. Raimudo plays a role that sharply contrasts with the role of the housewife that she performs in *Alfredo Alves*. Lying in bed, she demands of her husband: "Where's the coffee? Is there coffee?" She continues in this "macha" vein, complaining loudly that he has not laundered and ironed her clothes. In a documentary about this episode of *Fala São Paulo*, we see the TV Anhembi crew projecting this vignette on the video wall of their mobile production unit. Passing pedestrians on the busy São Paulo street stop to watch. The crew then turns the camera on the audience, soliciting responses to Raimudo's performance. These responses are simulcast on the video wall, allowing the audience members to watch themselves and hear one another's responses on the video display. The audience debates domestic relationships—how they are, how they should be. As the discussion unfolds, the crew uses specific responses as a springboard to project video segments on related issues produced by other community groups, thereby expanding the critiques of issues of gender roles and family life. Dividing the video wall, the crew combines live discussions of the telenovela vignette with tapes such as *Black Women of Brazil*, by the Lilith Women's Video Collective (a tape that includes interviews with women of color about how they are represented in the media), or TV dos Trabalhadores's *Todos os dias sao seus* (Everyday Is Theirs), a documentary about Brazilian women and AIDS. In this manner, TV Anhembi's crew creates a productive intersection of genres, an intersection that exceeds the potential of individual forms used: the telenovela, the variety show, and the community documentary.[11]

Cinema Novo, Broadcast Television, and Brazilian Video Activism

TV Anhembi was tailored to its political and viewing context; however, it also emerged from an established tradition of politically engaged film and television culture in Brazil. It was this convergence of an established discourse on film and video activism and the coalition politics of the Workers' Party that informed TV Anhembi's distinctive approach. TV Anhembi drew directly on two interrelated traditions of Brazilian media: Cinema Novo (the work of Glauber Rocha, Nelson Pereira dos Santos, Carlos Diegues, Joaquim Pedro de Andrade, and others), and Brazilian community video (groups including TV Viva, the Lilith Women's Video Collective, TV dos Trabalhadores, Video Memoria, and TV Brixiga).[12] The latter tradition emerged in part out of a crisis around

Cinema Novo's position of outright resistance to popular media forms, a crisis that took place after the military coup in 1964. The saga of Cinema Novo's relationship to popular cinema, and the strategies these directors developed to confront it, parallels in many ways the relationship between party and social movement politics.

Cinema Novo began as a critical response to the popular cinema of the 1950s and early 1960s. It was part of a broad cultural movement aligned with the rise of leftist political parties and opposing a liberal government. After the unexpected 1964 military coup, the newly established military regime implemented government communications policies that fostered a monopolistic mass communications system in Brazil. Throughout the subsequent decade, Cinema Novo lost ground through a failure to engage the diverse interests of various constituencies in their battle against mass entertainment policies and the government-fostered media enterprise, TV Globo (a component of the Globo communications monopoly that was consolidated by the early 1970s). Cinema Novo directors and leftist intellectuals were forced to rethink their relationship to popular media genres. At the same time, leftist oppositional parties were losing ground to local neighborhood groups and movements.

It was during this period of retrenchment that community video groups began to take over from Cinema Novo. Ingrid Sarti, in her study of independent video in Brazil, provides a concise analysis of the ambiguous and complex relationship between television and politics during this period. She explains that whereas "video technologies made possible the centralization of programming and hence the national television networks," these same technologies were also deployed as part of the vanguard challenge to the regime-fostered vertical structure of the television industry.[13] Thus community video was a part of the direct response to monopolistic private network entities like TV Globo. But it was also and more generally a historical solution to the crises that came up among Cinema Novo intellectuals around the problem of the popular. The disavowal of popular film genres by early Cinema Novo directors was an aesthetic formulation of a leftist, anti-imperialist political program. As Randal Johnson and Robert Stam point out, Cinema Novo directors and theorists formulated a philosophy and a practice aimed at developing a national culture and identity in the face of foreign (especially U.S.) economic and cultural imperialism. They asserted the political urgency of creating a film aesthetic that engaged the realities of underdevelopment and its causes—an aesthetic formulated in direct opposition to Hollywood and mainstream auteur cinema that dominated the Brazilian media.[14]

By the late 1960s, Johnson and Stam explain, Cinema Novo's filmmakers "realized that although their cinema was 'popular' in that it attempted to take the point of view of 'the people,' it was not popular in the sense of having a mass audience."[15] The films of Cinema Novo saw limited Brazilian distribution, in part because of government censorship and repression, but also because of the filmmakers' own embrace of an elite avant-garde aesthetic that did not attract enthusiastic audiences. Critical debate over these issues within the movement caused a radical rethinking of popular cultural forms. In his 1975 "Manifesto for a Popular Cinema," filmmaker Nelson Pereira dos Santos argued that by engaging with popular culture, film producers would reach a wider audience, address "the legitimate claims of the masses," and "defend popular political ideas." Moreover, he suggested that the use of popular cultural vernaculars would help break down distinctions between audience and producer.[16] Significantly, for Pereira dos Santos, popular vernacular included Afro-Brazilian and indigenous religious and cultural forms. This marked the emergence of a focus on the specifics of cultural identity. This had not been considered by early Cinema Novo's more totalizing and programmatic left agenda.

Cinema Novo's decline was also linked to the relative decline of film as a popular cultural form with the rise of television. Luiz Fernando Santoro suggests that Cinema Novo's inability to sustain its critique of popular forms and genres as manifestations of imperialist culture was symptomatic of the growing presence of domestically produced television. The productions of entities such as TV Tupi, TV Excelsior, and TV Globo increasingly overshadowed Hollywood and Brazilian mainstream cinema, outstripping its mass appeal after 1964.[17] As Carlos Eduardo Lins da Silva points out, "Television . . . experienced extraordinary growth after the military takeover and served as one of the instruments (ideological and instrumental) for the consolidation of monopolistic capitalism which it represented."[18] Thus Cinema Novo's biggest ideological contender was not other cinema forms but television.

Television was a qualitatively different kind of ideological force than the cinema. Unlike Brazilian cinema, which drew on U.S. and European productions, the Brazilian broadcast television industry was relatively autonomous. It grew up quickly under the wing of the repressive military government of the 1960s and 1970s and produced programs that were characteristically Brazilian.[19] As a popular media form, television increasingly drew on national cultural forms, politics, and social concerns as it sought to compete for the home market against U.S. and other Latin American media entities. This can be seen most clearly in the rise of the telenovela as a distinct genre, and not merely a reflection of the U.S. soap opera—a development that was the key to the ascendance of TV Globo as the leading television producer in Brazil.[20] Networks such as TV Globo used two strategies to create a genre with much broader appeal: they drew on national cultural traditions, and they made increasing reference to issues of contemporary social concern. Michèle and Armand Mattelart explain this dual strategy as having its origins in 1968 with *Beto Rockefeller*, the first popular Brazilian network telenovela to break significantly with U.S. conventions of melodrama:

> Since "Beto Rockefeller," the novella has never ceased to refer to certain problems of Brazilian Society: racial prejudice, the condition of women, the relations between Catholicism and Afro-Brazilian religions *(Umbandismo)*, industrial pollution, corruption, misery, urban violence, neighborhood struggles, and so forth. It has continued to take up the challenge of realism in a genre originally devoted to love triangles and affairs of the heart.[21]

The television industry, in its infusion of a melodramatic drama with strategies of realism, and in its increasing focus on national culture, successfully co-opted a central agenda of Cinema Novo directors: combating cultural imperialism. Despite its cultivation by the military state, Brazilian television's increasing treatment of national social, political, and cultural concerns throughout the 1970s was symptomatic of a broader tendency toward liberalization of dominant ideological and political mechanisms of power. Thus Cesar Guimarães and Roberto Amaral have argued that the television industry (and the Globo network in particular) played a crucial role in the eventual unseating of the military regime, realigning itself with the ascendant liberal government.[22] In terms of both party politics and mass media, left producers were challenged by a powerful new liberal opposition with a distinctly nationalist appeal.

As the first generation of alternative video producers began to take over and transform the media politics of Cinema Novo in the mid-1970s, they worked within a media landscape shaped by the Brazilian broadcast television industry. The new generation of media activists recast media politics by providing a communications venue for myriad local issues and points of view elided by the liberal broadcast television industry. Video activism, in effect, paralleled the widespread retreat from national party politics that marked the multiplication of localized social movements. Like the later Cinema Novo theorists, these producers embraced popular modes — but with a characteristically local, rather than national, focus. Sarti explains why video producers were at first more concerned about opposing mainstream media on the level of content rather than aesthetic form:

> Brazilian video producers . . . hung their hopes on the success of an original and decentralized type of production. By the early 1980s a young generation of producers with great creative force had emerged on the electronic media scene.
>
> The young producers knew their work would be seen by a public addicted to the TV Globo model of great technical virtuosity. They therefore tried to show what TV Globo hid from the population.[23]

Video technology allowed producers to achieve a more immediate and local form of media politics than could be achieved with film. Video production was less expensive, and distribution was less reliant on government (and commercially) regulated venue. This fact would seem to make video the ideal medium for carrying out the type of popular engagement and breaking down of distinctions between audience and producer later advocated by Cinema Novo directors such as Periera dos Santos. But as relatively inexpensive video equipment became available in the mid-1970s, it was not, for the most part, the directors of Cinema Novo who initiated political uses of the newly introduced medium but nonprofessionals from within the social movements themselves. As Alberto López, coordinator of the Brazilian Association of Popular Video (ABVP) recounts:

> En Brasil, existe una jerarquización peyorativa entre el cine y el video. Sin duda, hay algunos cineastas que han pasado a producir video; para ellos ese pasaje fue algo natural, porque el video se dio en los

movemientos sociales de una manera muy espontánea. Los movemientos sociales se aproprian del medio antes que los profesionales.

[In Brazil, there exists a pejorative hierarchy between cinema and video. Without doubt, there were some filmmakers who switched to video production; for them the change was natural, because video found its place so spontaneously in the evolving social movements. The social movements appropriated the medium before the professionals.][24]

The Brazilian video movement reflects a broader tendency throughout Latin America toward expanding the uses of the medium to meet the various needs of emerging social movements.[25] It also spans various levels of professional expertise and institutional affiliation. López describes a successive development of three modes of video production in emerging social movements.

There are basically three forms of community television at work: one that develops directly out of, and remains connected to, particular movements (for example in the favelas in Rio)—this work is quite primitive, yet always growing and becoming more professional; there is another type that occurs out of interrelations between independents, usually students of communication, and social movements; and finally there are those like TV Viva that are nongovernmental professional organizations, supported with international cooperation (funding), that produce tapes for various movements.[26]

López points out that there was an increase in community production aimed at broadcast venues in the early 1990s. What is absent from his account is that production of high-quality tapes directed at broadcast increased incorporation of independent producers from the nonprofit sector into the commercial broadcast sector. This shift also affected the content of work produced by nonprofit groups, such as TV Viva, that work for social movement groups but are trying to get their programs out to a broader public. Sarti notes that later independent videographers "became more concerned with the search for new languages and the development of the art of video than with their subject-matter. The technical experimentation and excellence of their productions had become the calling card for commercial television."[27]

For many of these independent videographers, she goes on to explain, this heightened focus on aesthetics and technique compromised their political engagement with community television production. But it is also possible to conclude that this situation allowed producers who were also working with community groups to get a foot in the industry door. This alternative take on Sarti's analysis suggests that higher production values can in some instances be a means of mainstreaming community video and community politics.

This is precisely the situation that we find with TV Anhembi. Almas, for example, notes that the tendency toward the professionalization of community video producers bears a direct relationship to the specific politics of TV Anhembi: "The industry is changing and opening its eyes to what community groups are doing. . . . Carlos Freitas, one of the founding members of TV Anhembi and our electrical engineer, went on to do work for MTV. And there are community video groups like TV Viva that are beginning to produce some programs for TV Globo."[28] Almas provides a narrative in which the industry does not simply co-opt independent talent. By incorporating its producers and programs, it learns the lessons of independent video and community politics. The industry's interest in purchasing community programming was a signal that it had become sensitive to the broadening appeal of local movement politics. This is not surprising, since the Brazilian television industry had adapted and rapidly transformed to account for political liberalization throughout the same period when independent and community video were coming into their own. This was a matter not only of the networks' increasing appeal to national cultural values but of their active incorpo-ration of popular discourse in their mode of production.

TV Anhembi and National Context

The idea of the incorporation of popular discourse into media texts brings us back to my discussion of the Brazilian telenovela. It allows me to return to my claim that TV Anhembi shows such as *Fala São Paulo* incorporated not only the genre of the electronic town meeting but also popular forms like the telenovela. As Mattelart and Mattelart explain, telenovelas are in a sense coscripted by their audiences: "The production system allows for . . . the participation of the audience in the develop-ment of the serial: the daily reactions of the audience influence the evolution of the characters and the outcome of the story."[29] Even more to the point, Mattelart and Mattelart propose that the telenovela is, for Brazilian culture, the equivalent of an "echo chamber of public debate."[30] As they explain, telenovelas are more than a central theme of everyday discussion, debate, and rumor; they are public events widely covered in the mainstream press. The television industry extends the strategic commandeering of popular responses to other forms of programming as well. They cite as evidence of this mode being participatory the fact that talk and variety shows often encourage home-audience telephone participation in the live show.

What distinguishes TV Anhembi from mainstream Brazilian media, as well as from antecedent community video organizations like DCTV, is its aggregate aesthetic and structural innovations, which linked local movement concerns and popular cultural forms to facilitate broader public debates. "Democratization of the means of communication" was for TV Anhembi more than the technical facilitation of TV production within the idealized public sphere of the urban streets. It was an array of strategies for bringing together community concerns and high-tech aesthetic values of art video and broadcast television. A particularly successful part of TV Anhembi's project was the development of strategies to appropriate and subvert broadcast genres—an aspect of its project that situates TV Anhembi at the cutting edge of postmodern media initiatives.

As I have suggested, TV Anhembi's form was intimately connected to the particular social and political milieu that swept Erundina's administration into office. The project was discontinued in 1992 when the Erundina administration was replaced by a less sympathetic city government. The history of TV Anhembi cannot be separated from the local, short-lived, and distinctive political administration that sponsored it. However, it is important to consider the legacy of TV Anhembi after 1992. The array of local social movements active in São Paulo in the 1990s constituted a considerable source of alternative media production. In 1993 Almas expressed uncertainty about the possibility of creating another TV Anhembi but nonetheless asserted that he would "continue to search for funding to form new groups like TV Anhembi. Without cable access, we need this sort of alternative venue in Brazil."[31]

I have used the example of TV Anhembi to stress the particularity of the Brazilian media landscape and its various distinct groups. But

TV Anhembi does provide a useful comparison or counterpoint to discussions about alternative media projects in other regional and national contexts. As U.S. community media organizations faced the reconfiguration and reregulation of communications networks (including the information superhighway and the cable and telephone conglomerates) in the 1990s, the example of TV Anhembi suggested the need to rethink terms such as "community" and "alternative media." TV Anhembi, by bringing together apparently contradictory techniques and approaches of local video activists, government agencies, and popular television forms, demonstrated the viability of some alliances and strategies. But TV Anhembi's short history also warns of some of the potential risks of conceiving community through state-subsidized alternative television production. As Almas notes, "TV Anhembi's heavy reliance upon the mayor for financial support was in the end a big problem. . . . There just weren't adequate alternative means of support in São Paulo to replace the resources that the Erundina administration had provided."[32]

911 Media Arts Center
117 Yale Ave. N
Seattle, WA 98109
phone: 206-682-6552
http://www.911media.org/
911 is Washington's premier nonprofit media center. It aims to increase participation in the media-making process through four program areas: *Create, Educate, Exhibit,* and *Distribute.*

Alliance for Community Media
666 11th Street NW, Suite 740
Washington, DC 20001–4542
phone: 202-393-2650
e-mail: acm@alliancecm.org
http://www.alliancecm.org
The Alliance for Community Media is a nonprofit national membership organization committed to ensuring everyone's access to electronic

media. The Alliance advances this goal through public education, a progressive legislative and regulatory agenda, coalition building, and grassroots organizing. Founded in 1976, the Alliance represents more than one thousand public, educational, and governmental (PEG) access organizations and community media centers throughout the country. It also represents the interests of millions of people who, through their local religious, community, and charitable groups, use PEG access to communicate with their memberships and the community as a whole.

American Indian Film Institute (AIFI)
333 Valencia Street, Suite 322
San Francisco, CA 94103
phone: 415-554-0525
http://www.AIFISF.Com
The American Indian Film Institute (AIFI) is a nonprofit media arts center founded in 1979 to foster understanding of the culture, traditions, and issues of contemporary Native Americans. Film has created and perpetuated enduring stereotypes that are at best tedious, and at worst profoundly erosive to the self-image of generations of Native Americans. AIFI aims to counter the tendency by using the power of film to heal and strengthen, to preserve and record Native American heritage, and to help Indians and non-Indians alike to "unlearn" damaging stereotypes and replace them with multidimensional images that reflect the complexity of Native peoples.

Appalshop, Inc.
91 Madison Ave.
Whitesburg, KY 41858
phone: 606-633-0108
e-mail: info@appleshop.org
http://ns.appalshop.org/
Appalshop is a media arts and cultural center located in Whitesburg, Kentucky, in the heart of the Central Appalachian Coalfields. Appalshop produces and distributes work that celebrates the culture and voices the concerns of people living in the Appalachian Mountains. Appalshop began in 1969 as a War on Poverty program to train mountain young people in media production skills.

ArtMattan Productions
535 Cathedral Pkwy., Suite 14b
New York, NY 10025
phone: 212-749-6020
e-mail: info@africanfilm.com
http://www.Africanfilm.com/
ArtMattan distributes films that focus on the experience of black people
in Africa, the Caribbean, North and South America, and Europe.

Asian Media Access
3028 Oregon Ave. S
Minneapolis, MN 55426
phone: 612-376-7715
e-mail: amamedia@amamedia.org
http://www.amamedia.org
Asian Media Access is a not-for-profit organization dedicated to meeting the media needs of the Asian American communities in the Twin
Cities. It works to promote the use of the media as an educational
and communicative tool, to present Asian American issues and perspectives in the mainstream media, to empower Asian American youth with
media production skills, and to expand the support network and job
market for Asian American media professionals.

Bay Area Video Coalition
2727 Mariposa Street, 2nd Floor
San Francisco, CA 94110
phone: 415-861-3282
e-mail: bavc@bavc.org
http://www.bavc.org
The Bay Area Video Coalition (BAVC) is the nation's largest nonprofit
media arts center dedicated to providing access to media, education,
and technology in the nonprofit sector. Founded in 1976, BAVC offers
broadcast-quality video services as well as access to new technologies in
all aspects of media production to independent producers, artists, and
nonprofit organizations. BAVC is a production facility, an affordable
training center, a pioneer in technology-based workforce development,
and a critical resource for independent media makers. It was coproducer
of the *Brothers* interactive video project (discussed in chapter 4).

California Newsreel
149 9th Street, Suite 420
San Francisco, CA 94103
phone: 415-621-6196
e-mail: contact@newsreel.org
http://www.newsreel.org
California Newsreel is a nonprofit documentary film and video production and distribution center that has been in operation since 1968. They distribute award-winning collections of African American video, African video, and video on the workplace, media, and society.

Children's Media Project
358 Main Street
Poughkeepsie, NY 12601
phone: 845-485-4480
http://www.childrensmediaproject.org/
Children's Media Project (CMP) is a nonprofit art and education organization focusing on technology and media. It gives children and youth, parents and teachers, artists and media makers a space, both literally and metaphorically, to use media critically and creatively. CMP teaches the skills, tools, and processes necessary for creative self-expression, critical thinking, and awareness.

Community Art Center's Teen Media Program
119 Windsor St.
Cambridge, MA 02139
phone: 617-868-7100 x15
e-mail: joe@communityartcenter.org
http://www.doityourdamnself.org
The Teen Media Program (TMP) was founded at the Community Art Center in 1970, offering black-and-white photography classes and filmmaking. Video production was introduced in 1986. Two years later CCTV, Cambridge's public access station, opened its doors and welcomed the Community Art Center as one of its first organizational members. TMP offers Cambridge teens the opportunity to explore the various issues in their lives through a media curriculum.

D*LAB (*Digital Movies)
P.O. Box 883683
San Francisco, CA 94188
phone: 415-822-2472
e-mail: RLight@aol.com
http://storyvault.org/dlabinfo.html
D*LAB is an arts-based youth program that teaches digital production skills as the basis for learning an emerging art form encompassing new media technologies and the expressive arts. Instruction focuses on digital moviemaking, where students learn to explore the potential for integrating aspects of the visual, dramatic, literary, and moving-image arts in a single production. D*LAB welcomes relationships with schools and after-school organizations serving at-risk youth, students with special needs, and underserved communities. In addition to on-site programs for youth, D*LAB provides teacher training, program development, and consulting services to emerging school-based programs in digital creativity and the media arts.

Deep Dish TV Network
339 Lafayette Street
New York, NY 10012
phone: 212-473-8933
e-mail: deepdish@igc.apc.org
http://www.igc.org/deepdish/
Deep Dish TV is a national satellite network linking access producers and programmers, independent video makers, activists, and people who support the idea and reality of a progressive television network. Deep Dish assembles material from producers around the world and transmits it to community television stations and home dish owners nationwide. Deep Dish TV is programmed on more than three hundred cable systems around the country as well as on selected public stations. Many stations run Deep Dish in several time slots each week, reaching audiences at various times on different days.

Downtown Community Television Center (DCTV)
87 Lafayette Street
New York, NY 10013
phone: 212-966-4510

e-mail: web@dctvny.org

http://www.dctvny.org

Downtown Community Television Center (DCTV) is a nonprofit community-based media arts center dedicated to teaching youth and emerging artists within low-income and minority communities to produce insightful and artistic electronic media. The center supports the belief that expanding public access to the electronic media arts invigorates democracy. Through its programs, DCTV encourages productions that are responsive to the needs of people, especially those who are often overlooked or stereotyped by mainstream media.

Educational Video Center (EVC)
120 W. 30th Street, 7th Floor
New York, NY 10001
phone: 212-465-9366
e-mail: goodman_steve99@hotmail.com
http://www.evc.org

The Educational Video Center (EVC) is a nonprofit community-based organization that teaches documentary video production and media analysis to students, educators, and community organizers. The center is dedicated to the creative and community-based use of video and multimedia as a means to develop the literacy, research, public speaking, and work preparation skills of at-risk youth. It supports this mission through four major programs: High School Documentary Workshop, YO-TV (Youth Organizers TV), CO-TV (Community Organizers TV), and Teacher Development. Since 1984, EVC students have produced more than seventy-five documentaries on issues such as media and youth culture, gun violence, race relations, and environmental pollution. These youth documentaries have been broadcast on the NBC, ABC, and PBS television networks. In addition, the center's tapes have won more than one hundred awards nationally and internationally, including an Emmy. EVC's work is discussed in chapters 3 and 4.

Five Points Media Center
2900 Welton Street, Suite 310
Denver, CO 80205
phone: 303-295-1357

e-mail: dmourning@5points.org
http://www.5points.org
The Five Points Media Center Corporation provides access to media and the Internet, including education, training, and placement opportunities for youth, people of color, and the economically disadvantaged, so that they may fully participate in the emerging communications marketplace.

Gay Men's Health Crisis (GMHC)
Dept. of Education
129 W. 20th Street
New York, NY 10011
phone: 212-367-1000
http://www.gmhc.org
Gay Men's Health Crisis, founded in 1981, is a model for AIDS care, education, and advocacy worldwide. GMHC provides compassionate care to New Yorkers with AIDS, educates to keep people healthy, and advocates for fair and effective public policies. GMHC's educational department produces and distributes educational media on AIDS and sexuality, including *It Is What It Is,* by Greg Bordowitz, discussed in chapter 3.

Global Action Project
4 W. 37th Street, 2nd Floor
New York, NY 10018
phone: 212-594-9577
e-mail: media@global-action.org
http://www.global-action.org/
The Global Action Project (GAP) is an educational organization that develops youth leaders through video production and peer education and promotes the inclusion of diverse youth voices on critical local and global issues. Global Action Project began in 1991 as a program of Global Kids, a New York City educational organization dedicated to preparing urban youth to become community leaders and global citizens. The project's videos focus on such critical issues as ethnic and sectarian conflict, violence prevention, human rights, community health, and civic participation. Its monthly youth-produced television program, *Urban Voices* (formerly called *Youth Agenda*), is one of the leading youth series on public access television. Through its international program,

GAP has produced videos with young people in Croatia, Ghana, Guatemala, the Middle East, and Northern Ireland.

gURL
1440 Broadway, 21st floor
New York, NY 10018
e-mail: gURLstaff@gURL.com
http://www.gurl.com
An on-line community for teenage girls, gURL.com is committed to discussing issues that affect the lives of girls age thirteen and up in a nonjudgmental, personal way. Through honest writing, visuals, and liberal use of humor, gURL tries to give girls a new way of looking at subjects that are crucial to their lives and to provide connection and identification in a way that is not possible in other media.

HIV Center for Clinical and Behavioral Studies
722 W. 168th Street
New York, NY 10032
phone: 212-543-5969
The HIV Center conducts innovative studies on reducing transmission of HIV in high-risk groups, improving the quality of life for HIV-positive persons, and determining the factors that reinforce unprotected sexual behavior in order to design sound interventions. The center engages in collaborative efforts with community service providers and distributes HIV/AIDS-related educational media, including *AIDS, Not Us,* by Sandra Elkin (discussed in chapter 3).

Jubilee Arts
84 High Street
West Bromwich, Sandwell
West Midlands
UK B70 6JW
phone: +44 (0)121-553-6862
http://www.jubilee-arts.co.uk/
Jubilee Arts is an independent community arts, media, and communications company based in the Borough of Sandwell in the West Midlands, U.K. Jubilee engages with its diverse publics in a wide range of

art forms and participatory activities, tackling issues of social exclusion, cultural identity, education, health, social sustainability, regeneration, and developing urban form. Throughout its history, Jubilee has been at the forefront of community arts development, creating a range of innovative exhibitions, performances, and cultural products ranging from books and guides to CD-ROMs and posters. Jubilee partners with organizations regionally, nationally, and internationally to create new projects, produce new work, and bring existing work and experience into Sandwell. Jubilee distributes its own media projects, including the interactive CD-ROM *Sex Get Serious* (discussed in chapter 4).

L.A. Freewaves
2151 Lake Shore Ave.
Los Angeles, CA 90039
phone: 323-664-1510
e-mail: freewaves@aol.com
http://www.freewaves.org/
L.A. Freewaves is a media arts network that produces festivals, workshops, curriculum materials, and a Web site to encourage artistic and social expression and serve the needs of artists and audiences alike.

Latin American Video Archive Database (LAVA)
124 Washington Place
New York, NY 10014
phone: 212-463-0108
e-mail: imre@igc.org
http://www.latinamericanvideo.org
Latin American Video Archive Database (LAVA) contains approximately six thousand Latin American and Latino-produced videotapes (and films on video) available in the United States and is accessible on-line with full search and order capabilities. The archive provides a monthly electronic newsletter and can run searches for hard-to-find titles on request. It publishes a guide to Latin American, Caribbean, and U.S.-made film and video, which contains more than four hundred Latin American and Latino titles that have been evaluated by academics. Their titles include work by TV Anhembi and other alternative Brazilian media discussed in chapter 7.

Media Alliance
c/o WNET
450 W. 3rd Street
New York, NY 10001
phone: 212-560-2919
e-mail: mediaall@thirteen.org
http://www.mediaalliance.org
Media Alliance is an advocacy and service organization dedicated to advancing independent media in New York State. Media Alliance members include media arts centers, distributors, exhibitors, museums, libraries, educators, cable access and public television programmers, and independent artists and producers. Media Alliance acts as an information clearinghouse on media arts for the New York region. Promoting values of equity and free expression, Media Alliance works to preserve and expand public and private resources for the media arts. It also plays a key leadership role in creating regional strategies for the preservation of video art and community video.

National Asian American Telecommunication Association (NAATA)
346 Ninth Street, 2nd Floor
San Francisco, CA 94103
phone: 415-863-0814
e-mail: naata@naatanet.org
http://www.naatanet.org
National Asian American Telecommunication Association (NAATA) is dedicated to presenting stories that convey the richness and diversity of the Asian Pacific American experience. The association funds, produces, distributes, and exhibits films, videos, and new media to the broadest audience possible.

OnRamp Arts
534 E. Edgeware Road
Los Angeles, CA 90026
phone: 213-481-2395
http://www.onramparts.org/
OnRamp Arts is a nonprofit digital arts studio whose mission is to provide opportunities for Central L.A. youth, encouraging the exploration of new media, empowerment through skills-based training, and commu-

nity dialogue within the development of arts and technology. OnRamp's programs are dedicated to giving youth specialized skills in a highly supervised yet exploratory, hands-on setting to which they would not otherwise have access.

Paper Tiger Television
339 Lafayette Street
New York, NY 10012
phone: 212-420-9045
e-mail: tigertv@bway.net
http://www.papertiger.org
Paper Tiger TV is a nonprofit volunteer video collective that has been pioneering media criticism through video since 1981. Paper Tiger TV works to illuminate the role of media in our society through the production and distribution of the Paper Tiger public access television series, as well as through media literacy and hands-on video production workshops and through advocacy and coalition work. Its programs analyze and critique issues involving media, culture, and politics. The shows feature scholars, community activists, critics, and journalists addressing the ideological assumptions and the social meanings of the mainstream media, as well as exploring the opportunities for alternative communications sources.

Rheedlen Centers for Children and Families,
Rise and Shine Productions (TRUCE)
147 St. Nicholas Ave., 3rd Floor
New York, NY 10026
phone: 212-663-0555
e-mail: lvural@ix.netcom.com
Rise and Shine Productions is the media literacy program of Rheedlen Centers for Children and Families, a multiservice youth organization. Rise and Shine creates opportunities for young people to develop communication, reading, artistic, and leadership skills. The program started as a dropout prevention program to motivate children to go to class and improve their academic performance through poetry writing, performance, scriptwriting, and video production. Through their cable TV program *The Real Deal*, teens from diverse communities come together to produce independent videos on race relations, violence, drugs, ma-

terialism, and the power of media. Their productions include *Blind Alley* (discussed in chapter 3), *Mending Wounds,* and *Stolen Innocence* (discussed in chapter 4). Videos are screened nationally and are widely recognized for their quality and authenticity.

Scribe Video Center
342 Cypress Street
Philadelphia, PA 19107
phone: 215-735-3785
e-mail: scribe@libertynet.org
http://www.libertynet.org/scribe/
Scribe Video Center, a Philadelphia-based nonprofit organization, is dedicated to advancing the use of video as an artistic medium and as a tool for progressive social change. Scribe aims to reach constituencies that traditionally have not had access to video training or production facilities, including people of color, women, young people, senior citizens, and those with limited economic resources. Scribe offers workshops in film and video production and oral history production. Scribe also offers artist's services such as fiscal sponsorship, equipment rental, and editing facilities. Scribe's ongoing programs include Community Visions, a video production program for community organizations; Street Movies, a free outdoor neighborhood-based screening series, and the Producer's Forum screening and lecture series of visiting artists and media activists. Additionally, Scribe produces the Youth History Project, an annual production workshop for middle school and high school students.

Street-Level Youth Media
1856 W. Chicago, 1st Floor
Chicago, IL 60622
phone: 773-862-5331
e-mail: admin@street-level.org
http://www.street-level.org
Street-Level Youth Media educates Chicago's inner-city youth in media arts and emerging technologies for use in self-expression, communication, and social change. Street-Level's programs build self-esteem and critical-thinking skills for urban youth who have historically been ne-

glected by government and mass media. Using video production, computer art, and the Internet, Street-Level's young people address community issues, access advanced communications technology, and gain inclusion in our information-based society.

TILT (Teaching Intermedia Literacy Tools)
1053B Valencia Street
San Francisco, CA 94110
phone: 415-401-8458
e-mail: tilt@tiltmedia.org
http://www.tiltmedia.org
TILT (Teaching Intermedia Literacy Tools) is a nonprofit that works within school programs and community organizations to teach the fundamentals of moviemaking, giving people a hands-on understanding of the tools and the language of media. TILT encourages students to write and produce videos with fictional content and narrative structure, trains students to be their own technicians and insist on high production values, and educates them about the language of media.

Third World Newsreel
545 Eighth Ave., 10th Floor
New York, NY 10018
phone: 212-947-9277
e-mail: twn@twn.org
http://www.twn.org/
Founded in 1967, Third World Newsreel is one of the oldest alternative media arts organizations in the United States. It is committed to the creation, distribution, and appreciation of independent and social-issue media by and about people of color, and the peoples of developing countries around the world.

The Video Activist Network
P.O. Box 40130
San Francisco, CA 94140
phone: 415-789-8484
e-mail: info@videoactivism.org
http://videoactivism.org/

The Video Activist Network (VAN) is an informal association of activists and politically conscious artists using video to support social, economic, and environmental-justice campaigns.

Video Data Bank
112 S. Michigan Ave.
Chicago, IL 60603
phone: 312-345-3550
e-mail: info@vdb.org
http://www.videodatabank.com/
Founded in 1976 at the inception of the media arts movement in the United States, the Video Data Bank is one of the nation's largest providers of alternative and art-based video, including *Pedagogue*, by Stuart Marshall (discussed in chapter 3). The collections include seminal works that, seen as a whole, describe the development of video as an art form originating in the late 1960s and continuing to the present.

Video Machete
1180 N. Milwaukee
Chicago, IL 60622
phone: 773-645-1272
http://www.videomachete.org/
Video Machete is a collective of community activists, artists, video producers, students, and youth committed to working toward positive social change with people and communities. Through the process of video production, theater, movement, and creative writing, Video Machete aims to develop skills that enable its constituencies to participate as critically thinking members of society.

VIDKIDCO
VIDKIDCO, Long Beach Museum of Art Video Annex
2300 E. Ocean Blvd.
Long Beach, CA 90803
phone: 562-439-2119
http://www.lbma.org
A program of the Long Beach Museum of Art, VIDKIDCO provides training in video, animation, and multimedia for at-risk teenagers. Through its programs, young people experience the technical and cre-

ative aspects of video firsthand. The program maintains an extensive video library for museum-site screenings or purchase.

Visual Communications
120 Judge John Aiso Street
Los Angeles, CA 90012
phone: 213-680-4462
e-mail: info@vconline.org
http://www.vconline.org
Visual Communications is a nonprofit media arts center dedicated to promoting intercultural understanding, and the creation, presentation, preservation, and support of media works by and about Asian Pacific Americans. The organization is one of the foremost multicultural media arts centers and has been operating continuously since its inception in 1970. Visual Communications' community workshop activities include the Frame by Frame: Youth Media Program. Its internship program and Open Studio L.A. provide opportunities for upcoming generations of young artists and Los Angeles arts organizations to learn and enhance their media production skills.

WireTap
WireTap c/o Independent Media Institute
77 Federal Street
San Francisco, CA 94107
http://www.alternet.org/wiretapmag/
WireTap is an independent information source produced for and by socially conscious youth. It showcases investigative news articles, personal essays and opinions, artwork, and activism resources that challenge stereotypes, inspire creativity, foster dialogue, and give young people a voice in the media. The WireTap Web portal gives a new generation of writers, artists, and activists a space to network, organize, and mobilize.

Women Make Movies
462 Broadway, Suite 500WS
New York, NY 10013
phone: 212-925-0606
fax: 212-925-2052

e-mail: info@wmm.com
http://www.wmm.com
Women Make Movies was established in 1972 to address the underrepresentation and misrepresentation of women in the media. A national nonprofit feminist media arts organization whose multicultural programs provide resources for both users and producers of media by women, it is the largest distributor of women's media in North America.

Youth Communication
224 W. 29th Street
New York, NY 10001
phone: 212-279-0708
http://www.youthcomm.org/
Youth Communication helps teenagers develop their skills in reading, writing, thinking, and reflection so that they can acquire the information they need to make thoughtful choices about their lives.

Introduction

1 Paolo Freire, *Pedagogy of the City* (New York: Continuum, 1973), 25.
2 Paolo Freire and Donaldo Macedo, *Literacy: Reading the Word and the World* (South Hadley, Mass.: Bergin and Garvey, 1987), 32, 94–119, 160–69.
3 Peter McLaren, "Contesting Capital: Critical Pedagogy and Globalism: A Response to Michael Apple," *Current Issues in Comparative Education* 1, no. 2 (30 April 1999). www.tc.columbia.edu/cice.
4 David Trend, *Cultural Pedagogy: Art/Education/Politics* (New York: Bergin and Garvey, 1992), 59.
5 Ira Shor, *Culture Wars: School and Society in the Conservative Restoration* (Chicago: University of Chicago Press, 1992), chap. 2. See also J. L. Kincheloe, *Toil and Trouble: Good Work, Smart Workers, and the Integration of Academic and Vocational Education* (New York: Peter Lang, 1995).
6 In a startling historical twist, the U.S. vo-tech track took an upward turn with the digital boom of the 1990s, placing the electronic classroom and technological career education at the cutting edge. In some cases educational technology made class transcendence possible for students who benefited from experimental programs introduced in low-income rural and urban schools.
7 U.S. Department of Education, *Getting America's Students Ready for the 21st*

Century: Meeting the Technology Literacy Challenge, Report to the Nation on Technology and Education (Washington, D.C.: GPO, June 1996). http://www.ed.gov/Technology/Plan/NatTechPlan/.

8 Ibid.

9 Todd Oppenheimer, "The Computer Delusion," *Atlantic Monthly,* July 1997, 45–62.

10 Readers may wonder why I do not consider museum education practices through the lens of my own curatorial practice. There are two answers to this question: I wrote the chapter on museum pedagogy prior to my tenure at the New Museum of Contemporary Art, and I wanted the museum education chapter to consider some of the more mainstream tendencies in museum education. The New Museum's program was exceptional and deserves its own analysis. I hope to take this up elsewhere in the future.

11 Pierre Bourdieu, *Distinction: A Social Critique of the Judgment of Taste,* trans. Richard Nice (Cambridge: Harvard University Press, 1984).

12 Tony Bennett, "The Exhibitionary Complex," *New Formations,* no. 4 (1988): 79.

13 The reader may look askance at my phrasing here. *Techniques,* not people, as agents of discipline is indeed the intended locution. This is grounded in Michel Foucault's broad contribution to theories of institutions and power. Power, Foucault suggests, is enacted across institutional contexts through techniques and relationships among subjects. Individual subjects do not wield power; it is a relational force enacted through them. See Michel Foucault, *Discipline and Punish: The Birth of the Prison,* trans. Alan Sheridan (New York: Vintage Books, 1979).

14 Jacques Derrida, *On Grammatology* (Baltimore: Johns Hopkins University Press, 1974).

15 David Lusted, "Why Pedagogy," *Screen* 27, no. 5 (1986): 2–3.

1 Media and Global Education

1 R. Murray Thomas, "The Rise and Decline of an Educational Technology: Television in American Samoa," *Educational Communication and Technology: A Journal of Theory Research and Development* 28, no. 3 (fall 1980): 156–57.

2 The commission was an international advisory organization to governments that controlled South Sea islands, dedicated to the social welfare of island peoples.

3 Wilbur Schramm, *ITV in American Samoa—after Nine Years* (Stanford, Calif.: Institute for Communication Research, Stanford University, 1973), 3.

4 The U.S. Department of Education budget went from $1.9 billion in 1953 to $52 billion in 1970. This was accompanied by a parallel increase in spending by foundations such as Ford and Carnegie, focused on national policy and standards. For a discussion of the close relation between increases in foundation and government spending in this area see Dennis C. Buss, "The Ford Foundation

in Public Education: Emergent Patterns," in *Philanthropy and Cultural Imperialism: The Foundations at Home and Abroad,* ed. Robert F. Arnove (Boston: G. K. Hall, 1980), 331–59; and Armand Mattelart, *Multinational Corporations and the Control of Culture: The Ideological Apparatus of Imperialism* (Sussex: Harvester Press, 1979), 155–56.

5   Herbert Marchl and Etienne Brunswick, "Educational Television in Developing Countries," *Educational Media International,* no. 2 (1977): 9–13.

6   Wilbur Schramm, Lyle M. Nelson, and Mere T. Betham, *Bold Experiment: The Story of Educational Television in Samoa* (Stanford, Calif.: Stanford University Press, 1981), 68.

7   Thomas, 155–67.

8   "Coming of (TV) Age in Samoa," *Life,* 15 November 1968; "For Samoa — a Barefoot Teacher from Oklahoma," *Look,* 13 May 1966, 88–90; " 'Talofa, Norma!' New York TV Teacher Is Hit with Youths on American Samoa," *Ebony,* January 1966, 54–58.

9   Martha L. Fiedler, "TV Goes Way Out and Brings the World to Samoa," *American Education* 3, no. 3 (March 1967): 15–17.

10 Mattelart, 159.

11 Wilbur Schramm, "Educational Television in American Samoa," in *New Educational Media in Action* (Paris: UNESCO, 1967), 13–14.

12 Ibid., 14–15.

13 Edward Beauchamp, "Educational Policy in Eastern Samoa: An American Colonial Outpost," *Comparative Education* 11, no. 1 (March 1975): 24.

14 Schramm, "Educational Television in American Samoa," 15.

15 Beauchamp, 29.

16 Ibid.

17 Armand Mattelart, *Mapping World Communication* (Minneapolis: University of Minnesota Press, 1994), 230.

18 Arjun Appadurai, "Disjuncture and Difference in Global Cultural Economy," *Public Culture* 2, no. 2 (spring 1990): 6, quoted in Mattelart, *Mapping World Communication,* 230.

19 American Samoan Department of Education, *A Co-operative Design for Instruction* (Pago Pago, May 1965), quoted in Schramm, "Educational Television in American Samoa," 17.

20 Lewis Rhodes, "A Trip to the Possible," *Educational Perspectives* 7, no. 3 (October 1968): 11.

21 "For Samoa — a Barefoot Teacher from Oklahoma," 88.

22 "Talofa, Norma!" 58.

23 Schramm, Nelson, and Betham, 21.

24 On home TV in Samoa, see Schramm, Nelson, and Betham, 148–73.

25 The Network Project, *The Fourth Network* (New York: Network Project, 1971), 7.

26   Buss, 331–32.

27   The Fund for the Advancement of Education, *Teaching by Television* (New York: Ford Foundation, 1961), 52–53, 58.

28   Serena Wade, "Hagerstown: A Pioneer in Closed Circuit Televised Instruction," in *New Media in Action: Case Studies for Planners—I* (Paris: UNESCO, 1967), 76.

29   Ibid.

30   The Network Project, 9–10.

31   Mary Ann Watson, *The Expanding Vista: American Television in the Kennedy Years* (New York: Oxford University Press, 1990), 185–86.

32   Ibid., 188.

33   Buss, 331–59.

34   John Walker Powell, *Channels of Learning: The Story of Educational Television* (Washington, D.C.: Public Affairs Press, 1962), 63.

35   R. Murray Thomas, "Scheme for Assessing Unmet Educational Needs: The American Samoa Example," *International Review of Education* 23, no. 1 (1977): 61.

36   For an in-depth account of the effect of the Sputnik crisis on educational policy see Barbara Barksdale Clowse, *Brainpower for the Cold War: The Sputnik Crisis and National Defense Education Act of 1958* (Westport: Greenwood Press, 1981). Also see Robert A. Divine, *The Sputnik Challenge* (New York: Oxford University Press, 1993).

37   Clowse, 15.

38   For a discussion of the evolution of the relationship between government and private R&D see Armand Mattelart, *Mapping World Communication*, 88–89.

39   The Network Project, 4–6.

2   Students as Producers

1   See Heather Hendershot, *Saturday Morning Censors* (Durham: Duke University Press, 1998), especially chap. 3, "Action for (and against) Children's Television."

2   Theodor W. Adorno and Max Horkheimer, *Dialectic of Enlightenment* (1944; New York: Continuum, 1982, especially "The Culture Industry: Enlightenment as Mass Deception," 120–67.

3   See Janice Radway, *Reading the Romance: Representing Women in Popular Culture* (Chapel Hill: University of North Carolina Press, 1984); John Fiske, *Understanding Popular Culture* (Unwin Hyman, 1989), and *Television Culture* (London: Methuen, 1987); Dick Hebdige, *Subculture: The Meaning of Style* (London: Methuen, 1979).

4   Stanley Aronowitz and Henry Giroux, *Postmodern Education* (Minneapolis: University of Minnesota Press, 1991), 165.

5   Ibid.

6   Warren Crichlow, "School Daze," *Afterimage* 18, no. 10 (May 1991): 17.

7   John Fiske, "Popular Discrimination," in *Modernity and Mass Culture*, ed.

James Naremore and Patrick Brantlinger (Indianapolis: Indiana University Press, 1991), 106.

8   Ibid., 108.

9   Fiske, *Understanding Popular Culture,* 25.

10 Meaghan Morris, "Banality in Cultural Studies," in *Logics of Television: Essays in Cultural Criticism,* ed. Patricia Mellencamp (Bloomington and Indianapolis: Indiana University Press, 1990), 23.

11 James Donald, review of *Television Culture,* by John Fiske, *Screen* 31, no. 1 (spring 1990): 114.

12 Stuart Hall, "The Whites of Their Eyes," in *Silver Linings,* ed. George Bridges and Rosalind Brunt (London: Lawrence and Wishart, 1981), 52.

13 Aronowitz and Giroux, 183.

14 Walter Benjamin, "Author as Producer," in *Reflections,* ed. Peter Demetz (New York: Harcourt, Brace, Jovanovich, 1978), 225.

15 On the history of Portapak video activism, see Marita Sturken, "Paradox in the Evolution of an Art Form: Great Expectations and the Making of a History," in *Illuminating Video: An Essential Guide to Video Art,* ed. Doug Hall and Sally Jo Fifer (San Francisco: Aperture, 1991), 100–121.

16 See Mary Ann Watson, *The Expanding Vista: American Television in the Kennedy Years* (Durham: Duke University Press, 1994), especially chap. 9, "A New Network Serving All the People," 185–202.

17 See the appendix for a listing of community TV organizations, many of which date to the early years of community television.

18 James Donald, "Media Studies: Possibilities and Limitations," in *Media Education: An Introduction,* ed. Manuel Alvarado and Oliver Boyd Barret (London: BFI and Open University Press, 1992), 116.

19 Ibid., 81.

20 Ian Connell and Geoff Hurd, "Cultural Education: A Revised Program," *Media Information Australia,* no. 53 (August 1989): 23–30.

21 Paula Giddings, *When and Where I Enter: The Impact of Black Women on Race and Sex in America* (New York: Bantam Books, 1984), 103.

22 Steven Goodman, "Talking Back: The Portrait of a Student Documentary on School Inequity," in *Experiencing Diversity: Toward Educational Equity,* ed. Frank Pignatelli and Susanna W. Pflaum (Thousand Oaks, Calif.: Corwin Press, 1994), 47.

23 Diana Agosta, "Mo' Better News," *Afterimage* 18, no. 4 (November 1990): 5.

24 Goodman, 63.

25 On the silencing and marginalization of students from low-income backgrounds in New York City schools, see Michelle Fine, "Silencing in the Public Schools," *Language Arts* 64, no. 2 (1987): 157–74.

26 Goodman, 67–68.

27 Youth Struggling for Survival was founded by Luis Rodriguez, author of *Always*

Running, La Vida Loca: Gang Days in L.A. (New York: Simon and Schuster, 1994).

28 Ramiro Rodriguez, "No One Should Have to Fight the Battle Alone!" *Tribuno del Pueblo*, August 1998. http://www.lrna.org/league/TP/TP.98.08/9808. ramiro.eng.html.

29 The videotape *Self-Protection: Teen Moms Expand Their Options* was produced by Sara Safford and directed by Alex Juhasz for the Brooklyn Perinatal Network.

3 Critical Pedagogy at the End of the Rainbow Curriculum

An earlier version of this chapter was published in *Afterimage* 20, no. 10 (May 1993), and was republished in *Art, Activism, and Oppositionality*, edited by Grant Kestor (Durham, N.C.: Duke University Press, 1998).

1 For a discussion of heteronormativity see Michael Warner, ed., *Fear of a Queer Planet: Queer Politics and Social Theory* (Minneapolis: University of Minnesota Press, 1993), xxi–xxv.

2 *It Is What It Is,* dir. Greg Bordowitz, New York, 1992, is distributed by Gay Men's Health Crisis (GMHC) Dept. of Education, (212) 337-3559, 129 West 20th St., New York, NY 10011.

3 As a member of the GMHC audiovisual staff, Bordowitz produced the tape in consultation with the New York City School Chancellor's Office—specifically, with Fernandez's material review committee. Well informed of concurrent developments within the public school system, he saw the tape as an opportunity to push the limits of authorized high school sexuality curriculum.

4 Office of the Chancellor, New York City Public Schools, *Children of the Rainbow* (1992), xii.

5 The quote is from Mary A. Cummins, president of District 24's school board, cited in Steven Lee Myers, "How a 'Rainbow' Curriculum Turned into Fighting Words," *New York Times,* 13 December 1992, 6. See also Myers, "Board in Queens Is Suspended in Battle over Gay Curriculum," *New York Times,* 2 December 1992, 1.

6 The curriculum guide is a set of general guidelines meant to aid individual teachers and schools in the development of curriculum advocating the acceptance of diversity. It is not a specific or mandatory set of lessons. Many on the religious Right erroneously claim that the attention that the Fernandez administration has given to the social issues represented by the Rainbow Curriculum has been at the expense of "academics."

7 The condom distribution program was adopted on 27 February 1991 by the New York City Board of Education in a four to three vote. The program is an addendum to the "HIV/AIDS Program Implementation Guidelines" instituted in accordance with a 1987 requirement by the New York State commissioner of education to form an advisory council on HIV/AIDS education.

8   As this chapter was being written, New Yorkers faced heated school board battles in many of the city's thirty-two districts. Led by groups such as Pat Robertson's Christian Coalition and armed with more money than registered voters, the religious Right has begun targeting local elections that normally have a low voter turnout (as low as 4 to 7 percent). As threatening as this "grassroots" backlash may seem, defeating the religious Right on their chosen ground of local electoral politics requires only a relatively small oppositional voting block. Indeed, groups such as People about Change in Education (PACE), the Gay and Lesbian Emergency Media Campaign, and the Campaign for Inclusive Multicultural Education have already begun to mount a broad-based opposition.

9   For further discussion see Jeffrey Weeks, *Against Nature* (London: Routledge, 1991); and Michel Foucault, *The History of Sexuality, Volume 1: An Introduction,* trans. Robert Hurley (New York: Vintage Books, 1980).

10   See Eve Kosofsky Sedgwick, "How to Bring Your Kids Up Gay," *Social Text* 29 (fall 1991); U.S. Department of Health and Human Services, "Report of the Secretary's Task Force on Youth Suicide," summer 1989; Friends of Project 10, Inc., *Project 10 Handbook: Addressing Lesbian and Gay Issues in Our Schools* (Los Angeles: Friends of Project 10, 1991), 11–16; Hetrick-Martin Institute, "Factfile: Lesbian, Gay, and Bisexual Youth," 1992.

11   Eve Kosofsky Sedgwick, *Epistemology of the Closet* (Berkeley: University of California Press, 1990), 1.

12   That there is a dire need for AIDS educational media that situate the problem in terms of diverse sexual practices and identities was driven home in my experience as a teacher (a straight, white, male teacher) in New York City elementary and junior high schools during the late eighties.

13   Alex Juhasz, *AIDS TV: Identity, Community, and Alternative Video* (Durham: Duke University Press, 1995), 51–53.

14   Michelle Fine, "Sexuality, Schooling, and Adolescent Females," *Harvard Educational Review* 58, no. 1 (February 1988): 49–50.

15   "Teaching of Sexual Concepts Stirs a Heated Debate among Officials," *New York Times,* 17 June 1992, B1, B2. The curriculum was later revised under pressure from conservative members of the city school board, omitting the mention of oral and anal sex, references implying gay relationships among youth, as well as the cleaning of hypodermic needles. See Joseph Berger, "Board Agrees on Teaching about AIDS," *New York Times,* 25 June 1992, B1, B4.

16   Resolution 33 of the New York City Board of Education, as noted in a school board public relations document titled "HIV/AIDS Including Condom Availability in NYC High Schools and Selected Special Education Programs: Commonly Asked Questions and Answers," October 1992, 3.

17   James Dao, "Critics Decry New AIDS Education Rules as Censorship," *New York Times,* 29 May 1992, B3.

18 *AIDS, Not Us,* dir. Sandra Elkin, New York, 1989, is distributed by HIV Center for Clinical and Behavioral Studies, 722 West 168th St., New York, NY 10032.

19 An important lesson learned from the widening struggle to develop effective AIDS prevention material has been the necessity of addressing explicitly the diversity of sexual practices in terms specific to all communities, and particularly those being hit hardest by the AIDS epidemic. This means organizations originally set up by and for gay communities are narrowcasting videos to straight and gay Latino/a and black urban communities (which are currently experiencing higher HIV infection rates), and to (primarily urban) youth. As a result, AIDS educational material produced by these organizations has begun to address sexuality as it is constituted within and across ethnic, class, and regional communities. In the context of public school institutions, these approaches represent a radical departure from curricula that have generally denied the centrality of sexual desire and sexual cultures as they are expressed through other cultural discourses.

20 Karen Harbeck, "Gay and Lesbian Educators: Past History/Future Prospects," in *Coming Out of the Classroom Closet,* ed. Karen Harbeck (New York: Routledge, 1991), 130.

21 Ronald Reagan, quoted in Harbeck, 129.

22 Sedgwick, "How to Bring Your Kids Up Gay," 20. Sedgwick points out that this designated disorder is in fact highly differentiated between boys and girls—whereas boys may be given this label if they display marked desire to participate in female-stereotyped activity or practice cross-dressing, it is applied to a girl only if she actually insists that she is anatomically male.

23 Nina Willdorf, "How to Be Gay (and Controversial)," *Chronicle of Higher Education,* 7 April 2000, A12.

24 Quoted in Simon Watney, "School's Out," in *Inside/Out: Lesbian Theories, Gay Theories* (New York: Routledge, 1991), 388.

25 *Pedagogue,* dir. Stuart Marshall, England, 1988. Distributed by Video Data Bank, 37 South Wabash Ave., Chicago, IL 60603, (800) 634-8544.

26 Viewers of the tape in the late 1990s and later may find this moment resonant with the gays-in-the-military controversy and the "don't ask, don't tell" policy instituted by the Clinton administration in 1993. Under the policy, military personnel are not supposed to be questioned about their sexual orientation but also cannot openly acknowledge their sexual orientation or participate in homosexual activities. Gay rights supporters have repeatedly challenged the policy in courts.

27 Watney, 300.

28 Nonetheless progressive pedagogical work retains the often contradictory nature of the political struggles that inform it. Thus educators need to marshal both minoritizing and universalizing claims within sexuality curricula. Although the notion of an innate or immutable sexuality may be necessary to pro-

tect some youth, without a curriculum that begins to break down the simple binary opposition between hetero and homo identities, educators cannot begin to dismantle the disciplinary mechanisms that reinforce homophobia.

29 Harbeck, 130.

30 *Blind Alley,* Rise and Shine Productions, Rheedlen Centers for Children and Families, 147 St. Nicholas Ave., 3d floor, New York, NY 10026.

31 *Free to Be Me.* Educational Video Center (EVC), 120 W. 30th Street, 7th floor, New York, NY 10001.

4 Peer Education and Interactivity

1 The research for this chapter was also the basis of *alt.youth.media,* an exhibition that I curated for the New Museum of Contemporary Art in New York City in 1996. The exhibition brought together hundreds of media works by youth, primarily teens and young adults, ranging from institutionally sanctioned media texts of videographers to more marginal productions of cyberpunks, riot grrrls, and zine editors. Researching and organizing the exhibition took more than two years and involved the development of a network of producers who previously had little or nothing to do with museums. The exhibition comprised numerous skateboard graphics and stickers, hundreds of alternative publications or zines, over sixty video tapes, and dozens of CD-ROMS, Internet-based projects, and zines. The work in these various media forms spans a variety of topics including cultural identity, race, sexuality, drugs, violence, community, gangs, family, and education. The idea behind the show was to look at how young people's agency is negotiated within media culture, and to examine how young people influence and are influenced by the media.

2 Channel One, launched by Whittle Communications in 1989, broadcasts a twelve-minute commercial newscast into thousands of classrooms daily.

3 Ann De Vaney, *Watching Channel One: The Convergence of Students, Technology, and Private Business* (Albany: State University of New York Press, 1994).

4 The discussion of the production of *Kept Quiet* is based on a series of interviews with Julia Meltzer and her students conducted by the author in spring 1995.

5 Anna Williams, "Domestic Violence and the Aetiology of Crime in *America's Most Wanted," Camera Obscura* 31 (1993): 97–118.

6 Mimi White, *Tele-advising: Therapeutic Discourses in American Television* (Chapel Hill: University of North Carolina Press, 1992), 182.

7 Ibid.

8 Janine Marchessault, "Amateur Video and the Challenge for Social Change," in *Mirror Machine: Video and Identity,* ed. Janine Marchessault (Toronto: YYZ Books, 1995), 17.

9 The following discussion of the production of *Mending Wounds* and *Stolen Innocence* is based on a series of interviews with Laura Vural, the director of Rise and Shine Productions, and her students conducted by the author in spring 1995.

10   The organization is funded by the New York Community Trust and New York Council for the Arts.

11   The discussion of the production of *Sex Get Serious* is based on a series of interviews with Ro Rai of the London-based ARTEC, and the staff of the Birmingham-based Jubilee Arts, conducted by the author in fall 1993.

12   Ibid.

13   The discussion of the production of *Brothers* is based on a series of interviews with David Bolt, executive producer of the project; Sally Fifer, director of the Bay Area Video Collective (BAVC); Steve Feeback of the National Task Force on AIDS Prevention, and Tony Glover, director of the Brothers Network (a subsidiary of the National Task Force on AIDS Prevention) conducted by the author in fall 1993.

14   Ibid.

15   The discussion of *gURL* is based on conversations and collaborative projects between Esther Drill, Rebecca Odes, and the author from spring 1996 through spring 1997. The *gURL* Web site can be found at www.gurl.com.

16   Ibid.

17   For an account of the New Museum of Contemporary Art's curatorial and exhibition politics, see Brian Goldfarb and Mimi Young, eds., *Temporarily Possessed: The Semi-permanent Collection* (New York: New Museum of Contemporary Art, 1995).

5 Museum Pedagogy

1   James Clifford, *The Predicament of Culture* (Cambridge: Harvard University Press, 1988), especially "Histories of the Tribal and the Modern" and "On Collecting Art and Culture"; Carol Duncan, *Civilizing Rituals: Inside Public Art Museums* (New York: Routledge, 1995); Alan Wallach, *Exhibiting Contradiction: Essays on the Art Museum in the United States* (Amherst: University of Massachusetts Press, 1998); Douglas Crimp, *On the Museum's Ruins* (Cambridge: MIT Press, 1993); Tony Bennett, *The Birth of the Museum: History, Theory, Politics* (New York: Routledge, 1995), and "The Exhibitionary Complex," *New Formations* 4 (1988).

2   Bennett, "The Exhibitionary Complex," 79.

3   See Pierre Bourdieu, "The Aristocracy of Culture," in *Distinction: A Social Critique of the Judgement of Taste* (Cambridge: Harvard University Press, 1984); and Duncan, "Public Spaces, Private Interests," in *Civilizing Rituals*.

4   Bourdieu, 30–31, 272–73.

5   Pierre Bourdieu and Jean-Claude Passeron, *Reproduction in Education, Society, and Culture,* 2d ed. (Newbury Park, Calif.: Sage, 1977), 51–52.

6   Charter of the Metropolitan Museum of New York, 1870. Cited in Hiroshi Daifuku, "The Museum and the Visitor," in *The Organization of Museums* (Paris: UNESCO, 1960), 73; italics mine.

7 Molly Harrison, "Education in Museums," in *The Organization of Museums*, 81.

8 Ibid., 92.

9 Bennett, 81.

10 Nancy Einreinhofer provides an account of the central role of Thomas Hoving, director of the Metropolitan Museum of Art (1967–1977) in the commercialization of museums and the development of blockbuster special exhibitions. See Nancy Einreinhofer, *The American Art Museum: Elitism and Democracy* (Washington, D.C.: Leicester University Press, 1997), 125–29.

11 Bennett, 81.

12 Einreinhofer, 185.

13 William Rubin, ed., *Pablo Picasso, a Retrospective* (New York: Museum of Modern Art, distributed by Thames and Hudson, 1980).

14 Carol Duncan and Alan Wallach, "The Museum of Modern Art as Late Capitalist Ritual: An Iconographic Analysis," *Marxist Perspectives* 1, no. 4 (winter 1978): 31.

15 Mark Lilla, "The Museum in the City," in *Public Policy and the Aesthetic Interest,* ed. Ralph Smith and Ronald Berman (Urbana: University of Illinois Press, 1992), 182.

16 Paul DiMaggio and Michael Useem, "The Arts in Class Reproduction," in *Cultural and Economic Reproduction in Education,* ed. Michael W. Apple (London: Routledge and Kegan Paul, 1982), 182.

17 Bourdieu and Passeron, 8–9.

18 DiMaggio and Useem, 183.

19 Michelle Wallace, "Modernism, Postmodernism, and the Problem of the Visual in Afro-American Culture," in *Out There,* ed. Russell Ferguson, Martha Gever, Trinh T. Minh-ha, and Cornel West (Cambridge: MIT Press, 1990), 41.

20 See Duncan and Wallach, 34–35; Duncan, *Civilizing Rituals,* 63–71.

21 William Rubin, *"Primitivism" in 20th Century Art: Affinity of the Tribal and the Modern* (New York: Museum of Modern Art, 1984).

22 Hal Foster, "The Primitive Unconscious of Modern Art, or White Skin Black Masks," in *Recodings: Art Spectacle, Cultural Politics* (Port Townsend, Wash.: Bay Press, 1985), 183. See also Clifford, "Histories of the Tribal and the Modern," in *Predicaments of Culture.*

23 From the title page of the catalog to MOMA's *Primitivism in 20th Century Art: Affinity of the Tribal and the Modern* (New York: Museum of Modern Art, 1984).

6   A Pedagogical Cinema

An earlier version of this chapter was published in *Iris,* no. 18 (spring 1995).

1 Richard Jenkins, *Pierre Bourdieu* (New York: Routledge, 1992), 24–44.

2 Pierre Bourdieu, *Algeria 1960: The Disenchantment of the World, The Sense of Honor, and The Kabyle House of the World Reversed: Essays* (New York: Cambridge University Press, 1979), 7, 30–31, 92–94.

3 Manthia Diawara, *African Cinema: Politics and Culture* (Bloomington and Indianapolis: Indiana University Press, 1992), 57.

4 Kwate Nee Owoo, "The Language of Real Life: Interview with Ousmane Sembéne," *Framework* 16 (1989): 84–85.

5 Françoise Pfaff, *The Cinema of Ousmane Sembene, a Pioneer of African Cinema* (Westport, Conn.: Greenwood Press, 1984), 182.

6 Johannes Fabian, *Time and the Other: How Anthropology Makes Its Object* (New York: Columbia University Press, 1983), 178. See also Fatimah Tobing Rony, "Those Who Squat, Those Who Sit: The Visualizing of Race in the 1895 Films of Félix-Louis Regnault," *Camera Obscura* 28 (January 1992): 263–83.

7 See Marcel Mauss, "Techniques of the Body," in *Incorporations*, ed. Jonathan Crary and Sanford Kwinter (New York: Zone Books, 1992).

8 Fabian, 121.

9 See, for example, Nancy Leys Stepan, "Race and Gender: The Role of Analogy in Science," *Isis* 77 (1986); and Stephen Jay Gould, *The Mismeasure of Man* (New York: W. W. Norton, 1981).

10 Arturo Escobar, "Imagining a Post-development Era: Critical Thought, Development, and Social Movements," *Social Text* 31–32 (1992): 24.

11 Tobing Rony, 265. Also see Ella Shohat, "Imaging Terra Incognita: The Disciplinary Gaze of Empire," *Public Culture* 3, no. 2 (spring 1991), for an extensive discussion of the intersection of the origins of cinema with the Western projects of social science and imperialism.

12 Edward Said confirms this point, clarifying the particular distinction of Western marshaling of representational practice: "All cultures tend to make representations of foreign cultures the better to master or in some way control them. Yet not all cultures make representations of foreign cultures *and* in fact master or control them. This is the distinction, I believe of modern Western cultures. It requires the study of Western Knowledge or representations of the non-European world to be a study of both those representations and the political power they express" (*Culture and Imperialism* [New York: Alfred A. Knopf, 1993], 100).

13 Fabian, 122.

14 Ashis Nandy also provides an insightful discussion of this tendency within the social sciences and particularly psychology, adding that "Freud's early disciples . . . went out to 'primitive' societies to pursue the homology between primitivism and infantility. They, too, were working out the cultural and psychological implications of the biological principle 'ontology recapitulates phylogeny,' and that of the ideology of 'normal,' fully socialized adult male." See Nandy, *The Intimate Enemy: Loss and Recovery of Self under Capitalism* (Delhi and Oxford: Oxford University Press, 1989), 13. Also see Octave Mannoni, *Psychoanalysis and the Decolonization of the Mind*, ed. J. Miller Freud (London: Weidenfeld and Nicholson, 1972), 86–95.

15 Jean Piaget, *The Moral Development of the Child* (New York: Free Press, 1965), 84–85, 340, 348.

16 Piaget, 186–96, 339–40.

17 Piaget, 188; Joseph H. Di Leo, *Young Children and Their Drawings* (New York: Brunner/Mazel, 1970), 40.

18 Piaget, 340.

19 Ibid., 348.

20 Pierre Erny, *The Child and His Environment in Black Africa: An Essay on Traditional Education* (New York: Oxford University Press, 1981), 161. Erny cites the work of R. Bastide, who criticizes Piaget's theories as being "based on a too-simplified and inexact conception of education amongst traditional peoples."

21 Nandy, *The Intimate Enemy*, 15. Nandy draws on aspects of Philippe Aries' thesis that the concept of childhood was expanded in seventeenth-century Europe, extending the scope and duration of pedagogic discipline, and that the child became increasingly viewed as inferior to, rather than simply smaller than, the adult.

22 Guari Viswanathan, *Masks of Conquest: Literary Study and British Rule in India* (New York: Columbia University Press, 1989).

23 Lizbeth Malkmus and Roy Armes, *Arab and African Film Making* (London: Zed Books, 1991), 37.

24 Françoise Pfaff provides a further description of *Emitai,* stressing the contradictions and opportunism of the French system in *The Cinema of Ousmane Sembene, a Pioneer of African Cinema,* 147. For a description of the connection between assimilationist policies and crisis in the West, see also Cornel West, "The New Cultural Politics of Difference," *October* 53 (summer 1990): 94–109.

25 David G. Scanlon, *Traditions of African Education* (New York: Teachers College Press, Columbia University, 1964). This book summarizes and discusses notable European governmental documents of the period that addressed the issue of education in colonial Africa, including "Das Schulwesen in den deutschen Schutzgebieten" (The School System in the German Colonies), 1911; the "Phelps-Stokes Report of 1922" (International/League of Nations); "Education Policy in British Tropical Africa," 1925; and "Reorganization of Education in French Equatorial Africa," 1925.

26 Malkmus and Armes, 37.

27 Said, 264.

28 Ibid.

29 Diawara, *African Cinema: Politics and Culture,* 1, 10, 14–17, 104.

30 Ibid.

31 Stuart Hall, "Cultural Identity and Cinematic Representation," in *Ex-iles: Essays on Caribbean Cinema,* ed. Mbye Cham (Trenton: Africa World Press, 1992), 222.

32 Noureddine Ghali, "An Interview with Sembene Ousmane," in *Film and Politics in the Third World,* ed. John H. D. Downing (New York: Autonomedia, 1987), 42.

33 Malkmus and Armes, 199.

34 Ghali, 49.

35 Manthia Diawara, "Oral Literature and African Film: Narratology in *Wend Kuuni*," *Presence African* 142 (1987): 38.

36 Ibid.

37 Leopold S. Senghor, *Nationhood and the African Road to Socialism* (Paris: Présence Africaine, 1962), and *Négritude et Humanisme* (Paris: Editions du Seuil, 1964).

38 Among them are Kenya's first president, Jomo Kenyatta, who wrote *Facing Mount Kenya* (1938, 1962); Ghanaian president Kwame Nkrumah's *Africa Must Unite* (1963); and Tanzanian leader Julius K. Nyerere's *Freedom and Socialism* (1968). For a more extensive bibliography, see George E. F. Urch, *Education in Sub-Saharan Africa* (New York: Garland, 1992), 8–9.

39 Diawara, "Oral Literature and African Film," 39.

40 The voice-over narrative recedes, only to appear twice more, once to remind viewers of the continued burden of Wênd Kûuni's voicelessness. Speaking for Wênd Kûnni, the narrator informs the viewer that though Wênd Kûnni is happy with his new family, he still bears grief within. The voice reemerges the final time, again speaking for Wênd Kûnni and foreshadowing his recovery of voice: "That day Wênd Kûnni awoke . . . with a strange foreboding. Throughout the day that feeling never left him."

41 Accounts of traditional African pedagogy that I draw on include Donald G. Burns, *African Education: An Introductory Survey of Education in the Commonwealth Countries* (London: Oxford University Press, 1965); Erny, *The Child and His Environment in Black Africa*; Scanlon, *Traditions of African Education*; and Urch, *Education in Sub-Saharan Africa*.

42 Benedict Anderson, *Imagined Communities: Reflections on the Origin and Spread of Nationalism* (New York: Verso, 1983), 119.

43 Ibid., 119.

44 Erny, 7, 56.

45 Ibid., 53.

46 Idrissa Ouedraogo's *Yaaba* (1989) is another example of the breakdown of film narrative according to intragenerational pedagogical relations. The prevalence of themes of generation conflict and transition in African cinema is indicative of both the significance of age-defined pedagogical spheres and the divisive effects of Eurocolonial education. Other examples of this include Sembéne's *Emitai*, Kaboré's *Rabi* (1991), and Souleymane Cissé's *Yeleen* (1987). These films' representations of youth function symbolically as a locus of hope and change, but

they take on a specifically historical and often literal significance as representations of the generation of national liberation.

7 Local Television and Community Politics in Brazil

An earlier version of this chapter was published in *Visible Nations: Latin American Cinema and Video*, edited by Chon Noriega (Minneapolis: University of Minnesota Press, 2001).

1   I draw on two sources for most of the descriptive and historical information on TV Anhembi: video footage from TV Anhembi's series *Fala São Paulo*; and an interview that I conducted in fall 1993 with Almir Almas, who was the coordinating producer of TV Anhembi throughout its existence. All quotations of Almas are drawn from this interview. A sample reel of TV Anhembi's work is available for rental from the International Medial Resource Exchange, 124 Washington Place, New York, NY 10014.

2   Other North American groups include Top Value Television (TVTV), Ant Farm, Paper Tiger, and Deep Dish Television (New York City), and Portable Channel (Rochester, N.Y.). See Deirdre Boyle, "A Brief History of American Documentary Video," in *Illuminating Video: An Essential Guide to Video Art,* ed. Doug Hall and Sally Jo Fifer (San Francisco: Aperture/Bay Area Video Coalition, 1990), 51–70.

3   Sandra Ventura, "O último programma da TV Anhembi," *Diário do comércio* (São Paulo, 8 January 1993).

4   Orlando Fals Borda, "Social Movements and Political Power in Latin America," in *The Making of Social Movements in Latin America: Identity, Strategy, and Democracy,* ed. Arturo Escobar and Sonia E. Alvarez (Boulder: Westview Press, 1992), 305.

5   Discussing the same situation with a less optimistic slant, Ruth Corrêa Leite Cardoso describes how political administrations have at times been able to play competing community groups off of one another, and how community groups have had to compromise their goals to form coalitions that "claimed to represent the 'true will' of the entire neighborhood." See Ruth Corrêa Leite Cardoso, "Popular Movements and Consolidation of Democracy in Brazil," in Escobar and Alvarez, 295.

6   Fals Borda, 305.

7   Ibid., 306.

8   Paolo Freire, *Pedagogy of the City* (New York: Continuum, 1993).

9   Almir Almas interview.

10 Nico Vink, *The Telenovela and Emancipation: A Study on Television and Social Change in Brazil* (Amsterdam: Royal Tropical Institute, 1988).

11 On the productive uses of combined genres: Chon A. Noriega, "Genre Blurring, Genre Bending: Willie Varela's *A Lost Man* (1992)," manuscript.

12 A detailed description of many of these groups is provided in Luiz Fernando Santoro's comprehensive history of popular video in Brazil, *A imagem nas mãos: O vídeo popular no Brasil* (São Paulo: Sumas Editorial, 1986). See also Karen Ranucci, *Directory of Film and Video Production Resources in Latin America and the Caribbean* (New York: Foundation for Independent Video and Film, 1989).

13 Ingrid Sarti, "Between Memory and Illusion: Independent Video in Brazil," in *Media and Politics in Latin America: The Struggle for Democracy,* ed. Elizabeth Fox (Newbury Park, Calif.: Sage Publications, 1988), 157.

14 Randal Johnson and Bob Stam, "The Shape of Brazilian Film History," in *Brazilian Cinema,* ed. Randal Johnson and Bob Stam (Austin: University of Texas Press, 1982), 30–36. See also Glauber Rocha's 1965 manifesto "Down with Populism," in *Twenty-five Years of the New Latin American Cinema,* ed. Michael Chanan (London: British Film Institute, 1983), 15–16. Rocha's manifesto is representative of early arguments for an avant-garde aesthetic that refused popular tastes. In it, he described popular culture as a form of illiteracy fostered by the United States and Europe with the aim of fostering underdevelopment in Latin America.

15 Johnson and Stam, 36.

16 Julianne Burton, "Nelson Pereira dos Santos: Toward a Popular Cinema," in *Cinema and Social Change in Latin America: Conversations with Filmmakers,* ed. Julianne Burton (Austin: University of Texas Press, 1986), 135.

17 Santoro, 62–63, 85.

18 Carlos Eduardo Lins da Silva, "Transnational Communication and Brazilian Culture," in *Communication and Latin American Society,* ed. Rita Atwood and Emile G. McAnany (Madison: University of Wisconsin Press, 1986), 104.

19 Cesar Guimarães and Roberto Amaral, "Brazilian Television: A Rapid Conversion to the New World Order," in *Media and Politics in Latin America: The Struggle for Democracy,* ed. Elizabeth Fox (Newbury Park, Calif.: Sage Publications), 124–37.

20 Ana López, "The Melodrama in Latin America: Films, Telenovelas, and the Currency of a Popular Form," *Wide Angle* 7, no. 3 (1985): 5–13. Lopez notes three differences between Latin American telenovelas and U.S. soap operas: "Unlike American soaps, *telenovelas* always have clear cut stories with definite endings that permit narrative closure; they are shown during prime-time viewing hours; and they are designed to attract a wide viewing audience of men, women and children" (8).

21 Michèle Mattelart and Armand Mattelart, *Carnival of Images: Brazilian Television Fiction,* trans. David Buxton (New York: Bergin and Garvey, 1990), 79.

22 Guimarães and Amaral, 125–37.

23 Sarti, 160.

24 Alberto López, interview with *VideoRed,* "Universos Diversos y Puntos de Encuentro en la Produccion Audiovisual Brasilera," *VideoRed: Revista del audio-*

visual latinoamericano (Lima, Peru: IPAL) 4, no. 17 (October–December 1992): 15; translation mine.

25 Rafael Roncagliolo, "The Growth of the Audio-visual Imagescape in Latin America," in *Video the Changing World,* ed. Nancy Thede and Alain Ambrosi (New York: Black Rose Books, 1991), 22–29. Roncagliolo classifies these uses within five overlapping categories: (1) video records—the use of video to gather the history of a community to support the community's organizing processes that form both its subject and its object; (2) group video—the use of video for education within groups, as a communication link between villages and generally as a mechanism for obtaining feedback within movements; (3) special events video—the use of video at public events as a mechanism of outreach and mobilization; (4) counternews video—video aimed at a broader public, with the purpose of "confronting the 'official [televised] version' of events" through the establishment of alternative video cassette distribution networks; (5) mass broadcast video—the production of video programming from the perspective of social movements explicitly for broadcast television.

26 Alberto López, interview with *VideoRed,* 15–16; translation mine.

27 Sarti, 160.

28 Almir Almas interview.

29 Mattelart and Mattelart, 131.

30 Ibid., 79.

31 Almir Almas interview.

32 Ibid.

Abrash, Barbara, and Catherine Egan, eds. *Mediating History: The Map Guide to Independent Video*. New York: New York University Press, 1992.

ACT UP/ New York. *Women, AIDS, and Activism*. Boston: South End Press, 1990.

Adam, Roy. "Education and Politics in Developing Countries." *Teachers College Record* 70, no. 6 (March 1969).

Adams, Dennis, and Mary E. Hamm. *Media and Literacy: Learning in an Electronic Age*. Springfield, Ill.: Charles C. Thomas, 1989.

Adler, Richard R. *Aspen Notebook: Cable and Continuing Education*. New York: Praeger, 1973.

Agosta, Diana. "Mo' Better News: A Discussion on Media Education." *Afterimage* 18, no. 4 (November 1990): 5–8.

Altbach, Philip. "Education and Neocolonialism." *Teachers College Record* 72, no. 4 (May 1971): 543–58.

——. "Servitude of the Mind? Education, Dependency, Neocolonialism." *Teachers College Record* 79, no. 2 (December 1997): 187–204.

Althusser, Louis. *Lenin and Philosophy and Other Essays*. Trans. Ben Brewster. New York: Monthly Review Press, 1971.

Alvarado, Manuel, Edward Buscombe, and Richard Collins, eds. *The Screen Education Reader*. New York: Columbia University Press, 1993.

Alvarado, Manuel, and John Thompson, eds. *The Media Reader*. London: BFI, 1990.

Alvarado, Manuel, and Oliver Boyd-Barrett, eds. *Media Education: An Introduction*. London: British Film Institute and Open University, 1992.

Ambrosi, Alain, and Nancy Thede, eds. *Video the Changing World*. New York: Black Rose Books, 1991.

Amey, Lorne J. *Visual Literacy: Implications for the Production of Children's Television Programs*. Halifax: Dalhousie University, School of Library Service, 1976.

Anderson, Benedict. *Imagined Communities: Reflections on the Origin and Spread of Nationalism*. New York: Verso Press, 1983.

Appadurai, Arjun. "Disjuncture and Difference in Global Cultural Economy." *Public Culture* 2, no. 2 (spring 1990).

———. "Global Ethnoscapes: Notes and Queries for a Transnational Anthropology." In *Recapturing Anthropology,* ed. Richard G. Fox. Santa Fe: School of American Research Press, 1991.

Apple, Michael. *Official Knowledge: Democratic Knowledge in a Conservative Age*. New York: Routledge, 1993.

Armes, Roy. *Third World Film Making and the West*. Berkeley and Los Angeles: University of California Press, 1987.

Arnove, Robert F., ed. *Philanthropy and Cultural Imperialism: The Foundations at Home and Abroad*. Boston: G. K. Hall, 1980.

Aronowitz, Stanley, and Henry Giroux. *Postmodern Education: Politics, Culture, and Social Criticism*. Minneapolis: University of Minnesota Press, 1991.

Atwood, Rita, and Emile G. McAnany, eds. *Communication and Latin American Society: Trends in Critical Research, 1960–1985*. Madison: University of Wisconsin Press, 1986.

Barkan, Debby. "Hidden Talents." *Afterimage* 18, no. 4 (November 1990): 4.

Baughman, James L. *The Republics of Mass Culture: Journalism, Filmmaking, and Broadcast in America since 1941*. Baltimore: Johns Hopkins University Press, 1970.

Bazalgette, Cary, Evelyne Bevort, and Josiane Savino. *New Directions: Media Education Worldwide*. London: British Film Institute, 1992.

Beauchamp, Edward. "Educational Policy in Eastern Samoa: An American Colonial Outpost." *Comparative Education* 11, no. 1 (March 1975).

Benjamin, Walter. *Reflections*. Ed. Peter Demetz. New York: Harcourt, Brace, Jovanovich, 1978.

Bennett, Tony. "The Politics of 'The Popular' and Popular Culture." In *Popular Culture and Social Relations,* ed. Tony Bennett, Colin Mercer, and Janet Woollacott. Philadelphia: Open University Press, 1986.

———. "The Exhibitionary Complex." *New Formations* 4 (1988).

————. *The Birth of the Museum: History, Theory, Politics.* New York: Routledge, 1995.

Berger, Joseph. "Board Agrees on Teaching about AIDS." *New York Times,* 25 June 1992, B1, B4.

Bigelow, William. "Inside the Classroom: Social Visions and Critical Pedagogy." *Teachers College Record* 91, no. 3 (spring 1990): 437–48.

Boddy, William. "Alternative Television in the United States." *Screen* 31, no. 1 (spring 1990): 91–101.

————. "The Seven Dwarfs and the Money Grubbers: The Public Relations Crisis of U.S. Television in the 1950s." In *Logics of Television,* ed. Patricia Mellencamp. Bloomington and Indianapolis: Indiana University Press, 1990.

————. "The Beginnings of American Television." In *Television: An International History,* ed. Anthony Smith. New York: Oxford University Press, 1995.

Bourdieu, Pierre. *Algeria 1960: The Disenchantment of the World.* New York: Cambridge University Press, 1979.

————. *Distinction: A Social Critique of the Judgement of Taste.* Trans. Richard Nice. Cambridge: Harvard University Press, 1984.

————. *Homo academicus.* Trans. Peter Collier. Stanford, Calif.: Stanford University Press, 1988.

————. *The Love of Art: European Art Museums and Their Public.* Stanford, Calif.: Stanford University Press, 1990.

Bourdieu, Pierre, and Jean-Claude Passeron. *Reproduction in Education, Society, and Culture.* 2d ed. Newbury Park, Calif.: Sage, 1977.

Bowles, Samuel, and Herbert Gintis. *Schooling in Capitalist America: Educational Reform and the Contradictions of Economic Life.* New York: Basic Books, 1976.

Boyle, Dierdre. "Guerilla Television." In *Transmission,* ed. Peter D'Agostino. New York: Tanam Press, 1985.

————. "A Brief History of American Documentary Video." In *Illuminating Video: An Essential Guide to Video Art,* ed. Doug Hall and Sally Jo Fifer. San Francisco: Aperture/Bay Area Video Coalition, 1990.

————. "From Portapak to Camcorder: A Brief History of Guerrilla Television." *Journal of Film and Video* 44, nos. 1–2 (spring–summer 1992): 67–80.

Bratlinger, Patrick. *Crusoe's Footprints: Cultural Studies in Britain and America.* New York: Routledge, 1990.

Britzman, Debra. *Practice Makes Practice.* Albany: State University of New York Press, 1991.

Brookfield, Stephen. "Media Power and Literacy." *Harvard Educational Review* 59, no. 3 (May 1986): 297–324.

Buckingham, David, and Julian Sefton-Green. *Cultural Studies Goes to School: Reading and Teaching Popular Media.* London: Taylor and Francis Publishers, 1994.

Burger, Maurice. *How Art Becomes History.* New York: Harper Collins, 1992.

Burke, Richard C. *Instructional Television: Bold New Venture*. Bloomington: Indiana University Press, 1971.

Burnes, E. Bradford. *Latin American Cinema: Film and History*. Los Angeles: University of California Press, 1975.

Burns, Donald G. *African Education: An Introductory Survey of Education in the Commonwealth Countries*. London: Oxford University Press, 1965.

Burton, Julianne. "Women behind the Camera." *Heresies* 16 (1983).

———. "Don (Juanito) Duck and the Imperialism of Patriarchal Unconscious: Disney Studios, the Good Neighbor Policy, and the Packaging of Latin America." In *Nationalisms and Sexualities*, ed. Andrew Parker et al. New York: Routledge, 1992.

———, ed. *Cinema and Social Change in Latin America: Conversations with Filmmakers*. Austin: University of Texas Press, 1986.

———, ed. *Social Documentary in Latin America*. Pittsburgh: University of Pittsburgh Press, 1990.

Buss, Dennis C. "The Ford Foundation in Public Education: Emergent Patterns." In *Philanthropy and Cultural Imperialism: The Foundations at Home and Abroad*, ed. Robert F. Arnove. Boston: G. K. Hall, 1980.

Butler, Judith P. *Gender Trouble: Feminism and the Subversion of Identity*. New York: Routledge, 1990.

———. *Bodies That Matter: On the Discursive Limits of "Sex."* New York: Routledge, 1993.

Caldwell, John Thornton. *Televisuality: Style, Crisis, and Authority in American Television*. New Brunswick: Rutgers University Press, 1995.

Carnegie Commission on Higher Education. *The Fourth Revolution: Instructional Technology in Higher Education*. A Report and Recommendations by the Carnegie Commission on Higher Education. New York: McGraw-Hill, 1972.

Carnes, Alice, and John Zurzan, eds. *Questioning Technology: Tool, Toy, or Tyrant*. Santa Cruz: New Society, 1991.

Carter, Erica, and Simon Watney, eds. *Taking Liberties: AIDS and Cultural Politics*. London: Serpents Tail, 1989.

Cassirer, Henry R. *Television Teaching Today*. Paris: UNESCO, 1960.

Castaño, Eleonora Ferrieira, and João Paulo Castaño. *Making Sense of the Media: A Handbook of Popular Education Techniques*. London: Monthly Review Press, 1993.

Cham, Mbye, ed. *Ex-Iles: Essays on Caribbean Cinema*. Trenton: African World Press, 1992.

Clifford, James. *The Predicament of Culture: Twentieth Century Ethnography, Literature, and Art*. Cambridge: Harvard University Press, 1988.

Clignet, Remi. "Damned If You Do, Damned If You Don't: The Dilemmas of Colonizer-Colonized Relations." In *Education and the Colonial Experience*, ed. Philip Altbach and Gail Kelly. New Brunswick: Transaction Books, 1984.

Clowse, Barbara Barksdale. *Brainpower for the Cold War: The Sputnik Crisis and National Defense Education Act of 1958.* Westport, Conn.: Greenwood Press, 1981.

Collins, Ava. "Intellectuals, Power, and Quality Television." In *Between Borders Pedagogy and the Politics of Cultural Studies,* ed. Henry A. Giroux and Peter McLaren. New York: Routledge, 1994.

"Coming of (TV) Age in Samoa." *Life,* 15 November 1968.

Connel, Ian, and Geoff Hurd. "Cultural Education: A Revised Program." *Media Information Australia,* no. 53 (August 1989).

Cooney, Stu. "American Samoa: In Our Image." *Audiovisual Instruction* 18, no. 8 (October 1973).

Craggs, Carol E. *Media Education in the Primary School.* London: Routledge, 1992.

Crichlow, Warren. "School Daze." *Afterimage* 18, no. 10 (May 1991).

Crichlow, Warren, and Cameron McCarthy, eds. *Race, Identity, and Representation in Education.* New York: Routledge, 1993.

Crimp, Douglas. "Mourning and Militancy." *October* 51 (winter 1989).

———. "Portraits of People with AIDS." In *Cultural Studies,* ed. Lawrence Grossberg, Cary Nelson, and Paula A. Treichler. New York: Routledge, 1992.

———. *On the Museum's Ruins.* Cambridge: MIT Press, 1993.

———, ed. *AIDS: Cultural Analysis, Cultural Activism.* Cambridge: MIT Press, 1989.

Crimp, Douglas, and Adam Rolston. *AIDS Demo Graphics.* Seattle: Bay Press, 1990.

Curtin, Michael. *Redeeming the Wasteland: Television and Cold War Politics.* New Brunswick: Rutgers University Press, 1995.

D'Agostino, Peter, ed. *Transmission: Theory and Practice for a New Television Aesthetics.* New York: Tanam Press, 1985.

Daifuku, Hiroshi. "The Museum and the Visitor." In *The Organization of Museums.* Paris, UNESCO, 1960.

Dao, James. "Critics Decry New AIDS Education Rules as Censorship." *New York Times,* 29 May 1992, B3.

Deitcher, David. "Social Aesthetics." In *Democracy,* ed. Brian Wallis. Seattle: Bay Press, 1990.

Delpit, Lisa. *Other People's Children: Cultural Conflict in the Classroom.* New York: New Press, 1995.

Derrida, Jacques. *On Grammatology.* Baltimore: Johns Hopkins University Press, 1974.

Deutsch, Roslyn. "Alternative Space." In *If You Lived Here,* ed. Brian Wallis. Seattle: Bay Press, 1991.

De Vaney, Ann. "Instructional Television without Educators: The Beginning of ITV." In *The Ideology of Images in Educational Media: Hidden Curriculums in the Classroom,* ed. Elizabeth Ellsworth and Mariamne Whatley. New York: Teachers College Press, 1990.

———. *Watching Channel One: The Convergence of Students, Technology, and Private Business.* Albany: State University of New York Press, 1994.

Diamond, Robert M., ed. *A Guide to Instructional Television.* New York: McGraw-Hill, 1964.

Diawara, Manthia. "Oral Literature and African Film: Narratology in *Wend Kuuni.*" *Presence African* 142 (1987): 38.

———. *African Cinema: Politics and Culture.* Bloomington and Indianapolis: Indiana University Press, 1992.

Di Leo, Joseph H. *Young Children and Their Drawings.* New York: Brunner/Mazel, 1970.

DiMaggio, Paul, and Michael Useem. "The Arts in Class Reproduction." In *Cultural and Economic Reproduction in Education,* ed. Michael W. Apple. London: Routledge and Kegan Paul, 1982.

Divine, Robert. *The Sputnik Challenge.* New York: Oxford University Press, 1993.

Dizard, Wilson P. *Television: A World View.* Syracuse, N.Y.: Syracuse University Press, 1966.

Donald, James. "A Review of John Fiske's *Television Culture.*" *Screen* 31, no. 1 (spring 1990).

———. "Media Studies: Possibilities and Limitations." In *Media Education: An Introduction,* ed. Manuel Alvarado and Oliver Boyd Barrett. London: BFI and Open University Press, 1992.

Dow, Peter B. *Schoolhouse Politics: Lessons from the Sputnik Era.* Cambridge: Harvard University Press, 1991.

Downing, John D. H., ed. *Film and Politics in the Third World.* New York: Autonomedia, 1987.

Drummond, Phillip, and Richard Paterson. *Television in Transition.* London: British Film Institute, 1986.

Duncan, Carol. *Civilizing Rituals: Inside Public Art Museums.* New York: Routledge, 1995.

Duncan, Carol, and Alan Wallach. "The Museum of Modern Art as Late Capitalist Ritual: An Iconographic Analysis." *Marxist Perspectives* 1, no. 4 (winter 1978).

"Education: Growing Up in Samoa." *Time,* 4 December 1964.

Ellsworth, Elizabeth, and Mariamne Whatley, eds. *The Ideology of Images in Educational Media: Hidden Curriculums in the Classroom.* New York: Teachers College Press, 1990.

Erny, Pierre. *The Child and His Environment in Black Africa: An Essay on Traditional Education.* New York: Oxford University Press, 1981.

Escobar, Arturo. "Imagining a Post-development Era: Critical Thought, Development, and Social Movements." *Social Text* 31–32 (1992).

―――. "Notes on the Anthropology of Cyberculture." *Current Anthropology* 35, no. 3 (June 1994).

Fabian, Johannes. *Time and the Other: How Anthropology Makes Its Object.* New York: Columbia University Press, 1983.

Fals Borda, Orlando. "Social Movements and Political Power in Latin America." In *The Making of Social Movements in Latin America: Identity, Strategy, and Democracy,* ed. Arturo Escobar and Sonia E. Alvarez. Boulder: Westview Press, 1992.

Fanon, Franz. *The Wretched of the Earth.* New York: Grove Press, 1963.

Farber, Paul, Eugene Provenzo Jr., and Gunilla Holm, eds. *Schooling in the Light of Popular Culture.* Albany: State University of New York Press, 1994.

Fee, Elizabeth, and Daniel Fox, eds. *AIDS: The Burdens of History.* Berkeley: University of California Press, 1988.

Feldman, Douglas A., ed. *Culture and AIDS.* New York: Praeger Books, 1990.

Feldstein, Martin, ed. *The Economics of Art Museums.* Chicago: University of Chicago Press, 1991.

Fiedler, Martha L. "TV Goes Way Out and Brings the World to Samoa." *American Education* 3, no. 3 (March 1967).

Fine, Michelle. "Sexuality, Schooling, and Adolescent Females." *Harvard Educational Review* 58, no. 1 (February 1988): 49–50.

―――. *Framing Dropouts: Notes on the Politics of an Urban Public High School.* Albany: State University of New York Press, 1991.

Fiske, John. *Television Culture.* London: Methuen, 1987.

―――. *Understanding Popular Culture.* Boston: Unwin Hyman, 1989.

Fontana Unified School District. *The Use of Closed Circuit Television to Improve Teacher Effectiveness: A Research Project Using Closed Circuit Television as a Medium for Classroom Observation.* Fontana, Calif.: Fontana Unified School District, 1961.

Ford Foundation. *Teaching by Television: A Report from the Ford Foundation and the Fund for the Advancement of Education.* New York: Ford Foundation, 1959.

Fornewt, Ambrosia, ed. *Cine, literatura, sociedaded.* Havana: Editorial Letras Cubanas, 1982.

"For Samoa—a Barefoot Teacher from Oklahoma." *Look,* 13 May 1966.

Foster, Hal. *Recodings: Art Spectacle, Cultural Politics.* Port Townsend, Wash.: Bay Press, 1985.

Foucault, Michel. *The Birth of the Clinic: An Archaeology of Medical Perception.* Trans. A. M. Sheridan Smith. New York: Vintage Books, 1973.

―――. *Discipline and Punish: The Birth of the Prison.* Trans. by Alan Sheridan. New York: Vintage Books, 1979.

―――. *The History of Sexuality, Volume 1: An Introduction.* Trans. Robert Hurley. New York: Vintage Books, 1980.

———. *Language, Counter-Memory, Practice: Selected Essays and Interviews.* Ed. Donald Bouchard. New York: Pantheon, 1980.

———. *Power/Knowledge: Selected Interviews and Other Writings, 1927–1977.* Ed. Colin Gordon. New York: Pantheon, 1980.

Fox, Elizabeth, ed. *Media and Politics in Latin America: The Struggle for Democracy.* Newbury Park, Calif.: Sage, 1988.

Freire, Paolo. *Pedagogy of the City.* New York: Continuum, 1993.

Freire, Paolo, and Donaldo Macedo. *Literacy: Reading the World and the Word.* South Hadley, Mass.: Bergin and Garvey, 1987.

Friends of Project 10, Inc. *Project 10 Handbook: Addressing Lesbian and Gay Issues in Our Schools.* Los Angeles: Friends of Project 10, 1991.

Fuller, Linda K. *Community Television in the United States.* Westport, Conn.: Greenwood Press, 1994.

Fundacion Mexicana de Cineastas. *Hojas de cine: Testimonios y documentos del nuevo cine Latinoamericano, volumen I Centro and Sudamerica.* Mexico: Universidad Autonoma Metropolitana, 1988.

Fuss, Dianna. *Essentially Speaking: Feminism, Nature, and Difference.* New York: Routledge, 1991.

———, ed. *Inside/Out: Lesbian Theories, Gay Theories.* New York: Routledge, 1991.

Gans, Herbert. *The Uses of Television in Education.* New York: Center for Urban Education, 1968.

Garcia Espanosa, Julio. *Un imagen recorre el mundo.* Havana: Editorial Letras Cubanas, 1979.

Gardener, Howard. "Cracking the Codes of Television: The Child as Anthropologist." In *Transmission,* ed. Peter D'Agostino. New York: Tanam Press, 1985.

Garman, J. F. "HIV/AIDS Education: A Comparison of Public and Non-public Secondary Instruction Effectiveness." *Education* 117 (spring 1997): 361–370.

Garver, Marjorie, Jann Matlock, and Rebecca Walkowitz, eds. *Media Spectacles.* New York: Routledge, 1993.

Gattengo, Caleb. *Towards a Visual Culture: Educating through Television.* New York: E. P. Dutton, 1969.

Geever, Martha. "Meet the Press: On Paper Tiger Television." In *Transmission,* ed. Peter D'Agostino. New York: Tanam Press, 1985.

Geever, Martha, John Greyson, and Pratibha Parmar. *Queer Looks: Perspectives on Lesbian and Gay Film and Video.* New York: Routledge, 1993.

Ghali, Noureddine. "An Interview with Sembene Ousmane." In *Film and Politics in the Third World,* ed. John H. D. Downing. New York: Autonomedia, 1987.

Giddings, Paula. *When and Where I Enter: The Impact of Black Women on Race and Sex in America.* New York: Bantam Books, 1984.

Giroux, Henry A. *Theory and Resistance in Education: A Pedagogy for the Opposition.* New York: Bergin and Garvey, 1983.

———. "Radical Pedagogy and the Politics of Student Voice." *Interchange* (Ontario Institute for Studies in Education) 17, no. 1 (1986): 48–67.

———. *Teachers as Intellectuals.* Westport, Conn.: Bergin and Garvey, 1988.

———. *Border Crossings: Cultural Workers and the Politics of Education.* New York: Routledge, 1992.

Giroux, Henry A., and Peter McLaren, eds. *Between Borders Pedagogy and the Politics of Cultural Studies.* New York: Routledge, 1994.

Giroux, Henry A., Roger Simon, and contributors. *Popular Culture, Schooling, and Everyday Life.* New York: Bergin and Garvey, 1989.

Goodwin, Andrew, and Gary Whannel, eds. *Understanding Television.* New York: Routledge, 1990.

Gordon, Beverly M. "The Necessity of African American Epistemology for Educational Theory and Practice." *Boston Journal of Education* 172, no. 3 (1990): 88–106.

Gore, Jennifer. *The Struggle for Pedagogies: Critical Feminist Discourses as Regimes of Truth.* New York: Routledge, 1993.

Gore, Jennifer, and Carmen Luke, eds. *Feminisms and Critical Pedagogy.* New York: Routledge, 1992.

Gould, Stephen Jay. *The Mismeasure of Man.* New York: W. W. Norton, 1981.

Greenfield, Patricia Marks. *Mind and Media: The Effects of Television, Video Games, and Computers.* Cambridge: Harvard University Press, 1984.

Greninger, Edwin. "Eyes and Ears in Foreign Lands: A Comparison of Educational Approaches." *Educational Screen and Audiovisual Guide* 49, no. 4 (April 1970).

Guimarães, Cesar, and Roberto Amaral. "Brazilian Television: Rapid Conversion to the New Order." In *Media and Politics in Latin America,* ed. Elizabeth Fox. Newbury Park, Calif.: Sage, 1988.

Gurevitch, Michael, Tony Bennett, James Curran and Janet Woollacott, eds. *Culture, Society, and the Media.* London: Routledge, 1982.

Hall, Clarence. "Samoa: America's Shame in the South Seas." *Reader's Digest,* July 1961, 111–16.

Hall, George. "Samoa: The Nonconformist." *Educational Screen and Audiovisual Guide* 48, no. 5 (May 1969).

Hall, Stuart. "The Whites of Their Eyes: Racist Ideologies and the Media." In *Silver Linings,* ed. George Bridges and Rosalind Brunt. London: Lawrence and Wishart, 1981.

———. "Cultural Identity and Cinematic Representation." In *Ex-iles: Essays on Caribbean Cinema,* ed. Mbye Cham. Trenton: Africa World Press, 1992.

Halloran, James, and Marsha Jones. "The Inoculation Aproach." In *Media Education: An Introduction,* ed. Manuel Alvarado and Oliver Boyd-Barrett. London: British Film Institute and Open University, 1986.

Harbeck, Karen M., ed. *Coming Out of the Classroom Closet: Gay and Lesbian Students, Teachers, and Curricula.* New York: Harrington Park Press, 1992.

Harrison, Molly. "Education in Museums." In *The Organization of Museums.* Paris: UNESCO, 1960.

Head, Sydney W. *Broadcasting in Africa.* Philadelphia: Temple University Press, 1974.

Hebdige, Dick. *Subculture: The Meaning of Style.* London: Methuen, 1979.

Hendershot, Heather. *Saturday Morning Censors: Television Regulation before the V-Chip.* Durham: Duke University Press, 1999.

Hetrick-Martin Institute. "Factfile: Lesbian, Gay, and Bisexual Youth." Hetrick-Martin Institute, 1992.

Husen, Torsten. *Education and the Global Concern.* New York: Pergamon Press, 1990.

Huyssen, Andreas. *After the Great Divide.* Bloomington and Indianapolis: Indiana University Press, 1986.

Jhally, Sut, and Justin Lewis. *Enlightened Racism: The Cosby Show, Audiences, and the Myth of the American Dream.* Boulder: Westview Press, 1992.

Johnson, Randal. "The Rise and Fall of Brazilian Cinema, 1960–1990." *Iris* 13 (summer 1991).

Johnson, Randal, and Robert Stam, eds. *Brazilian Cinema.* Austin: University of Texas Press, 1982.

Juhasz, Alex. *AIDS TV: Identity, Community, and Alternative Video.* Durham: Duke University Press, 1995.

Kadesch, Rollen B. "Businessmen Learn via Hagerstown CCTV: Government, Business Groups, and Educators Collaborate." *NAEB Journal* 21, no. 10 (November–December 1962): 44–46.

Karp, Ivan, Christine Mullen Kreamer, and Steven D. Lavine, eds. *Exhibiting Cultures: The Poetics and Politics of Museum Display.* Washington, D.C.: Smithsonian Institution Press, 1992.

Karp, Ivan, and Steven D. Lavine. *Museums and Communities.* Washington, D.C.: Smithsonian Institution Press, 1991.

Katz, Elihu, and George Wedell. *Broadcasting in the Third World: Promise and Performance.* Cambridge: Harvard University Press, 1977.

Kelly, Gail P. "The Relation between Colonial and Metropolitan Schools: A Structural Analysis." *Comparative Education* 15, no. 2 (June 1979): 209–15.

———. "Colonialism, Indigenous Society, and School Practices: French West Africa and Indochina, 1918–1938." In *Education and the Colonial Experience,* ed. Philip Altbach and Gail Kelly. New Brunswick: Transaction Books, 1984.

Killian, James, Jr. *Sputnik, Scientists, and Eisenhower.* Cambridge: MIT Press, 1977.

Kinder, Marsha. *Playing with Power in Movies, Television, and Video Games.* Berkeley: University of California Press, 1991.

Klein, Susan Shurberg, ed. *Sex Equity and Sexality in Education*. New York: State University of New York Press, 1992.

Klusacek, Allan, and Ken Morrison. *A Leap in the Dark: AIDS, Art, and Contemporary Cultures*. Montreal: Véhicule Press, 1992.

Koeng, Allen, and Ruane Hill, eds. *The Farther Vision: Educational Television Today*. Madison: University of Wisconsin Press, 1967.

Kozol, Jonathan. "Whittle and the Privateers: Corporate Raid on Education." *Nation*, 21 September 1992, 272–78.

Lankshear, Colin, and Peter L. McLaren, eds. *Critical Literacy: Politics, Praxis, and the Postmodern*. New York: State University of New York Press, 1993.

Lather, Patti. *Getting Smart: Feminist Research and Pedagogy with/in the Postmodern*. New York: Routledge, 1991.

Latour, Bruno. *Science in Action*. Cambridge: Harvard University Press, 1987.

Leeming, Owen. "TV in Senegalese Adult Education." *School and Society* 96, no. 2312 (November 1968): 442–44.

Lefranc, Robert. "Problems Created by the Development of the Use of Media in Industrialized Countries." *Educational Media International* no. 4 (1978): 6–15.

Lilla, Mark. "The Museum in the City." In *Public Policy and the Aesthetic Interest*, ed. Ralph Smith and Ronald Berman. Urbana: University of Illinois Press, 1992.

Lins da Silva, Carlos Eduardo. "Transnational Communication and Brazilian Culture." In *Communication and Latin American Society*, ed. Rita Atwood and Emile G. McAnany. Madison: University of Wisconsin Press, 1986.

Livingston, David, and contributors. *Critical Pedagogy and Cultural Power*. New York: Bergin and Garvey, 1987.

López, Ana. "The Melodrama in Latin America: Films, Telenovelas, and the Currency of a Popular Form." *Wide Angle* 7, no. 3 (1985): 5–13.

Lunn, Eugene. *Marxism and Modernism*. London: Verso, 1982.

Lusted, David. "Why Pedagogy?" *Screen*, no. 27 (September–October 1986): 2–14.

Magat, Richard. *The Ford Foundation at Work: Philanthropic Choices, Methods, and Styles*. New York: Plenum Press, 1979.

Malkmus, Lizbeth, and Roy Armes. *Arab and African Film Making*. London: Zed Books, 1991.

Mander, Jerry. *Four Arguments for the Elimination of Television*. New York: Morrow, 1978.

Mankekar, D. R. *Whose Freedom? Whose Order? A Plea for a New Information Order by the Third World*. Delhi: Clarion Books, 1981.

Mannoni, Octave. *Psychoanalysis and the Decolonization of the Mind*. Ed. J. Miller Freud. London: Weidenfeld and Nicholson, 1972.

———. *Prospero and Caliban: The Psychology of Colonization*. Trans. Pamela Powesland. Ann Arbor: University of Michigan Press, 1990. "First published in 1950 by Editions du seuil Paris, under the title *Psychologie de la colonisation*."

Marchessault, Janine. "Amateur Video and the Challenge for Social Change." In

Mirror Machine: Video and Identity, ed. Janine Marchessault. Toronto: YYZ Books, 1995.

Marchl, Herbert, and Etienne Brunswick. "Educational Television in Developing Countries." *Educational Media International,* no. 2 (1977).

Masland, Lynn, and Grant Masland. "The Samoan ETV Project: Some Cross-Cultural Implications of Educational Television—Part 1." *Educational Broadcasting* 8, no. 2 (March–April 1975): 13–16.

———. "The Samoan ETV Project: Some Cross-Cultural Implications of Educational Television—Part 2." *Educational Broadcasting* 8, no. 3 (June 1975): 23–28.

Mattelart, Armand. *Multinational Corporations and the Control of Culture: The Ideological Apparatuses of Imperialism.* Atlantic Highlands, N.J.: Humanities Press, 1979.

———. *Mapping World Communication.* Minneapolis: University of Minnesota Press, 1994.

Mattelart, Armand, and Michèle Mattelart. *The Carnival of Images: Brazilian Television Fiction.* New York: Bergin and Garvey, 1990.

———. *Rethinking Media Theory.* Trans. James Cohen and Marina Urquidi. Minneapolis: University of Minnesota Press, 1992.

Mattelart, Armand, and Seth Siegelaub, eds. *Communication and Class Struggle.* Vols. 1 and 2. New York: International General, 1979.

Mayo, John K., Robert C. Hornik, and Emile G. McAnany. *Educational Reform with Television: the Salvadorean Experience.* Stanford, Calif.: Stanford University Press, 1976.

McAnany, Emile. "Success or Failure of Communication Technology in the Third World: By What Criteria Shall We Judge." *Educational Media International,* no. 4 (1978): 16–23.

McLaren, Peter. "Contesting Capital: Critical Pedagogy and Globalism: A Response to Michael Apple." *Current Issues in Comparative Education* 1, no. 2 (30 April 1999). www.tc.columbia.edu/cice.

Mellencamp, Patricia. *Logics of Television: Essays in Cultural Criticism.* Bloomington and Indianapolis: Indiana University Press, 1990.

Meyer, Richard. "South Asian Broadcast Instruction: Some Recent Observations." *Educational Television* 2, no. 12 (December 1970): 7–9.

Michaels, Eric. *Bad Aboriginal Art: Tradition Media and Technological Horizons.* Minneapolis: University of Minnesota Press, 1994.

Molner, Alex. "Fears about Business Involvement." *Rethinking Schools* 7, no. 1 (autumn 1992). Reprinted in *Leadership News,* 31 May 1992.

Morris, Meaghan. "Banality in Cultural Studies." In *Logics of Television: Essays in Cultural Criticism,* ed. Patricia Mellencamp. Bloomington and Indianapolis: Indiana University Press, 1990.

Murphy, Judith, and Ronald Gross. *Learning by Television.* New York: Fund for the Advancement of Education, 1966.

Myers, Steven Lee. "Board in Queens Is Suspended in Battle over Gay Curriculum." *New York Times,* 2 December 1992, 1.

———. "How a 'Rainbow' Curriculum Turned into Fighting Words." *New York Times,* 13 December 1992, 6.

Naficy, Hamid. "Narrowcasting and Nationality: Middle East Television in Los Angeles." *Afterimage* 20, no. 7 (February 1993): 9–11.

Nandy, Ashis. *The Intimate Enemy: Loss and Recovery of Self under Colonialism.* Delhi and Oxford: Oxford University Press, 1989.

The Network Project. *The Fourth Network.* New York: Network Project, 1971.

Newsom, Carroll. *A Television Policy for Education: Proceedings of the Television Programs Institute.* Washington, D.C.: American Council on Education, 1952.

New York City Public Schools, Office of the Chancellor. *Children of the Rainbow.* New York City Public Schools, 1992.

Noriega, Chon A. "Genre Blurring, Genre Bending: Willie Varela's *A Lost Man* (1992)." Manuscript.

Oakes, Jeannie. *Keeping Track: How Schools Structure Inequality.* New Haven: Yale University Press, 1985.

Okigbo, Charles. "Africa: Television and National Independence." In *Television: An International History,* ed. Anthony Smith. New York: Oxford University Press, 1995.

Oppenheimer, Todd. "The Computer Delusion." *Atlantic Monthly,* July 1997, 45–62.

Owens, Craig. *Beyond Recognition.* Berkeley: University of California Press, 1992.

Owoo, Kwate Nee. "The Language of Real Life: Interview with Ousmane Sembéne." *Framework* 16 (1989): 84–85.

Paper Tiger Collective. *The Paper Tiger Guide to Media Activism.* New York: Paper Tiger Collective, 1991.

Patton, Cindy. *Inventing AIDS.* New York: Routledge, 1990.

———. "Safe Sex and the Pornographic Vernacular." In *How Do I Look? Queer Film and Video,* ed. Bad Object Choices. Seattle: Bay Press, 1991.

Pfaff, Françoise. *The Cinema of Ousmane Sembene, a Pioneer of African Cinema.* Westport, Conn.: Greenwood Press, 1984.

Piaget, Jean. *The Moral Development of the Child.* New York: Free Press, 1965.

Philo, Greg. *Seeing and Believing: The Influence of Television.* London: Routledge, 1990.

Pick, Zuzana M. *The New Latin American Cinema: A Continental Project.* Austin: University of Texas Press, 1993.

Pines, Jim, and Paul Willeman, eds. *Questions of Third Cinema.* London: BFI, 1989.

Posner, George. "Models of Curriculum Planning." In *The Curriculum: Problems,*

Politics, and Possibilities, ed. Landon E. Breyer and Michael Apple. Albany: State University of New York Press, 1988.

Postman, Neil. *Amusing Ourselves to Death.* New York: Penguin Books, 1985.

———. *Conscientious Objections: Stirring Up Trouble about Language, Technology, and Education.* New York: Vintage, 1988.

Potter, Rosemary Lee. *The Positive Use of Commercial Television with Children.* Washington, D.C.: National Education Association of the United States, 1981.

Powell, John Walker. *Channels of Learning: The Story of Educational Television.* Washington, D.C.: Public Affairs Press, 1962.

Price, Monroe E. *Television, the Public Sphere, and National Identity.* New York: Oxford University Press, 1995.

Provenzo, Eugene F. *Video Kids: Making Sense of Nintendo.* Cambridge: Harvard University Press, 1991.

Raboy, Marc, and Peter A. Bruck, eds. *Communication for and against Democracy.* New York: Black Rose Books, 1989.

Radway, Janice. *Reading the Romance: Representing Women in Popular Culture.* Chapel Hill: University of North Carolina Press, 1984.

Ranucci, Karen. *Directory of Film and Video Production Resources in Latin America and the Caribbean.* New York: Foundation for Independent Video and Film, 1989.

Rhodes, Lewis. "A Trip to the Possible." *Educational Perspectives* 7, no. 3 (October 1968).

Rideout, William, Jr. "Education in Senegal: Two Promising Reforms." In *Cultural Identity and Educational Policy,* ed. Colin Brock and Witold Tulasiewicz. New York: St. Martin's Press, 1985.

Rocha, Glauber. "Down with Populism." In *Twenty-five Years of the New Latin American Cinema,* ed. Michael Chanan. London: British Film Institute, 1983.

Roncagliolo, Rafael. "Transnational Communication and Culture." In *Communication and Latin American Society,* ed. Rita Atwood and Emile G. McAnany. Madison: University of Wisconsin Press, 1986.

———. "The Growth of the Audio-visual Imagescape in Latin America." In *Video the Changing World,* ed. Nancy Thede and Alain Ambrosi. New York: Black Rose Books, 1991.

Rosler, Martha. *If You Lived Here.* Ed. Brian Wallis. Seattle: Bay Press, 1991.

Rubenstein, Anne. "Seeing through AIDS: Media Activists Join Forces with the NYC Department of Health." *Independent* 16, no. 1 (January–February 1993): 13.

Rushkoff, Douglass. *Playing the Future: How Kids Can Teach Us to Thrive in the Age of Chaos.* New York: Harper-Collins, 1996.

Ryan, Charlotte. *Prime Time Activism.* Boston: South End Press, 1991.

Saalfield, Catherine. "Pregnant with Dreams: Julia Barco's Visions from Latin America." *Independent* 14, no. 10 (December 1991).

Saettler, Paul. *A History of Instructional Technology*. New York: McGraw-Hill, 1968.

Said, Edward. *Culture and Imperialism*. New York: Alfred A. Knopf, 1993.

Sanjines, Jorge. *Theory and Practice of a Cinema with the People*. Trans. Richard Schaaf. Willimantic, Conn.: Curbstone Press, 1989.

Santoro, Luiz Fernando. *A imagen nas mãos: O vidoe popular no Brazil*. São Paulo: Summus Editorial, 1989.

Sarti, Ingrid. "Between Memory and Illusion: Independent Video in Brazil." In *Media and Politics in Latin America: The Struggle for Democracy,* ed. Elizabeth Fox. Newbury Park, Calif.: Sage Publications, 1988.

Scanlon, David G. *Traditions of African Education*. New York: Teachers College Press, Columbia University, 1964.

Schneider, Cynthia, and Brian Wallis, eds. *Global Television*. Cambridge: MIT Press, 1989.

Shor, Ira. *Culture Wars: School and Society in the Conservative Restoration*. Chicago: University of Chicago Press, 1992.

Schramm, Wilbur. "Educational Television in American Samoa." In *New Educational Media in Action: Case Studies for Planners—I*. Paris: UNESCO, 1967.

———. *ITV in American Samoa—after Nine Years*. Institute for Communication Research, Stanford University, 1973.

Schramm, Wilbur, Jack Lyle, and Ithíel de Sola Pool. *The People Look at Educational Television*. Stanford: Stanford University Press, 1963.

Schramm, Wilbur, Phillip Coombs, Friedrich Kahnert, and Jack Lyle. *The New Media: Memo to Planners*. International Institute for Educational Planning. Paris: UNESCO, 1967.

Schultz, Victoria. "Nicaragua Journal." In *Heresies 16: Film and Video*. New York: Heresies Collective, 1983.

Schwoch, James, Mimi White, and Susan Reilly. *Media Knowledge: Readings in Popular Culture, Pedagogy, and Critical Citizenship*. New York: State University of New York Press, 1992.

Sedgwick, Eve Kosofsky. *Epistemology of the Closet*. Berkeley: University of California Press, 1990.

———. "How to Bring Your Kids Up Gay." *Social Text 29* (fall 1991).

———. *Tendencies*. Durham: Duke University Press, 1993.

Sherman, Daniel, and Irit Rogoff, eds. *Museum Culture: Histories, Discourses, Spectacles*. Minneapolis: University of Minnesota Press, 1994.

Shohat, Ella. "Imaging Terra Incognita: The Disciplinary Gaze of Empire." *Public Culture 3*, no. 2 (spring 1991).

Sholle, David, and Stan Denski. *Media Education and the (Re)Production of Culture*. Westport, Conn.: Bergin and Garvey, 1994.

Siepmann, Charles Arthur. *TV and Our School Crisis*. New York: Dodd Mead, 1958.

Simon, Roger. *Teaching against the Grain: Texts for a Pedagogy of Possibility.* New York: Bergin and Garvey, 1992.

Simon, Roger, John Brown, Enid Lee, and John Young. *Decoding Discrimination: A Student Based Approach to Anti-racist Education Using Film.* Ontario: Althouse Press, 1988.

Simpson, Phillip, ed. *Parents Talking Television.* London: Comedia, 1987.

Skornia, Harry J. "Some Lessons from Samoa." *Audiovisual Instruction* 14, no. 3 (March 1969).

Smith, Ralph A., ed. *Cultural Literacy and the Arts.* Urbana and Chicago: University of Illinois Press, 1990.

Spigel, Lynn. *Make Room for TV: Television and the Family Ideal in Postwar America.* Chicago: Chicago University Press, 1992.

Stam, Robert. *Subversive Pleasures: Bakhtin, Cultural Criticism, and Film.* Baltimore: Johns Hopkins University Press, 1989.

———. "Mutual Illuminations: A Cross-Cultural Approach to Racial Representation in Brazilian Cinema." *Iris,* no. 13 (summer 1991).

Stepan, Nancy Leys. "Race and Gender: The Role of Analogy in Science." *Isis* 77 (1986).

Stoler, Ann Laura. *Race and the Education of Desire.* Durham: Duke University Press, 1995.

Stuckey, J. Elspeth. *The Violence of Literacy.* Portsmouth: Boynton/Cook Publishers, 1991.

Swing, Elizabeth Sherman. "Colonials, Subordinates or Superordinates: Puerto Ricans and Educational Policy on the United States Mainland." In *Cultural Identity and Educational Policy,* ed. Colin Brock and Witold Tulasiewicz. New York: St. Martin's Press, 1985.

Tagg, John. *The Burden of Representation: Essays on Photographies and Histories.* Minneapolis: University of Minnesota Press, 1993.

" 'Talofa, Norma!' New York TV Teacher Is Hit with Youths on American Samoa." *Ebony* 12, no. 3 (January 1966).

Tapscott, Don. *Growing Up Digital: The Rise of the Net Generation.* New York: McGraw-Hill, 1988.

"Teaching of Sexual Concepts Stirs a Heated Debate among Officials." *New York Times,* 17 June 1992, B1, B2.

Thomas, R. Murray. "Scheme for Assessing Unmet Educational Needs: The American Samoa Example." *International Review of Education* 23, no. 1 (1977).

———. "The Rise and Decline of an Educational Technology: Television in American Samoa." *Educational Communication and Technology: A Journal of Theory Research and Development* 28, no. 3 (fall 1980).

Tickton, Sidney G. "Instructional Technology in the Developing World." *Educational Broadcasting Review* 6, no. 2 (April 1972): 97–104.

Tobing Rony, Fatimah. "Those Who Squat, Those Who Sit: The Visualizing of

Race in the 1895 Films of Félix-Louis Regnault." *Camera Obscura* 28 (January 1992).

Trend, David. "To Tell the Truth: Strategies of Media Literacy." *Afterimage* 18, no. 8 (1991).

———. *Cultural Pedagogy: Art/Education/Politics*. New York: Bergin and Garvey, 1992.

———. "Rethinking Media Activism." *Socialist Review* 23, no. 2 (1993): 5–34.

Tunstall, Jeremy. *The Media Are American: Anglo-American Media in the World*. New York: Columbia University Press, 1977.

Twitchin, John, ed. *The Black and White Media Show Book*. Stoke-on-Trent, England: Trentham Books, 1988.

Urch, George E. F. *Education in Sub-Saharan Africa*. New York: Garland, 1992.

U.S. Department of Education. "Getting America's Students Ready for the 21st Century: Meeting the Technology Literacy Challenge." Report to the Nation on Technology and Education. Washington, D.C.: U.S. Department of Education, June 1996. http://www.ed.gov/Technology/Plan/NatTechPlan.

U.S. Department of Health and Human Services. "Report of the Secretary's Task Force on Youth Suicide." U.S. Department of Health and Human Services, summer 1989.

U.S. Department of the Interior. *Annual Report of the Governor of American Samoa to the Secretary of the Interior*. 1961–1966, 1970. Washington, D.C.: Government Printing Office, 1961–1966, 1970.

Ventura, Sandra. "O último programma da TV Anhembi." In *Diário do comércio*. São Paulo, 8 January 1993.

Vieyra, Paulin Soumanou. "African Cinema: Solidarity and Difference." In *Questions of Third Cinema*, ed. Jim Pines and Paul Willeman. London: BFI, 1989.

Vink, Nico. *The Telenovela and Emancipation: A Study on Television and Social Change in Brazil*. Amsterdam, Netherlands: Royal Tropical Institute, 1988.

Viswanathan, Gauri. *Masks of Conquest*. New York: Columbia University Press, 1989.

Wade, Serena. "Hagerstown: A Pioneer in Closed Circuit Televised Instruction." In *New Educational Media in Action: Case Studies for Planners—I*. Paris: UNESCO, 1967.

Walkerdine, Valerie. "On the Regulation of Speaking and Silence: Subjectivity, Class, and Gender in Contemporary Schooling." In *Language, Gender, and Childhood*, ed. Carolyn Steedman, Cathy Unwin, and Valerie Walkerdine. Boston: Routledge and Kegan Paul, 1985.

Wallace, Michelle. "Modernism, Postmodernism, and the Problem of the Visual in Afro-American Culture." In *Out There*, ed. Russell Ferguson, Martha Gever, Trinh T. Minh-ha, and Cornel West. Cambridge: MIT Press, 1990.

Warner, Michael, ed. *Fear of a Queer Planet: Queer Politics and Social Theory.*
Minneapolis: University of Minnesota Press, 1993.

Watney, Simon. "School's Out." In *Inside/Out: Lesbian Theories, Gay Theories.*
New York: Routledge, 1991.

Watson, Mary Ann. *The Expanding Vista: American Television in the Kennedy
Years.* New York: Oxford University Press, 1990.

Weeks, Jeffrey. *Against Nature.* London: Routledge, 1991.

Weiler, Kathleen, and Candace Mitchell, eds. *What Schools Can Do: Critical
Pedagogy and Practice.* Albany: State University of New York Press, 1992.

Wells, Alan. *Picture Tube Imperialism? The Impact of U.S. Television on Latin
America.* New York: Orbis Books, 1972.

White, Mimi. *Tele-advising: Therapeutic Discourses in American Television.* Chapel
Hill: University of North Carolina Press, 1992.

Wilhelm, Donald. *Global Communications and Political Power.* New Brunswick:
Transaction Publishers, 1990.

Williams, Anna. "Domestic Violence and the Aetiology of Crime in *America's Most
Wanted.*" *Camera Obscura* 31 (1993).

Williams, Frederick, and Geraldine Van Wart. *Carrascolendas: Bilingual Education
through Television.* New York: Praeger, 1974.

Williams, Raymond. *Television: Technology and Cultural Form.* New York:
Schocken Books, 1974.

———. "Metropolitan Perceptions and the Emergence of Modernism." In *The
Politics of Modernism.* Originally published in *Unreal City: Urban Experience in
Modern European Literature and Art,* ed. Edward Timms and David Kelly.
Manchester: Manchester University Press, 1985.

———. "The Practice of Possibility." Interview with Terry Eagleton. *New
Statesman* 7 (August 1987): 21.

———. "Culture and Technology." In *The Politics of Modernism.* New York: Verso,
1989.

Williamson, Judith. *Consuming Passions: The Dynamics of Popular Culture,* 1986.

Winston, Brian. *Misunderstanding Media.* New York: Routledge and Kegan Paul,
1986.

Wolff, Janet. *The Social Production of Art.* New York: New York University Press,
1984.

———. *Feminine Sentences.* Berkeley and Los Angeles: University of California
Press, 1990.

Woodring, Paul. *Investment in Innovation: An Historical Appraisal of the Fund for
the Advancement of Education.* Boston: Little, Brown, 1970.

Zerzn, John, and Alice Carnes, eds. *Questioning Technology.* Santa Cruz, Calif.:
New Society Publishers, 1991.

Brian Goldfarb is Assistant Professor of Communication
at the University of California, San Diego.

Library of Congress Cataloging-in-Publication Data
Goldfarb, Brian.
Visual pedagogy : media cultures in and beyond the
classroom / Brian Goldfarb.
p. cm.   Includes bibliographical references and index.
ISBN 0-8223-2936-0 (cloth : alk. paper)
ISBN 0-8223-2964-6 (pbk. : alk. paper)
1. Mass media and education.   2. Audiovisual education—
Social aspects.   3. Critical pedagogy.   I. Title.
LB1043 .G57   2002   371.335—dc21   2002001692